Falkirk

*The Battle of Falkirk Muir
17 January 1746*

GEOFF B. BAILEY

JOHN DONALD PUBLISHERS LTD
EDINBURGH

On the eve of battle Lord George Murray,
Commander of the Jacobite forces,
declared he 'would either ly in town or in Paradice'

Cover design
based on the painting *The Battle of Falkirk*, by Lionel Edwards

A companion volume:
The Life and Times of Falkirk by Ian Scott. John Donald Publishers

© Geoff B. Bailey 1996
All rights reserved. No part of this
publication may be reproduced in any
form or by any means without the
prior permission of the publishers,
John Donald Publishers Ltd
138 St Stephen Street, Edinburgh
EH3 5AA

ISBN 0 85976 431 1

A catalogue record for this book is available from the British Library

Printed and bound in Great Britain by Bell & Bain Ltd, Glasgow

Preface

On a dark, icey cold winter's evening 250 tears ago the drenched figure of Lord George Murray, commander of all the Jacobite forces of Prince Charles Edward Stuart, surveyed the little hill upon which huddled the flimsy houses of the small town of Falkirk. Around him gathered a confused group of fierce highland soldiers whose very survival on that bitter night seemed in jeopardy despite the seeming success on the battlefield just a few hours before. To spend the night on the moor in wretched weather conditions or to storm the town with all the attendant dangers? Lord George loudly and firmly declared that 'he would either ly in town or in Paradice' and the fate of the small band was sealed. The town fell to the Jacobites. Of course many of today's bairns would ask whether or not Falkirk actually is paradise? Perhaps for the historian it is, as it surely possesses a greater share of Scotland's history than its size might indicate.

Falkirk has played a central role in the history of the Scottish nation. The pages of Ian Scott's recent book on Falkirk are replete with incidents which altered the course of the nation's progress. More than on any other occasion this is true of the 1745 Jacobite campaign. To this dramatic episode Falkirk was central both geographically and strategically. Between the raising of the standard at Glenfinnan on 19th August 1745 and the humiliating defeat at Culloden on 16th April the following year, the huge Jacobite Army spent a period of 24 days in the town, from the 4th to the 28th January. There were many thousands more in the town than occupied Edinburgh the previous autumn, and the long delay in Falkirk lost them the initiative which their previous rapid motions had secured. More particularly, it threw away the immense advantage won on Falkirk Muir on the 17th January when they encountered and routed the Hanovarian army. This was no minor skirmish but perhaps the largest battle of the entire uprising. There were only three battles in which Bonnie Prince Charlie was involved - the first at Prestonpasns was fought before either side had fully assembled their forces and barely lasted five minutes. The last, at Culloden, took place when the Jacobite forces were on the wane and scattered. At Falkirk, however, the Jacobites were at full strength whilst the army that faced them was a regular professional force. There were over 18 thousand combatants on the field of battle that day leaving plenty of room for heroism, confusion and cowardice. The story which follows contains many examples of all three and I hope readers will share something of the excitement of these great events as the tale unfolds from those first stirrings in August 1745.

Falkirk, 1995   G.B.B

Acknowledgements

As a child I was taken around this and many other battlefields by my enthusiastic parents and it is to them that I owe my interst in such affairs. Their encouragement has led to the historic research upon which this book is based. It is due to Roy Earle's vision that the publication is in the form of a book and to Ian Scott's hard work that the book takes the present physical shape. I owe them all a debt of gratitude. I have been associated with the Falkirk Local History Society since I came to the area ten years ago and am delighted that the Society has acted as enabling agent in arranging for the publication of the book by John Donald of Edinburgh. During the quest for information I have trawled the shelves of many libraries and archives. The bulk of the search was carried out in the Central Library and the National Library of Scotland, both in Edinburgh and I would like to thank the staff of both for their forbearance at the time. The illustrations are provided and reproduced here by courtesy of the Trustees of the National Library, the National Portrait Gallery, the National Museum of Scotland, the Duke of Atholl and Roy Earle. I am also very grateful to Central Regional Council for financial assistance in the preparation of the publication.

Contents

Preface		iii
Acknowledgements		iv
1.	The Storm Clouds Gather *1st August - 21st September 1745*	1
2.	The Eye of the Storm *22nd September - 25th December 1745*	19
3.	The Storm Approaches *26th December 1745 - 12th January 1746*	43
4.	The Storm Begins *12th January - 16th January 1746*	70
5.	The Tempest *17th January 1746*	91
6.	The Storm Rages *17th January 1746*	121
7.	Storm Damage *18th January - 22nd January 1746*	157
8.	The Aftermath *22nd January - 14th April 1746*	183
9.	Mopping Up *14th April and After*	211
10.	A Tale to Tell, a Yarn to Spin	220
Notes		232
General Bibliography		241
Index		245

CHAPTER 1

The Storm Clouds Gather
1st August - 21st September 1745

By the beginning of August in the year 1745 the whole of the county of Stirlingshire was deeply immersed in rumours of a landing by a member of the exiled Stuart monarchy and a force of Frenchmen. Prince Charles, as he was styled, had audaciously travelled to the Highlands to set alight the flame of rebellion in the hope of regaining his father's kingdom. The people of the shire listened intently to the stories of travellers in an attempt to glean news of the events which seemed incredibly to be unfolding far away in the Highlands.

The Trysts were just starting again for the year. These were the great cattle fairs of Scotland, held on the high pasture just three miles to the south-east of the small market town of Falkirk. On this common land the vast herds had congregated annually for almost half a century. The open moor became a hive of activity as thousands of cattle were led down from the Highlands and the northern Islands. They were attracted by the presence of dealers from England who brought with them much needed hard currency. The field thronged with animals, while men busily sought out the best bargains. No where else in Scotland would you find such a mixture of cultures at one time. People from distant lands met and parted at this the country's largest assembly.

To the inhabitants of the little town of Falkirk below it also spelled prosperity. They catered to the needs of the strangers in their midst and took their share of the dues. The English merchants appeared aloof to them; but the dirty Gaelic speaking Highlanders were just as alien, and the townsfolk must have felt as though they were living in a frontier town acting as a trading post. This year it all seemed so familiar, and yet there was something in the air. The Highland drovers spoke of a stirring in the north, of secret meetings, men moving about in bands: tales of all sorts began to circulate. Then government troops from Edinburgh and the east started to pass through the district. Something was afoot.

The curious watched as the infantry marched behind the beating drums along the dusty roads. The soldiers were confident, exchanging words with the onlookers. Still, Falkirk had grown accustomed to an army presence over the years. Regiments were often billeted in the town's dwellings as it lay on a strategic road from Edinburgh and Linlithgow to either Stirling and the north or to Glasgow and the west. It was very much doubted whether what enemy there might be would even have the stomach for a fight. One thing was sure, what ever action there might be would take place well away from Falkirk.

The older townsfolk remembered how, some thirty years before, the local laird, James Livingston of Callendar, had marched out of the town at the head of a poorly armed but fiercely loyal force consisting of 300 of Falkirk's bairns.[1] How, after a few short weeks, that band had been dispersed and its leader exiled. Slowly many of them had drifted back to the town of their birth, but the laird had never returned to his ancestral seat at Callendar House just to the east of the town. He had died in France, the last of a long and distinguished line, leaving only his daughter to administer the forfeited estate. All his property now lay in the hands of an English business called the York Buildings Company.

Times had indeed changed since that last rebellion, and the York Buildings Company was an ever present reminder of that. It had loosened the old feudal ties which had bound the people in formalised servitude to their local laird. It had introduced an economic exploitation of the land to develop commerce; cranking up the engine which was to power the industrial revolution. It had provided an element of change in a previously stagnant world. The spark of rebellion in this area was not as strong as it had been on that earlier occasion which had ended almost where it had begun, in the fiasco at Sheriffmuir not far away. Few of the people of southern Scotland saw any reason to support the old cause of an estranged monarchy that most had never known. The majority of them were busy getting on with their own lives and resented the prospect of any disruption.

Yet, the urgent movements of regular troops along the rough roads of the shire indicated that the situation might be serious. After them went endless convoys of supplies in covered wagons, and a herd of cattle - fresh meat on the hoof. There were also two

The Storm Clouds Gather

regiments of dragoons, about 600 in number. Well equipped and smartly dressed they made an impressive spectacle on their big finely groomed mounts. At their head was Colonel James Gardiner, a man well known in the locality, and who in his turn knew the area well. His father was Patrick Gardiner of nearby Torwood-Head, and his mother was Mary Hodge of Gladsmuir (Prestonpans). He himself had been born at Burnfoot, Carriden, and educated at Linlithgow Grammar School. Like many of his family he was a professional soldier and had served abroad where he had seen much action. His military experience was therefore considerable. He was well respected by the soldiers, and indeed his kindness and humanity had won him many friends in the area. He was acquainted with the new occupants of Callendar House, William Boyd the Earl of Kilmarnock, and Anne Livingston his wife. A more congenial relationship existed with the reverend John Adams, the minister of the parish church. With his wife and eldest daughter Gardiner called in on his friend, discussing the momentous events that were occurring. Gardiner was now 57 years of age and had not been keeping good health. While in former days he might have relished the prospect of an encounter with the villainous

Colonel James Gardiner
(1688-1745)

A Trooper in Gardiner's
Dragoons in 1742

band that he saw as a threat to the tranquility of his beloved country, on this occasion he was relatively sombre.[2]

Rev Adams was greatly disturbed by Gardiner's analysis of the situation. Most of the British army was abroad fighting the French forces and their allies on the continent, and a major uprising in Scotland strongly supported by the French might make considerable headway against the remaining small force of regular soldiers and the hurriedly raised local militias. However, Adams dismissed this gloomy prognosis as the pessimism of an old friend. The Minister was a busy man and in his travels had seen no reason to believe that the Jacobite cause could be revived. Only the year before he had been made Moderator of the General Assembly and had taken the opportunity to speak to men from all over the country. He was sure that the presbyterian church was as strong as ever and that through its influence a Catholic monarchy would not be tolerated again.

Gardiner did not dally long in Falkirk. He had business in Stirling and his host had work to attend to. Part of this work was the supervision of the construction of a new manse to the east of the old decaying church. The new building was to be a dwelling in keeping with the Minister's status and a sign of the burgh's recent prosperity. Already on the site on Vicar's Loan, just inside the ancient port which hung over the road, masons were hard at work The walls were progressing well and the building was due to be completed by the following summer. From the upper floors there would be a magnificent view to the north picturing the River Forth winding its way through the flat carselands with the Ochil Hills behind. The carse was rich and productive land yielding fine crops of wheat as well as barley and beans. It contrasted sharply with the barren hills beyond the river, which rose almost vertically from the plain, dictating the lines of communication to the north. It was hoped to make enough progress on the manse to have a roof on it before the worst of the winter weather came.

The government troops gradually assembled at Stirling. By the 19th August a respectable force of some 1400 infantry and 600 cavalry had been drawn together under the over all command of General Sir John Cope. Everything was in readiness, and the next day, after much discussion, the foot started the long hard slog northwards to meet the unseen enemy as promptly as possible to

The Storm Clouds Gather

Falkirk from the south-west in 1830. The church and steeple are the main features. The Forth Estuary lies in the background with the Ochils beyond.

nip the rising in the bud. They hoped to recruit support on the way, and by intercepting the Jacobite army as soon as they could it was thought, in official circles, that they would halt the rising before it had gathered a full head of steam.

Colonel Gardiner and the dragoons were left behind as there was no grazing for their horses in the north at that time of year. Instead they were delegated to protect the strategic stronghold of Stirling and to stop any Jacobites from slipping southwards. From here they commanded the whole of central Scotland, as the Duke of Argyll had done in 1715. The small force in the castle had been reprovisioned and reinforced under the command of General Blakeney. Its heavy artillery dominated the crossing of the Forth by Stirling Bridge and the Abbot's Ford; and towered over the royal burgh below. Here Blakeney set about strengthening the town's security by patching its defensive wall and by instructing the people of Stirling. A militia was raised from volunteers armed with weapons provided from the castle's arsenal. The regular garrison gave what training they could to these enthusiastic gentlemen and helped to guard the town's gates at night. Recruitment was greatly aided by the exertions of Reverend Ebenezer Erskine of the Secession Church. He firmly believed that a return of the Stuarts would result in oppression and was an ardent supporter of

A view of Stirling Castle by Captain John Slezer

the Hanoverian regime. Back at Falkirk his nephew, Henry Erskine, the minister of the Secession church there, was kept apprised of the comings and goings. From time to time messengers from Cope's army rode into Stirling with news and instructions. The populace waited with a high degree of expectation as they heard first one rumour and then another. The fortnight since the army's departure produced a growing sense of unease. Daily the sentries at the castle gazed across the river through their telescopes, but the north held on to its secrets. Then, unexpectedly, news arrived that Cope had been outmanoeuvred and had withdrawn to Inverness leaving the way south open to the Jacobite supporters. On 3rd September intelligence was received of their arrival at Perth. Their destination was as yet unknown; it might be either the capital at Edinburgh, or the wealthy undefended city of Glasgow. The latter was evidently the softer target, but the former was the seat of government in Scotland and carried more prestige. The officials at Edinburgh made plans to provide themselves with more protection. The Jacobites might be delayed at Stirling if they were unable to bypass it to the east by crossing the Forth in boats. From Perth their obvious route to Edinburgh was by Alloa or Kincardine. Orders were therefore issued by the Lord Advocate to remove all vessels from the upper reaches of the Forth and its tributaries so that they would not fall into enemy hands. By confining the Jacobites to the north shore of the Forth their advance might be contained for long enough for Cope to return.

Walter Grossett, a customs officer from Alloa, was given the task of removing those vessels on the north side of the river to the harbours of Dunbar, Leith, Queensferry and Bo'ness on the south side and well out of reach of the enemy. These ports also had the considerable advantage of containing many loyal whig supporters. Indeed, Bo'ness was fervently anti-Jacobite in sentiment. The town depended for its livelihood on the recent freeing of trade and had flourished under the Hanoverians. Many in the town could still remember the destruction of a trading fleet by the French as it made its way from Bo'ness to Holland.[3]

> THE LORD ADVOCATE TO WALTER GROSSETT AND OTHERS. These are ordering and enquiring you and each of you to concur in sending all Vessels of whatever kind upon the North and South sides of the Firth from Stirling to Kinghorn to the Harbours of Leith and Borristouness and in case of resistance you are to use force in making the Order effectual. Given under my Hand at Edinburgh this ninth day of Sepr 1745 yeare...

Grossett employed the constables and tide surveyors as well as the admiralty sailors at Dunbar, Kirkcaldy, Leith, Queensferry, Bo'ness and Alloa. Even with all these men it was a major undertaking and they were kept gainfully employed "Night and Day therein for ten Days".[4] Walter Grossett's brother, Alexander, a tobacco merchant, zealously joined in the frenetic activity which "keeped me so closely imploy'd that I was there three Days & three Nights without geting off my Boots".[5] The scheme was indeed a success in that it effectively prevented the Jacobite army from circumnavigating the blockading force at Stirling. The resultant delay gave the government time to get messages through to Cope at Inverness and for transports to be sent to Aberdeen from Leith to collect the army. Could Cope's army be brought back by sea before the Jacobite army reached Stirling? Or would it have to land at one of the other ports along the Forth? The people of the town braced themselves for the storm to come.

Grossett was a very able man and was proving to be quite energetic in the Hanoverian cause. He immediately began to gather intelligence concerning the movements of the Jacobite army from Perth and kept track of its remorseless march towards Stirling. His employment at Alloa had given him the contacts amongst traders which proved to be invaluable for this purpose. A network for transmitting reports was quickly established, and relays kept the Lord Justice Clerk in Edinburgh informed. General Blakeney and Colonel Gardiner at Stirling were fitted into this web of information, increasingly aware of the gathering storm that threatened to overwhelm them. Exaggerated reports of the size of the Highland horde were now reaching Stirling directly. Doubtless some of these were the result of deliberate misinformation; propaganda spread by Jacobite sympathizers. Whatever, they made the dragoons feel uneasy and Gardiner grew increasingly tense. The waiting was almost over, but the shadow cast by the still invisible enemy was immense and his men's spirit was breaking. Gardiner was concerned about their willingness to enter into combat and about their declining effectiveness as a fighting force. Many of the rank and file were Irish with little relish for a civil war. Nor were there any longer two complete regiments at Stirling as Hamilton's had been redeployed to Edinburgh to help with its defence. Gardiner sought instructions from Cope and from the Lord Justice Clerk.

The intelligence reaching the Jacobite army suggested that the dragoons would in fact fiercely oppose any attempted crossing of the river Forth[6]. Nevertheless, they made for the Fords of Frew, just over 7 miles upstream from Stirling, where they believed that they could force a passage. There were some knowledgeable sympathizers in that area who could guide them across one of the numerous fords. On 12th September Gardiner wrote to Rev John Adams "The rebels are advancing to cross the Forth; but I trust in the almighty God who doth whatsoever he pleases, in the armies of heaven, and among the inhabitants of the earth".[7]

Early on the 13th September the Highland army duly appeared. The dragoons carefully monitored their approach and prepared themselves. However, the Forth here is full of shallows and fords which the highly mobile lightly armed irregulars of the Highland forces could readily exploit, especially as the river was quite low at that season. Whilst the dragoons kept a watchful eye on various parties of the Highlanders at some of these, the main force of Jacobites crossed successfully elsewhere. Gardiner, unable to further control the situation, withdrew to Stirling.[8] This decision was much criticized. The historian Henderson, with hindsight, stated that Gardiner should have acquired two cannon from the castle which would have been sufficient to cover the crossings.[9] This was not the case, for they would have fallen easy prey under the cover of darkness and Gardiner was right to try to preserve his force intact.

Conscious of his burdensome responsibility for the safety of lowland Scotland, Gardiner now understood that he was too weak to make a stand that would halt the enemy's advance. If he remained at Stirling he ran the risk of either being bypassed, or of being cooped up in the town - unsuitable terrain for cavalry. The dragoons therefore evacuated the King's Park below the castle rock whilst their colonel bid farewell to his wife and daughter whom he desired to remain behind with the castle garrison. As his wife watched the scene below she had a premonition that she would never see her life friend again; but this was war and such insights are not uncommon in these circumstances. Gardiner rode down from the fortress and with his regiment made an orderly withdrawal to Falkirk, encamping for the night at Carmuirs on the south side of the river Carron.[10] Here he was able to keep watch over the bridge at Larbert with the hope perhaps of making a stand. Knowing that the enemy was still a day's march away he was able to make a hurried visit to Falkirk to get Adams to draft a message to Edinburgh requesting urgent assistance. In particular, he wanted the regiment at Edinburgh to advance to join his small force. Together he felt confident that he could face the foe and halt their progress.[11] Without them he was uncertain. His presence spread alarm amongst the people of Falkirk.

Meanwhile, the Jacobites were being very cautious. They could hardly believe their luck in crossing the Forth unopposed.[12] To them it was like the crossing of the Rubicon - now there was no turning back. Their immediate aim was to consolidate their bridgehead and that night the army encamped between Touch and Sauchie.[13] The Prince himself stayed at Touch House whilst the situation was surveyed. Information gathered that night brought news of the retreat of the dragoons and of the consequent weakness of the resolve of the town of Stirling. At this stage in the campaign the town without the castle was of no strategic value to the highland army and it was seen to be necessary to keep the initiative that they had already gained by continuing with their speed of movement.

It had been this very mobility that had so unsettled the opposition thus far. A written demand for money and supplies was therefore all that was required. Another such request was delivered to the city of Glasgow signed by Charles Edward in person. It now seemed evident that this was to be their next destination.

The next morning envoys were sent into Stirling to see if the magistrates there had complied with the demands. The army resumed its march and made a lively showing with colours flying and pipes playing. As they came within the extreme range of the castle's guns a few defiant cannon shots were fired at them. Some of the balls whistled harmlessly over their heads and were answered by loud cheers, but the march continued. By mid-day the army had skirted around Stirling and halted at Bannockburn. Here they were brought the barrels of beer, bread, cheese and other assorted victuals that had been the price that the burgh's magistrates had been willing to pay to avoid direct contact.[14] Charles Edward dined at Bannockburn House.

After a rest of about two hours the Highland army resumed its movements by way of Torwood, passing through Falkirk only two hours after the dragoons had left. Gardiner, it seems, had now received orders to rendezvous with Cope at Edinburgh. There the united force would fight the Jacobites, and in the meantime Gardiner was not to imperil his small force.[15] Gardiner was undoubtedly relieved to have these instructions as he no longer trusted his dragoons to stand and fight on their own. Gone was their bravado of only a week before, their quick retreat before the inexorable advance of the enemy had greatly impressed them with a deep sense of foreboding.

That evening the Jacobite army halted "upon a learge field of Broom on the east side of the Parks of Calendar" adjacent to the highway to Linlithgow.[16] Some, the officers amongst them, were quartered in the town where they made a point of paying for their accommodation. Most of the officers were familiar with the place from earlier visits. The Prince occupied Callendar House [17] where his men were able to profit from the discovery of a "store of arms", of which they were in desperate need.[18] It is noteworthy that these

Callendar House as it would have appeared in 1745. The two wings were rendered and whitewashed.

arms were not voluntarily declared by the household, but were sought out as a result of information received from a butcher in the town, by the name of MacGregor. He reported the existence of the cache to Captain Evan MacGregor who then took forty men to the house to conduct the search. "he got twenty guns and fifteen swords and all very good, and thought ourselves very happie".[19]

Like many of the other Scottish nobles the Earl of Kilmarnock and his wife were not willing to commit themselves to either side at this early stage in the rebellion. They made placating noises to the government and made sure that they were absent when the Jacobites arrived on their doorstep. Anne had travelled to the distant safety of Paisley where she stayed with their Ross family relatives who were strong supporters of the Hanoverian regime. The Earl himself had departed with the dragoons to Linlithgow. Here they had encamped between the bridge over the river Avon and the town; once again choosing to guard a bridgehead where they might still plausibly make a stand.

Kilmarnock seems to have been struck by the fear that was now evident amongst the dragoons and by Gardiner's gloomy analysis of his predicament. Aware of his need to appear neutral until the impasse was broken he decided to return to his home and ensure its safety. Having dined with the colonel at his new camp he therefore left about 6 pm and headed back to Callendar House and an uncertain reception.[20] When he arrived he was introduced to the Prince for the first time and given a polite greeting. Undoubtedly the Prince and his advisors would have attempted to recruit the lowland lord to their cause, offering him the restoration of the Livingston lands as well as financial inducements. Kilmarnock diplomatically indicated his sympathy for the cause, but stopped well short of enlisting.[21] He was, however, able to demonstrate his tacit support by informing the Jacobite command of Gardiner's location and of his determination to hold Linlithgow Bridge. There was indeed no rush of enthusiasm for the Jacobite cause in the district despite Prince Charles' presence and their ranks were not swollen by volunteers. James Graham the younger of Airth, a tall man of medium build and 20 years of age, was a friend of Kilmarnock's eldest son and took this unique opportunity to visit the family. Eager for excitment he met the earl and his wife in the presence of John Vere and hinted at his interest in the adventure but was advised to bide his time.[22]

Walter Grossett had been informed of the crossing of the Forth and immediately perceived that the vessels off the seaports of Bo'ness and Queensferry were at risk. Many of these ships carried cannon, small arms and ammunition for their own protection - just the commodities desperately required by the Jacobite army. He promptly started to have these vessels and their crews removed further down the coast to Leith.[23] Aware that the dragoons still lay between him and the enemy he set about the task methodically with a sense of reasonable security. The priority was to get the ships away, and only then to clear the customs house of weapons that might be seized by a small force.

Later that evening Kilmarnock's information concerning the dragoons was confirmed by other witnesses and a council of war was convened and decided upon a night march of five miles in order to surprise Gardiner. Such nocturnal movements were to become a feature of Jacobite battle manoeuvres. It was considered too risky for Charles Edward to hazard his life at this undertaking and so Lord George Murray was given command of a hand-picked task force.

He chose a 900 strong contingent of the men he personally knew to be the most reliable. This consisted of the best Highlanders; Lochiel's, Keppoch's, Clanranald's, young Glengarry's and Ardshiel's.[24] It was quite dark between 1 and 2 am as they first formed up and then set out heading for a ford on the river Avon

The Storm Clouds Gather

Linlithgow Palace about 1678, from an engraving by Captain John Slezer

half a mile above the bridge. Once across this they would attack the dragoons in the flank at dawn, hopefully taking them unawares. In absolute silence the task force trudged along the high road, guided towards Linlithgow. Their breath hung heavily in the cold air as each man concentrated on holding their column formation in the blackness. They were in the right frame of mind for a fight and at last they would meet the elusive dragoons. Progress was slow, but there was no hurry for it would be another four hours before the first glimmer of daylight appeared. They had been marching for about an hour when they were met on the road by a lone traveller. The river and the cold drenching they expected still lay ahead of them. Then the news was passed back down the line - Gardiner had pulled back yet again.[25] The air of anticipation was dissipated. The Highlanders felt cheated. Gardiner had, in fact, decamped at 7 pm the previous evening, just one hour after Kilmarnock had left him.[26] Perhaps he had foreseen the danger of a night attack from an enemy quartered so close by.

As the first light of day dawned Lord George took possession of the abandoned bridge and then entered the royal burgh of Linlithgow. The town lay besides a small loch, on the bank of which was one of the old Stewart palaces. As Lord George entered its lofty but empty rooms he must have been reminded of the former grandeur of that family and thought it a good omen of things to come. A rider was sent back to Falkirk to apprise Charles Edward of the situation. The town's militia had rapidly and discreetly disbanded upon the withdrawal of the dragoons and the Jacobite task force was able to rest. Parties were organized to search for weapons. It was 10 am before the vanguard of the main army arrived, and noon when the Prince himself appeared. Together they now encamped a mere two miles to the east of Linlithgow. Once again they had crossed a river, and once again the dragoons had fled before them. They had good reason for optimism, but still they exercised extreme caution. Indeed, some of their senior officers, Lord George among them, believed that they were being too wary and were giving the government too much time to react.[27]

It was now Sunday afternoon on 15th September, and the country round about seemed as peaceful as ever. Lord George utilized the momentary break to despatch parties to the neighbouring seaports to search for further arms and ammunition.[28] Bo'ness was the main target, lying only 3 miles to the north with Erngath Hill between them. There was no armed opposition and the Highlanders strolled down the hill to the port with their pipers playing. As they neared they could see that Bo'ness was "a long Town, consisting only of one straggling Street, which is extended along the Shore, close to the Water".[29] There were still a few vessels remaining in the harbour. Grossett had been very busy, toiling through much of the night to clear the anchorage. News of the approach of the Highlanders took him by surprise. He was astonished at the speed of the Jacobite advance from Stirling, though it was now clear that Edinburgh and not Glasgow was their destination. As the advance party of the Jacobites entered the town Grossett's ship left the harbour with his work not fully accomplished.[30] The custom house at the east end of the main street still contained a large number of sword blades and cutlasses, part of a shipment from Germany, which he had not had time to recover. They were immediately seized by the Jacobite force, as was the rest of the building's contents.[31] Other weapons were also discovered: "we got information that a great store of powder and ball was at Burrowstoneness, waiting the enemy; we took as much as we could make use of ".[32]

Many of the town's burghers had fled towards Edinburgh, or else had set sail with Grossett, having first made plans for the security of their belongings. Not a few gardens and yards had

Bo'ness from the south around 1890. Sailing ships can be seen in the harbour.

been dug up to bury all manner of goods to hide them from the marauding highlanders. Even so, many possessions fell into their hands, liberated as taxation in kind to help to pay for the campaign. They also took the opportunity to provide themselves with victuals; taking fowls, meal, milk and butter. Though they offered the consolation that they would bring the townsfolk "a braw new King".

Glasgow too had been in turmoil, believing that the Jacobite army intended to pay them a visit after having issued its threat from Stirling. The confused atmosphere of near hysteria is admirably captured in this letter from Agnes Colquhoun:

AGNES COLQUHOUN, GLASGOW, TO ROBERT COLQUHAIRN, DUNBARTON.Sepr 16, 1745/6.

....our whole ears went a tingling, and each thought they heard the firing of great guns. The imagination was so strong that many persons took horses to goe see the engagement; and the magistrates and most part of the inhabitants went to the High Church yaird and steeples, who, when on the bartizans, thought they heard firing; but to our great surprise an allarm was that they were at the toun head. So all the people came doun the High Street, like mad folks, each making more hideous crys than another, and severall folks left the toun (this was occasioned by some persons clearing the way for an express). We did

16 *Falkirk or Paradise*

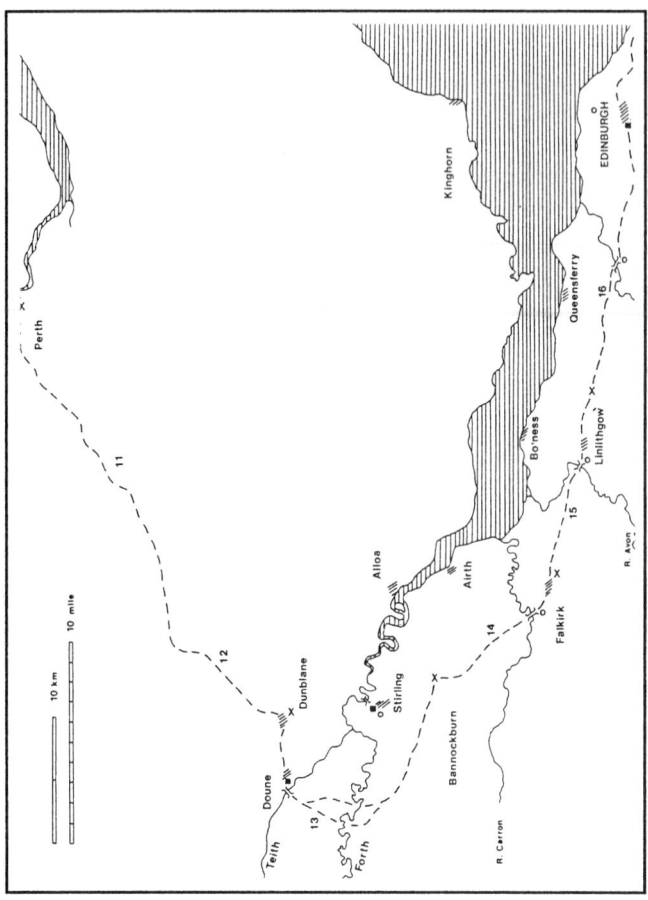

Map showing the march of the Jacobite Army. The numbers refer to the dates in September 1745 with an X marking the night stops. An O denotes Colonel Gardiner's camps.

not settle till about four at night, when some of our gentlemen who went out met the Earll of Kilmarnock, who told them that the Prince lodged in his house all night, and that the army marched for Edinburgh, and that they would encamp at Kirkliston. This day we had expresses that 2000 of the Rebells passed the Freugh, headed by Lord Nairn. They were to ly at Falkirk this night, and were to be succeeded by 2500 more. [33]

Again the size of the Jacobite army was being greatly exaggerated, but no one knew for certain! The Earl of Kilmarnock must have remained at Callendar House just long enough to ensure that the building and its few contents were secure from the ravages of an occupying army. In fact, he had little reason to worry on this account as Charles Edward and his party were trying to woo followers to their cause by courteous behaviour. The Earl had then set off to join his wife by way of Glasgow, bringing with him the fortunate news (for Glasgow) of the Jacobite move towards Edinburgh. The only thing taken from Callendar House that day had been a large heavy gun, some 8 feet long. It was labouriously dragged towards the anticipated siege of Edinburgh by the Clan Gregor.[34]

Throughout the day scouting parties of dragoons kept a watchful eye upon the Jacobite army's activities.[35] Gardiner was now camped at Kirkliston beside the River Almond. Slowly the main action had moved eastward, away from the the Falkirk district. The people there breathed a sigh of relief knowing that they had been fortunate to have had only a fleeting visit. All eyes were now on Edinburgh.

General Cope landed at Dunbar with the Government foot soldiers on 16th September. However, it took almost two days to disembark the troops. These were joined by Gardiner's dragoons who had deserted Edinburgh as they had Stirling before. Their sudden and unexpected departure had all but sealed the fate of that city. Abandoned by the military Edinburgh's civil authorities lost their resolve to fight and a combination of circumstances contrived to give the Jacobites possession of Scotland's capital on 17th September. The swiftness of its capitulation left the city intact and the inhabitants unharmed. It also left the Jacobite army free to manoeuvre against Cope's army.

On 19th September Cope began to advance on Edinburgh in the hope that Charles Edward would issue from its defensive walls to meet him. That night the government army lay at Haddington. The next day they resumed their march, intending to reach Musselburgh. They had only ventured as far as the small village of Prestonpans when their scouts brought news that the Jacobite army had unpredictably crossed the River Esk and were heading towards them. A little surprised by this turn of events Cope perceived that the flat ground around the village was eminently suited to his army's fighting needs. The Forth Estuary lay to his back preventing any flanking movements. He therefore decided to wait for the enemy there. Lord George Murray's priority was to obtain the high ground above the government army and this he quickly achieved by a rapid advance. Both armies had marched about eight miles that day and a little after noon faced each other across an intervening marsh. As the Jacobite army manoeuvred for position their moves were countered in turn by Cope, so that as dusk descended neither side had gained a definite advantage. Despite this Cope's men lost some of their former confidence. They had acted in a defensive manner all afternoon and had clearly lost the initiative. Even their partial success in driving some of Lochiel's men out of the nearby church by shooting at them with their artillery was overshadowed by the Jacobites own use of artillery which they had been led to believe was not possible. The large gun from Callendar House had been brought up late in the evening and Captain Evan MacGregor was given the privilege of the first shot; Duncan MacGregor the second; and Gregor MacGregor the third. The Jacobites were elated at the results, the government troops further disheartened.[36]

Few of the government soldiers got much rest that night. Colonel James Gardiner had time to reflect upon his hasty retreat from Stirling which he termed "a foul flight". In contemplative discussion with one of his friends he said that the dragoons "have not recovered from their panic; and I'll tell you in confidence that I have not above ten men in my regiment whom I am certain will follow me".[37] He was right, for the following day as the morning mist began to lift the Highlanders charged the front line of Cope's army from close in, and the dragoons fled in the ensuing onslaught. The cover of night and mist had allowed the Jacobites to approach to within a short distance without being subjected to fire. Once in amongst the enemy they were able to use their broadswords very effectively, inflicting heavy casualties in a matter of minutes. Gardiner did not follow the example of his men. He stayed to support the beleaguered infantry and was hacked to pieces. His second in command, Colonel Whitney, remained with him and was shot in the arm before he managed to escape. The battle, it is said, lasted for only four minutes!

CHAPTER 2

The Eye of the Storm
22nd September - 25th December 1745

After the success of Prestonpans which did so much to raise the spirits of the closet Jacobite supporters, the government was in considerable disarray. The Scottish whigs kept their heads down and former volunteers sought refuge with their country relatives. The Jacobites now had control of central Scotland, except for the two important fortresses at Stirling and Edinburgh. These were insignificant thorns at this stage in the campaign for such strongholds could be easily by-passed in a war that was to rely upon mobility. However, there was now a pause while the Jacobites considered their next move. The time was spent consolidating what had already been achieved and in increasing support for the cause ready for the inevitable next step. The two main areas of activity were thus the raising of money, and the raising of new recruits.

Much money came from the imposition of a levy on the towns, particularly those like Glasgow and Bo'ness with their Hanoverian sympathies. These taxes were exacted under considerable duress as few saw Prince Charles and his council as the legitimate government of their country. Further financial gain came about by the seizure of all the goods which had been impounded in the customhouses of Leith and Bo'ness. These articles were then sold back to the very smugglers from whom they had been confiscated.[1] A wide range of goods were smuggled on the Forth in the eighteenth century as is illustrated by the following long list:

> aniseed; cassia; pepper; aqua vitae; brandy; cordial waters; gin; rum; wine; vinegar; butter; chocolate; currants; figs; liquorice; prunes; raisins; sugar; cambric; damasks; handkerchiefs; lace; linen; muslin; silks; china; coal; combs; feathers; gunpowder; paper; pearl ashes; playing cards; salt; soap; starch; train oil; wool; coffee; tea; snuff; tobacco.[2]

Aid, both pecuniary and military, was also sought from France to augment the little already given. Glowing reports of the Highlanders' fighting skills were sent to the French court in the hope of persuading them of the great potential there was of a successful outcome to the entire venture. More immediately, the victory at Prestonpans did bring some wavering Scots over to the cause. More were needed. On the 24th September Alexander Macleod of Muiravonside, a cousin of young Clanranald, was despatched as a messenger to the Isle of Skye to enlist the help of Sir Alexander Macdonald and the Laird of Macleod. In this he was not successful. He then went on to Castle Downie where he had more joy in negotiation with the undecided Lord Lovat. It was agreed that Lovat's son should raise the Fraser clan for Charles.[3]

As the Highland clans slowly mustered they each made their way to Edinburgh. Perth became a rallying point for many and a regular stop on the route for the rest. From here they proceeded to the Forth at Alloa. The castle at Stirling was still held by government troops which could sally out whenever they chose to maul the small bodies of men now on the move and so the eastern route was the safest. It also saved the long trek around Stirling by the Fords of Frew along poor roads. Small boats took the rebels to the south shore at Airth or Higgins' Neuck, and the ferries were kept busy. A handful of sympathisers helped with this operation. John Simpson, a brewer and maltster in Falkirk, was described as "Very active in procuring boats for the rebels to pass to the Forth". In this he was aided by another man of the same trade, William Baad of Letham, who "Assisted the rebels as a guide, carried their arms & secured boats for them to pass the Forth".[4]

The road from Airth through Falkirk and Linlithgow to Edinburgh was under Jacobite control and the bold men from the north trickled down it on their way to the main army at Dalkeith. On 3rd October Lord Ogilvy with 600 men arrived at Edinburgh; Gordon of Glenbucket and 400 more arrived there shortly afterwards; Lord Pitsligo on the 9th and Lord Lewis Gordon on the 16th.[5] Further support eventually swelled the Jacobite army to over 5,000. On their way to Edinburgh these forces actively sought out further recruits by various means, as is attested by the people involved:

> John Scott, aged 10 years from the parish of Logganrat, Perth - "sometime after ye Battle of Preston Pans as he was driving ye plough Allan

Stewart Major to Col. Roy Stewarts Regt came into ye ffield with his Company & took ye Examt away & three of ye Horses out of ye plough & made ye Examt drive a Baggage Cart to Falkirk where he joined ye rest of Col Roy Stewarts Regt & Marched them altogether to Edinburgh''

Robert Adam of Kilsyth parish - "about a fortnight after ye Battle of Preston Pans last Peter Stewart of Col Roy Stewarts Regt come to his mod. House with sevl of his men & pressed one of his mstrs Horses & carried him to Falkirk & promised to send him back again, & the Exam's master sent him to fetch back ye Horse & he went with yr horse which was loaded with Baggages to Falkirk & when here at them he desired yt Capt Stewart to let him have yr horse back again but he was told he shd have it at ye next Town & so on ..."

Ellen Primerrow, wife of John McKenzie, Falkirk - "at ye last Harvest when the Rebels were at Edinburgh she & her Husband were at Work in a ffield near Falkirk when some of Glengarrie's Men came into yr fields & took her Husband away with them to Edinburgh ..."

James Begg, Falkirk - "on Saturday before Martinmass Day last he was going between Dalkeith & Edinburgh when he was met by some Highlanders who drew their Swords & Swore he shd go with them ..."

Adam Southerland, Sutherland, on his way to Falkirk Tryst - "sometime after ye Battle of Prestonpans he was going with his sd mstr assisting him in driving Cattle into ye Low Country to sell them between Falkirk & Linlithgow he was stopt by Capt McKenzie of Lochgarie's Regt & a party of his men & asked to go with them which he refusing they drew their Dirks ...".[6]

Lord Lewis Gordon represented his brother, the Duke of Gordon, who was keeping out of the affair personally. By doing so he knew that if anything should go wrong with the venture then the family, having seemed to have backed both sides, would not come unstuck. This had been the same ploy as that used by the devious Lord Lovat when he had sent his son to Charles Edward and a letter of support to the Lord President, Duncan Forbes. Indeed, this cautious posture was commonly adopted. In cases where the head of a family and proprietor of an estate went out he would previously make over his property to his eldest son, who remained at home in possession. When the father, on the contrary, was averse to active partisanship, a son went out, along with all the resources both in men and money which the house could contribute. He thus ensured that, although the youth might fall or be attainted, he still had brothers to inherit the patrimonial property for the family.

James Lord Boyd, the eldest son of the Earl of Kilmarnock, already had a commission as subaltern with the Scots Fusiliers. Another son, William, likewise served with Commodore Barnet in the King's navy. So, it may have been to preserve the political balance that Charles, the third son at the tender age of 17 years, joined the rebels on 12th October.[7] He soon found a place in Lord Balmerino's Horse Guards.[8] The Earl himself was on the edge of a crucial decision.

Already in his fortieth year, Lord Kilmarnock had all the appearance and bearing of a classical hero. His tall and slender frame was carried with great grace and he always appeared well groomed. His manners were pleasant and his actions and conversation possessed a quiet dignity combined with wit and intelligence. Behind him were many years of toil which had long since curbed the exuberance of youth. He had been only twelve when his father's death gave him added responsibilities, and his mother's obsessive gambling had caused him further problems. Nevertheless, he had graduated from Glasgow University and married well. His own family were growing up and two of his sons already had settled futures. His confidence made him popular with those whom he met. "I never heard so great an orator as Lord Kilmarnock" Lord Leicester is said to have exclaimed. A point confirmed by Horace Walpole.[9]

During the meeting with Charles Edward at Callendar House on the 14th September the Earl had given him his tacit support. This was natural enough, after all the house and estate were occupied at the time by an army of highlanders. However, he had stopped well short of actively pursuing the venture, thus leaving his options open. As a sign of his goodwill he had aided the Jacobite cause by reporting Colonel Gardiner's dispositions at Linlithgow Bridge, but these would have been discovered anyway, and he could always claim coercion should any charge be levelled against him. He does not appear, however, to have voluntarily surrendered the store of arms hidden in Callendar House noted earlier.

The Eye of the Storm 23

William Boyd
Earl of Kilmarnock
(1721-1746)

Anne Livingston
Lady Kilmarnock
(1709-1747)

As Charles Edward and the Highlanders moved eastward, Lord Kilmarnock heard news of the fall of Edinburgh, soon followed by the Jacobite victory over the only government army in Scotland. He was reminded of Colonel Gardiner's gloomy predictions and of the sparse disposition of Hanoverian troops in England. Could Gardiner have been right? One quick bold thrust by the Jacobites might catch the Hanoverian establishment off guard. Would England now rise for the Prince?

All these questions were on his mind as from the windows of Callendar House he watched the processions of reinforcements heading east to augment the already victorious Jacobite army. Even from a distance he felt some of their zeal for the crusade ahead. Some of the officers probably paid him a visit on their travels. He knew many of them personally as they moved in the same social circles. Some were episcopalians like his wife, and others, such as Lords Elcho and Ogilvy were members of the King's bodyguard, the honourable Royal Company of Archers, of which he was an officer.[10] The house was a convenient stopping place and the opportunity of strengthening the commitment of this Lowland laird was not to be missed. Lord Kilmarnock epitomised the well educated Lowlander, and if he were persuaded others might join.

Lord Kilmarnock also seems to have come into the acquaintance of Andrew Alves, a staunch Jacobite who had influenced the surrender of Edinburgh on 16th September.[11] There must have been much lively discussion between these two men. Some of this would have focused around the Earl's dire financial situation. According to Horace Walpole son of the former Prime Minister, "Lord Kilmarnock is a Presbyterian, with four earldoms in him, but so poor since Lord Wilmington's stopping a pension that my father had given him, that he often wanted a dinner".[12] The pension had been awarded for his family's aid to the government in the 1715 uprising. Letters to the authorities had failed to elicit help and he must have been tired of empty promises and failed intentions. Perhaps if he threw his lot in with Charles Edward he might have a chance of securing the earldoms of Callendar and Linlithgow which his father-in-law had forfeited in 1715.

During this period he was isolated from the counsel of his wife or his relatives in the west. His main contact was with the Jacobites who seemed to move about the country as freely as they wished. They also paid him many compliments and did him the honour of taking him into their confidence. By 15th October he was writing to his wife well aware of the advance dispositions of a good part of their army.[13]

Dearest Nanny

Since you still seem not to understand me in what you are so good as to be very anxious about, I must tell you That it is as it ought to be and that it will probably continue as it is till it is proper it should be otherwise: and in the mean time you need be in no pain about it. I hope, with a little Recollection, this will let in to the Truth and make you easy.

It gives me the greatest Pain to hear that my Dearest Life and Love is not well. Let me beg of you, my Heart's Delight, not to indulge your self in Meloncholy. God, who orders every thing as it ought to be, must be trusted in, and he will bring every thing about for the best. Let us pray to him, thank him, and resign our selves to his Will. Let me beg of you to go abroad often: you know that is your only and never failing Medicine; and if you love me, you will take it.

The Sermon in the Churches in Edr last Sunday is no more than a morning Exercise in the Trone Kirk.

The Arms Ammunition and money are expected this way tomorrow with a Guard and the rest of 1200 Men.

A Gentleman from Dundee this Day brings Account that Nine ships were seen coming in to the Harbour of Montrose Yesterday and nine more at some Distance steering that way.

May the Almighty Power Preserve protect and help my Dearest only Life and Love.

Octr 15th 1745   Lord Kilmarnock [14]

The same letter saw him preparing the ground with Anne. Then, on 18th October he revealed his intentions and informed her "that I am now in my Boots to join the Prince". His decision was already known to the Jacobites and he had been able to secure safe passage for his family within the Jacobite held territory.[15]

Dearest Nanny.

I am very sencible of the Pain the first sight of this Letter must give to her it is most my Duty to make Happy and my greatest Enjoyment is to please. I need not after this tell my Love and Life that I am now in my Boots to join the Prince, and have prevailed with Alves, in spite of business he has in Town on Saturday, to wait on you hither

Believe me my Dearest Angel, there was an absolute necessity for this step, and, if matters dont turn out against all Manner of Probabilitys, and almost against Probabilitys, it is the wisest and most lucky one, for my Dearest Nanny, I ever made in my Life, as I shall satisfy you fully when I am again blest with my dearest Girl, which will be in a few Days, for I shall be here again Monday or Teusday. It is now both proper and necessary for you to be here. Alves will come along with you and you'll get the Loan of Lord Rose's horses all the Length. I would have sent your own with a neighbour's help to meet you half way, but I could get no Coachman, I could trust, to drive you; and the inclosed & Protection in John Lowries Pocket will secure the horses here and back again. Receive eight guineas from Alves, which will defray the first Brush, and next week there shall be no want of money, beside that the house and Parks are fully provided in every thing you can have for use and in case I dont come out Saturday, Jim Lieshman has the key of the Wine Cellar. Now my Dearest Nanny, allow me for once to lay the Commands of a Husband on you, for the first time in my Life, to be home on Saturday. It is quite necessary for both our Good, and as you know the anxiety I have for every thing that concerns you, let nothing hinder your being here tomorrow. I shall say nothing of the Cause I am going in but that every Scots man in his senses will go the same way, and there are no graven Images concerned in it. Make my most affectionate and dutifull Compliments to good Lord Rose my Lady and my Cousins. I hope soon to have it in my power to do him material Service. All I can now is to apply for a Protection for all his houses horses and Estates, which I'll do as soon as I am able. May the Almighty Power protect preserve and bless my Dearest Dearest only Love and Life

Calender Octr 18th 1745 [16]

Lord Kilmarnock's letters indicate that Anne was not fully behind his decision. She was a staunch protestant and had done much to promote the episcopalian cause.[17] Her ideals had brought her into conflict with the presbyterian church and she was worried that her hard won gains in this area would be lost by her husband's active support of a catholic monarch. Even if he were successful what did this catholic outsider offer the episcopalians? Kilmarnock reassured her that the sermons being preached in the Tron Kirk were "no more than a morning Exercise". Later on he explained to her that "there was an absolute necessity for this step ... as I shall satisfy you fully", adding "I shall say nothing of the Cause I am going in but that every Scots man in his senses will go the same way, and there are no graven Images concerned in it".

Anne was not keeping good health when she found herself in this dilemma. Was her husband about to go down the same road as her late father and would it lead the same way? She had not been at Callendar House during Prince Charles's sojourn there, but she is said to have met him in Edinburgh early in October.[18] This would also have been the occasion upon which she heard those scornful sermons in the Tron Kirk. From Edinburgh she went straight to Paisley to stay with the Ross family once again.

Perhaps she felt safer away from the Jacobite influences. It was whilst she was away that Lord Kilmarnock made his fateful decision. Whether she had any sympathy with the Jacobite cause or not, it is clear that she did not want her beloved spouse to participate actively in the present hazardous adventure.

Anne returned to Callendar House on 20th October, too late to persuade her husband to be more cautious.[19]

TO THE RIGHT HONOURABLE THE COUNTESS OF LINLITHGOW AND KILMARNOCK AT CALENDER

I am so hurryed that I have hardly time to welcome my dearest Nanny home and to tell you I am in very good health. I'll be blest with my Love and Life teusday Night, May Heavens protect my heart's Delight

Edr Octr 20th 1745. [LORD KILMARNOCK][20]

That very day Lord Kilmarnock sealed his fate by attending Charles Edward at Holyrood. He was then given a commission to raise a troop of Horse Grenadiers.[21]

There was now no turning back, though evidently Anne persisted in her views. According to Lord Kilmarnock "tho' she was bred in different sentiments ... he thought her now more inclined to whiggish than jacobite principles ... instead of exciting him to, she had dissuaded him from entering into the ... rebellion".[22] So why did he engage in the rebellion? It was, as he readily admitted, "in Opposition to my own Principles, and to those of my Family, in Contradiction to the whole Tenor of my Conduct".[23] He later declared (though one may question his reasons for so doing) that his motives could be attributed to the great and pressing difficulties into which he had brought himself by extravagance and dissipation. The "exigency of his affairs was in particular very pressing at the time of the rebellion; and that, besides the general hope he had of mending his fortune by the success of it, he was also tempted by another prospect of retrieving his circumstances, if he follow'd the pretender's standard".[24]

Fully committed, Lord Kilmarnock set about raising his regiment. As the muster point was at Edinburgh he went first to his estates in Kilmarnock and then to those at Falkirk. At Kilmarnock his attempts at recruitment met with dismal failure. Only his elderly coal grieve, Charles Sheddon, joined up. He was 63 years of age, and was told by Lord Kilmarnock that he would "only take care of his Baggage Waggon".[25] Most of the inhabitants wanted nothing to do with the foolish exercise and some even suggested that if they were to take up arms it would be against him.[26]

At Falkirk he fared little better. The abortive attempt in 1715 when Anne's father, James Livingston, had led 300 tenants out in support of the Prince's father, James Stewart, had dampened their ardour. Since then the feudal ties had been loosened and the Livingston family no longer owned the land. Whilst the Earl of Kilmarnock had been active in promoting trade in the burgh town he was still regarded as an outsider by many. He owed money to most of the town's tradesmen and his financial problems were so notorious that many must have questioned his motives on this occasion. Perhaps the more realistic approach had come from Anne who would have foreseen these problems. Lord Kilmarnock expressed the circumstances himself: "I am not one of those dangerous Persons, who can raise a Number of Men when they will, and command them on any Enterprize they please: My Interests lie on the South side of Forth, in the well inhabited and well affected Counties of Kilmarnock and Falkirk ... These Places are so well affected (and, perhaps, partly thro' my Means) that any Influence I, or any other, could have on them to the contrary, would be very small ... at Falkirk, I did not raise a single Man."[27]

Despite this claim he was able to secure the services of a handful of people from the Falkirk area. His own household still had close bonds of duty to him and from them came George Boyd, "Servant of Lord Kilmarnock for many years" at Callendar House; William McCulloch, another servant at the House; David Davert, the gardener there; and William Wyce, another gardener. William Baird, "coal hewer to Kilmarnock" at Falkirk also joined up and became one of his three sergeants. On the other hand, John Denothy of Callendar House, the French wig-maker and servant to Charles Boyd, the son of Lord Kilmarnock, joined the French Service because of his nationality. The quartermaster of Kilmarnock's troop was from Linlithgow Bridge, where he had been an innkeeper - suitable training. From Bo'ness came James Semple, a humble weaver. The youngest recruit was John Auld of Falkirk. A boy of only 14 years of age "he acted as a drummer to Kilmarnock's Horse, but was forced thereto by his stepfather".[28] Kilmarnock's Horse was not a significant force, numbering about 30 in all.[29]

So poor was the response in Falkirk that Lord Kilmarnock even approached some of the dragoons that had been captured at Prestonpans and were then being held in Edinburgh. He offered the simple choice, service with his regiment or a lengthy detention in the Highlands. Robert Proctor of Hamilton's Dragoons joined up, but he was the only one.[30] Lord Kilmarnock had only joined the Jacobites at a late stage and it had been the last week in October before he started to muster his regiment. By then the few adventurous souls from Falkirk who had been willing to perform the role of cavalrymen had already joined the other units as they had passed through. The Life Guards were the most popular with their blue coats with red facings. James Graham, the rather rash son of the advocate of that name who owned Airth Castle estate, was one of the first to show enthusiasm and join them. Their household servant, James Gardner, went along to keep an eye on him. John Aitkenhead, younger of Jaw near Slamannan also joined the regiment; as did Alexander Dalmahoy, son to Sir Alexander Dalmohoy of Thirleston near Bo'ness with his gardener William Donaldson from nearby Grangepans; James Ogston, a weaver neighbour in Grangepans, carried arms in the Life Guards; from Bo'ness was Thomas Glassford, the son of a ship master; returning to Falkirk there was Andrew Porteous of Burnfoot who served in Balmerino's troop alongside Lord Kilmarnock's son; and last on this list of local men was the Falkirk postmaster with the evocative name of James Livingston.

All these men were provided with horses from their parental estates. Not for them the hazards of fighting on foot along with the clans. They were lowlanders, and even the servants did not mix easily with the men from the north. With the high spirits and optimism of the moment this seemed to matter little and most of the new recruits adopted the highland dress by wearing tartan along with a blue bonnet bearing a white cockade. Cavalry provided useful services for the Jacobite army, acting as scouts and messengers, and providing an essential screen during the march. Another important skill was provided by Walter Graham, surgeon in Falkirk. His father of the same name had been the town's surgeon and had prospered enough to buy an old property on the High Street nearly opposite to the Steeple. On his death his son inherited not only the building, but also his Jacobite principles. The Old Lodging, as the building was known, was left in his mother's hands whilst young Walter followed his calling with the Jacobite army.

So, although Lord Kilmarnock personally brought few men with him there were a small number from the area in the army as a whole. More important was the kudos of Lord Kilmarnock's name. It was felt that his defection was significant because he was a well known and learned lowland lord able to persuade others in the south of Scotland and in England to follow his example. No longer was it merely a highland rising. Kilmarnock's house continued to be used as the local headquarters. His son, Charles, and James Livingston were temporarily quartered there with the Life Guards. When these two were patrolling at Kersie near to Airth, they came across Thomas Christie whom they recognized as the Deputy Collector of cess for Stirlingshire. He was seized straight away and carried to Callendar House as a prisoner. His knowledge of the local tax system would be useful to the Jacobites as they tried to raise more money.[31]

Between the 7th and the 19th October four French ships had managed to pass by the patrolling fleet of the British government and landed at Montrose and Stonehaven. They brought money, artillery, ammunition and stores with which to sustain the rebellion. The first of these ships also carried the Marquis D'Eguilles, who became known as the French ambassador. He must have passed quickly through Falkirk, for within a week he was at Edinburgh. The artillery had to make a much slower and more arduous progress. On 15th October Lord Kilmarnock knew that "The Arms Ammunition and money are expected this way tomorrow with a Guard and the rest of 1200 Men".[32] Perhaps it was this which made him say "next week there shall be no want of money".[33] The artillery was escorted by the Athollmen and Cluny Macpherson's clan.[34] A small Jacobite garrison was left at Alloa and Airth to receive them and to assist the crossing of the Forth. On the 23rd October Lord George Murray was at Alloa to check on progress and found the guard there much alarmed at the reports reaching them of government ships off Bo'ness.[35]

LORD GEORGE MURRAY TO THE DUKE OF ATHOLL

Alloa, 23 Octr 1745.

Dr Brother,

We came very well here this evening, and found our partys much upon their guard, and alarm'd. I have seen Gentlemen who can be depended upon, who observ'd the Happy Janet, with two Kinghorn boats they had man'd, come up the lenth of Borostuness, with an intent to disturb this passage. ... send up the Swedish Cannon & Guners with an Escort & amunition, for otherways our Friends may be afronted here.

He therefore sent Colonel Kerr to the port to secure the river passage and to conduct the artillery on to Edinburgh.[36] Kerr was a very competent and experienced soldier; by the 26th he had prepared batteries on either side of the Forth and requested that the lighter guns be sent on ahead of the convoy so that they could be mounted on them.[37]

COLONEL KERR TO THE DUKE OF ATHOLL

Alloway, ye 26th Octr, 1745.

As Lord George is not to return to this place, his Royal Highness sent me here in order to secure the passage here for your Grace's passing , ... if the Cannon could be forwards, in order to place on the batteries, prepaird for secureing the passage which is of the utmost importance, wou'd be of great service ...

P.S.: It's hop'd that your Grace will let me know from time to time your Grace's motions, that Carriages may be ready on the other side of the water, who waits for nothing but the hour of your Grace's arivel.

Coll: Kerr, at Elphinston

THE DUKE OF ATHOLL TO COLONEL KERR.

I hope to be up time enough to morrow at Aloa, so that the convoy may be able to pass the river before night; therefore.... be so good as to have boats, carriages, and every thing ready for marching forward.

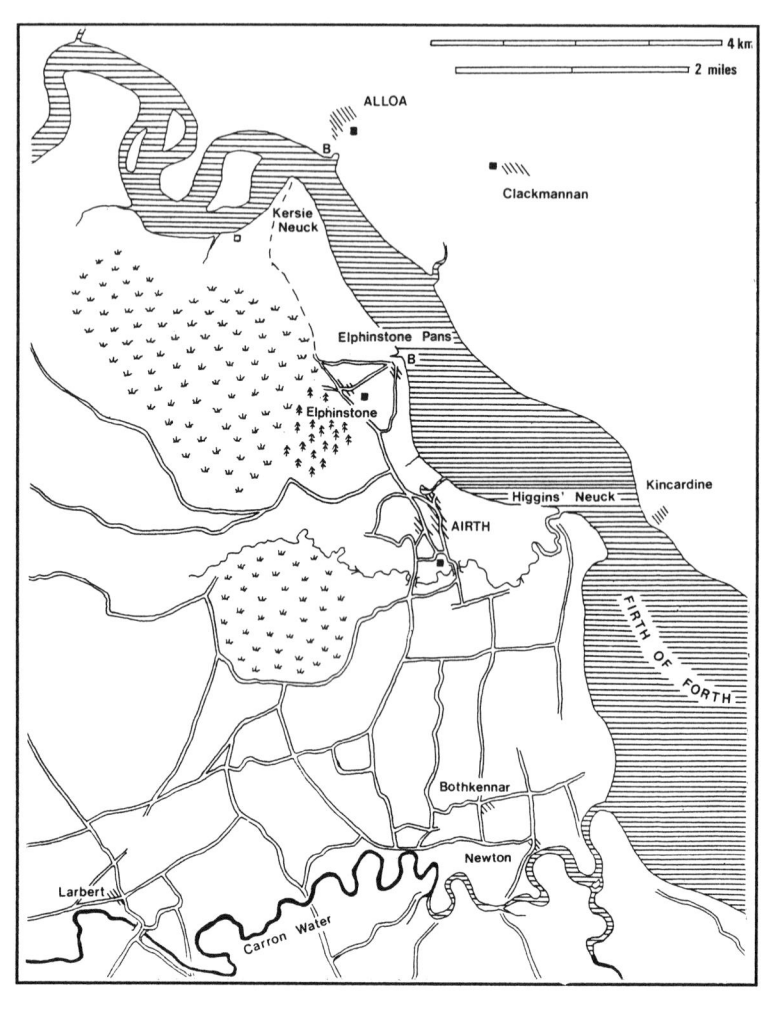

Map showing the middle reaches of the River Forth.
Large areas of marsh lay to the west of Airth

Six cannon were then placed on the battery on the quayside at Alloa[38], and four or five taken across the water to the Higgins' Neuck battery.[39] The Alloa guns were commanded by Colonel Richard Warren, an Irishman, who prepared furnaces in which to heat the cannonball before use so that they would set the ships on fire on hitting them.[40]

The government ships with the 'Happy Janet' at their head proceeded up the river and made several attempts to dislodge the rebel guns. In this they failed and were forced back. Shortly afterwards the supply convoy was successfully transported to the south bank of the Forth landing at the established crossing points of Elphinstone Pans, Airth, Carsie Nook and Higgins' Neuck. The one hundred or so carts and wagons then converged on the small town of Airth where they were reunited with the artillery and proceeded on to Falkirk.[41]

The swollen Jacobite army had been gathering around Edinburgh impatiently waiting for the next move in the campaign. If they were to head into England, as some thought they should, the supplies now at Falkirk were essential to them. About eighty-five carts were commandeered and dispatched from Edinburgh to meet the convoy at Falkirk, presumably with the intention of transferring some of the stores to them so that they could share the burden and hence hasten the journey. On their outward leg from Edinburgh they carried part of the army's sick and wounded who were to be transported northwards to their homes. The government supporters were uncertain about the meaning of what they saw. Was the apparent movement of the Jacobite baggage to Falkirk a sign of a retreat, or was it merely a feint?[42]

They knew that something momentous was about to happen. The Edinburgh carts probably arrived at Falkirk on the 29th October. Amongst the items that they collected were some newly made ramrods. James Whyte, a joiner in the town, had been making his way home with his bag of tools after the end of a hard day's work the previous Saturday. Before he reached it, however, his tools betrayed his trade and he was seized by two armed men and taken into Bailie Watt's Red Lion Inn in the High Street. Here he was ordered by an officer to immediately make ramrods to the number of one hundred and thirty two as the regiment would be moving on as soon as possible. This was a tall order to undertake at such a late hour, and, remembering how strict the Secession Church authorities were regarding the observance of the Sabbath and that the next day he would be performing his duties as "Uptaker o' the Psalm" there, he informed the Highlanders that he could not undertake the work that night as there was insufficient time. No doubt he also had at the back of his mind the great opposition which his church had made to the Jacobite cause, but this he did not mention. Whyte, apprehending the precariousness of his predicament, then offered to take the highlanders to some other joiners whom they might employ in his stead. This did little to satisfy them and he was told that he "Behoved" to go himself. There were mutterings about Whyte's life and those of his family, as well as of setting Falkirk to the torch. The threats were not needed, already fearful of the consequences Whyte went and employed James Warden and John Moir to share the burden of the work. Whyte completed his allocation about 2 o'clock on the sabbath morning, and four hours later the three joiners went to the highland camp and delivered the hurriedly manufactured ramrods. For James Warden and James Whyte, however, the relief of being rid of the Jacobites was muted by the censure of the church that they knew that they could look forward to from the minister and the kirk session.[43]

Lord Kilmarnock knew that the army was poised for the advance. He swiftly seized horses from the district around Falkirk for his troop of Grenadiers and collected the taxes from the town.[44] He would then have escorted the convoy to Dalkeith where he arrived on 31st. The Life Guards left at the same time, taking prisoners on their way to serve in their army.[45] They were just in time to march south the next day. Their destination was London, the seat of government.

The Jacobites left behind them small garrisons at strategic locations in order to secure their supply route. Money and new recruits would be needed in England, whereas food would be obtained on the ground. The batteries at Airth and Alloa, which secured the important crossing of the Forth and prevented government ships from reaching Stirling, each retained a detachment. "they boast of a battery of cannon on each side the Forth, at Alloa, by which their convenient passage is secured" wrote a government supporter.[46] However, the ships stationed at Bo'ness were not disheartened by their earlier failure and returned once again to their task. In the first days of November the Alloa battery was devastated and the Jacobite control of the crossing terminated.[47] Emboldened by this success the garrison at Stirling Castle made several sorties. On the 5th November one party sallied from the castle killing two highlanders and taking fifteen prisoners.[48]

This was a good omen for the government and its supporters whose confidence and fortunes in central Scotland were now improving daily since the departure of the Jacobite army. By 13th November Edinburgh was back in government hands. The following day the remnants of Hamilton's and Gardiner's dragoons together with Price's and Ligonier's regiments of foot entered the city. The foot regiments had been reduced by illness but could still provide some 900 fighting men.[49] The Jacobites meanwhile were actively recruiting in the north and slowly a second army was emerging. The government lost no time in deciding their strategic response to this situation. They were to reimpose the blockade of the Forth and keep the two Jacobite armies apart.[50] The cavalry were immediately ordered back to Stirling where they had been waiting only two months before. Provost Cochrane of Glasgow was aware of the developing circumstances and offered to supply 1,000 men for militia service at Stirling. These were to be paid for by the city of Glasgow for a two month period. All he requested in return was the provision of arms from Edinburgh Castle for the volunteers. This was soon granted as it was considered that "The arms will be usefull to keep off straggling partys, who may return after a defeat, and who may be too small to deserve the marching of troops from this, and yet may be troublesome if you have no arms. As for those who are beyond the Forth, the troops here certainly overawe them and they will not think of crossing the Forth".[51] One thousand stands of arms were sent under an escort of 100 dragoons.

Within two weeks of making the offer the Glasgow Militia was on the road to Stirling. There was no shortage now of willing help and the regiment consisted of 500 Glaswegians and 160 volunteers from Paisley. The men were of varying calibre with people from all walks of life, including William Cross a professor of law who was made a junior officer. Field command was given to the Earls of Home and Glencairn. By 1st December they were billeted at Stirling.[52]

Finding support from amongst the inhabitants, the government had little trouble in gaining control of the territory up to Stirling. They soon set about the routine of mounting patrols along the southern shore of the Forth to intercept the rebels.[53] Price's and Ligonier's infantry joined the task. Whilst Ligonier's Dragoons (formerly Gardiner's) moved to Stirling on Sunday the 2nd December [54], a large detachment of Hamilton's Dragoons was stationed at Kinneil. This was at a useful distance from Stirling and Edinburgh. Just as importantly, fodder was now becoming scarce as the winter drew in and the parks at Kinneil provided useful grazing. Whilst their horses were secure in the estate's enclosures the dragoons took over the old church building next to the house. This had long since ceased being the parish church and now functioned as little more than a private chapel for the Hamilton family when they were in residence. To ameliorate the coldness of the season some of the old pews were broken up and burnt.[55] However, there were still some dissidents in the area who knew the parks better than the dragoons. James Ancrum, the Duke of Hamilton's own salt overseer from Bonhard Pans stole two of their horses from under their very noses for his own use. In this he was assisted by Alexander Dalmohoy of Thirleston and James Ogston of Grange Pans.[56]

Life at Falkirk had all but returned to normal. The bad weather was coming and the nights began to draw in, so on 25th November work on the new manse had halted for the winter. The timber and slates already procured for the task were stored in the church where Adams resumed preaching against the catholic invaders.[57] The situation was so quiet at Airth that on 4th December James Graham

The ruined Kinneil Kirk with the House behind.
It had been the parish church until 1649.

of Airth Castle, a senior advocate in the Scottish justiciary, invited the Lord Justice Clerk to "pass two or three days here where is not a Soul but my own family".[58]

Dr Hugh,

> Inter arma filent Leges; and therefore I am much of your Opinion of Staying here till matters shall turn to a more settled State. If business is rightly carried on for the support of the Government and good of the Lieges, it is of no consequence who does it; In the mean time I cannot be blamed, who have never been desired or acquainted to concur in any Measure, altho' I told my Ld Advocate before he went off that I was ready in my Station to do what Service should be requisite: Now indeed I can blame no body considering the wretched Step my Son has taken, and that as Charity now runs very low, this would be imputed to Me, altho' I knew no more of it than the Child unborn; However I must endure these misfortunes the best way I can, and to this end it would much contribute, if you would be so good as to pass two or three days here where there is not a Soul but my own family ...
>
> yours affectionately

Airth Decr 4th 1745   JAMES GRAHAM [59]

However, with his own son and servant on active duty in Balmerino's Troop of the Jacobite Army, he too was suspected of complicity. His absence from Edinburgh throughout the troubles did little to dissipate these doubts concerning his loyalty.

Soon afterwards the government command in the area received news that the remnants of Prince Charles' army was on its way back to Scotland from Derby which it had left on 6th December. A simple mopping up process would be required but in the meantime it was more essential than ever to stop any communication whatsoever between the two Jacobite armies. On the 8th orders were issued to remove all the boats, of whatever type, from the northern coast of the Forth between Stirling and St Andrews and to secure them at Bo'ness and Queensferry. Naval vessels and crews were used to take the boats forcibly and to destroy those they could not move. This was an impossible task as the Jacobites held much of this coastline.[60] On the 9th December Ligonier's foot was sent to Stirling to strengthen the town's garrison.

The northern Jacobite army was now quite sizeable, consisting of over 5,000 men. Lord John Drummond had just arrived from France with regular troops and extra supplies, including some large artillery pieces and a French engineer which would enable them to lay siege to any town or fortress which resisted. The strategic stronghold of Stirling was an obvious target for the use of this equipment as it would effectively achieve the main priority of uniting the two armies. Yet, Drummond was not prepared to commit his forces to a protracted encounter of this nature at this stage, nor did he want the responsibility of such independent action. Instead, as a professional soldier, he set about establishing the rules of engagement. Firstly he wanted to set up a mechanism for the exchange of prisoners with the government; and secondly, just as important, he was able to neutralize a force of almost 2,000 Dutchmen that the government was sending to Scotland, because an international agreement dictated that these soldiers were not to fight against France or her allies - which he now represented. All this took time, and his messenger or 'drum' was escorted through Stirling and Falkirk to Edinburgh by eight dragoons during the second week of December.

With the first Jacobite army approaching from the south Grossett realized that it would also be necessary to extend his sphere of action to the south shore of the Forth. He therefore started removing boats from Airth and the river Carron, but when requested to show his warrant it became obvious that he did not possess the necessary authority. He was forced to request a written extension to this and to await its arrival. He also conscientiously hired a Bo'ness ship to remove some large timbers from the harbour at Alloa which might conceivably have been used by the Jacobites to construct rafts for use as transports, or even for creating floating batteries.[61]

The government officers in Edinburgh were now very worried that the two Jacobite armies would unite on the south side of the Forth and march on that city again. Their agitation increased when they received intelligence reports that the Jacobites in the north were to attempt a crossing at Alloa in flat-bottomed boats that they were bringing over land from Loch Earn.[62] The government supporters at Bo'ness offered to fit out a ship at their own cost and to man it with their own sailors, provided that the government paid for the supplies and £650 in insurance.⁶³ Evidently Lieutenant-General Guest did eventually agree to these terms as the 'Pretty Janet' with Captain Pearson in charge went to the passage at Higgins Neuck.⁶⁴ At the same time the armed sloop 'Jean' took up position at Carsie Neuck.

Events were beginning to move apace. Reports arrived that the Jacobite army returning from England was still largely intact, and that they were marching rapidly up the west coast. Lieutenant-General Guest formulated new plans accordingly. It was decided that the dragoons still in Edinburgh would march to Linlithgow where they would join with those from Kinneil and move on to Falkirk. They would then rendezvous with General Blakeney and the force from Stirling at Bonnybridge either to intercept the rebels there or move on to Glasgow.⁶⁵ Whether these were ever serious plans we cannot tell; they may merely have been intended to reassure the provost and citizens of Glasgow. Blakeney certainly had no intention of leaving the key site of Stirling Castle.

On the 19th December orders were issued to "get all Stirling shire in Arms immediately".⁶⁶ Grossett therefore collected arms from Stirling Castle and supplied them to whigs in "that Part of Stirling Shire which lies next to the River".⁶⁷ Volunteers readily came forward. At least 600 men were found in Stirlingshire and 200 at Kilsyth.⁶⁸ Ebenezer Erskine and his followers had recovered from their earlier shock and returned to the town walls of Stirling. It was at this time, when troops were being rapidly redeployed to take account of the new situation that the Countess of Kilmarnock offered the stables at Callendar House for the use of the dragoons.⁶⁹ Falkirk was beginning to find itself at the centre of all this activity, but at that moment the dragoons had switched to patrolling the roads to the south of Edinburgh - the direction from which Prince Charles and his first army might approach. Behind them, at Kinneil, they left a smouldering church, for the building had accidentally caught fire.⁷⁰

LETTER TO THE COUNTESS OF KILMARNOCK.

Edinburgh 20th Decembr 1745

Madam   I have the honour of your Ladyships Command of the 18th. If your Laps is so good as to offer to lend your stables for the Dragoons Horses of they shou'd want them, it is all that will be required, however to prevent all Mistakes I will write to Major Preston to have a particular Regard to your Laps and all that belongs to you, but if your Laps notwithstanding this shou'd meet with any uneasyness, you will please to show this letter which I hope will be your Laps protection for I have the hounour to be

Madam,
Your Lapss most Obdt humble Servant

JOS: GUEST [71]

The boats on the south side of the river Forth were now impounded and transferred to Bo'ness. On 21st December these, together with those already at Bo'ness and Queensferry, were anchored off shore under the protection of the navy. The first Jacobite army was now too close for comfort. The 'Happy Janet' began to act as a supply vessel, taking biscuit from Leith to Bo'ness and ammunition to the 'Pretty Janet' and to Stirling Castle.

LIEUTENANT-GENERAL GUEST'S DIRECTIONS

Directions for the Master of the Boat that goes to Borrostouness.
Edinburgh 22d Decem. 1745.

He is to sail directly for Borrostouness, lye out in the Road of that place and send in his Boat or yawl, to Collector Grosett who is there and get directions from him how he is to dispose of his Cargo, part of which is to go to Stirling Viz. the 9 pounders Cannon Ball, Spunges, etc.
The Pouder and small Cannon Ball is for use of the Jean of Alloa, and Pretty Janet, that are stationed near that place or at Higgens Nuik. The Biscuit which is to be taken in at Leith from Mr. Walker is to be disposed of at Bosness as Mr. Grosett will direct. In case of any accident of your not meeting with Mr. Grosett, I desire Cap. Knight of the Happy Janet may forward imediately the 9 pound Cannon Ball, Spunges etc. to Stirling, where General Blakeney has present occasion for them.
JOS: GUEST.

To the Master of the Boat Order'd to sail for Borrostouness.[72]

Confirmation arrived in Edinburgh of the true circumstances regarding the return of Prince Charles and his army, and it reinforced the worst fears of the officials there. Far from having been harassed all the way back from Derby the chase had ended ineffectually at Carlisle and the enemy had survived almost unmolested. Panic returned to the capital as it became clear that once again the official forces could easily be overcome, particularly as they were now considerably outnumbered. Only a handful of troops had remained in that vulnerable city together with the Lothian volunteers and the town guard. The local men were absolutely determined to recover their dignity from the previous surrender by defending the reinforced town walls at all costs. So too was the Lord Justice Clerk. The reaction was rapid. On the 22nd orders reached Stirling that all the foot soldiers still there were to march for Edinburgh the next morning at 7am.[73]

LIEUTENANT-GENERAL JOSHUA GUEST TO GENERAL BLAKENEY AT STIRLING
Edinburgh 21st Decr 1745.

As it is likely, the Rebels on the North of the Forth, may move to join those that are coming south, of which as you are on the spot you'll be best able to judge _ You will consider in these circumstances what is most proper for you to do, whether with the King's Troops and Militia, you can maintain your post at Stirling; if you are able, you may remain with all your Forces at Stirling, if not, after leaving a sufficient Garrison for the Castle of Stirling, you'll order the rest of the Troops to march to morrow to Linlithgow and Borroughstoness .... I have recalled the Dragoons from Kilsyth and Falkirk, & order'd them to march for Edinburgh; should the Rebels march quicker this way than we expect, as it would endanger the Troops on the Road, I'll endeavour to embark them at Borrowstoness [74].

Prince Charles and his army had in fact crossed back into Scotland on 20th December. The people of central Scotland could only wait to see which way he would turn. There were the same two choices that he had had in September. They could head to the seat of government again, or to the wealthy city of Glasgow. Reports led the government to believe that they had made for the former and were closing in on Edinburgh. On the 23rd the infantry left Stirling leaving General Blakeney and the castle garrison to hold out on their own. To help isolate them one of the arches on Stirling Bridge was demolished. Over the previous week the government patrols along the south side of the Forth had helped to locate vessels which were to be removed from the many creeks and inlets. To many of the inhabitants these formed part of their livelihood and they doubtless hid them as best they could. Even on its hurried way to Edinburgh, having abandoned Stirling, the Glasgow militia kept a last watchful eye open for more boats. Sure enough, two vessels were spotted near to the mouth of the river Carron. These were reported by Lord Home to Grossett when he reached Linlithgow.[75] They were to be "secured or destroyed".

THE EARL OF HOME TO WALTER GROSSETT.

Linlithgow Decr 23 1745
Sir,- Having receiv'd information that John Liddel in Haugh of Dalderse lying in Newtown Pow hath a Boat, and that there are another Boat upon Carron Watter belonging to James Simpson on the west side of John Liddels in the Pow about the Slyde bank bridge, I desire you'l order them to be secured or destroyed as you think
proper.
          I am Sir Your Humble Serv.
            HOME[76]

These boats were concealed and as Grossett believed them to have been used to carry Jacobite dispatches they were destroyed later that month.[77]

Most of the government's infantry in central Scotland were now at Linlithgow, but such was the perceived threat that they still thought it likely that they would be intercepted before they reached the walls of Edinburgh. With a great sense of urgency they hurried that same evening to Bo'ness where Grossett had hired ships and boats laden with provisions to take them to Leith, and on to Berwick if required. In all, about one thousand men, tired after their rapid march, together with their baggage, were embarked. A little after midnight they set sail and with favourable conditions were able to land at Leith the next morning.[78] With other regular troops on their way to Edinburgh from Berwick the city was safe, but once again Stirlingshire lay wide open. On Christmas day the first parties of the Jacobite army entered Glasgow.

CHAPTER 3

The Storm Approaches
26th December 1745 - 12th January 1746

At Glasgow the Jacobites demanded and received clothes, provisions, horses and money. It was clear to the government that they would not delay there long and it was still expected that they would move on to Edinburgh. A very harassed Lord Justice Clerk issued an amazingly sweeping warrant to "all Gentlemen and Inhabitants of Stirling Shire" to arrest and detain anyone that they even suspected of Jacobite sympathies.[1]

WARRANT JUSTICE CLERK FOR SEIZING REBELS

Edinburgh 2d Jan 1745/6
Gentlemen,
I apprehend it would be greatly for his Majestys Service as well as for your Interest and the good of the Country in Generall that you take prudent methods for intercepting all Intelligence of the Rebells, and of seizing some principally concerned with Rebellion as you beli. can till they be brought before the proper Judge to be by him Examined & dealt with according to Law for wch this shall be a sufficient warrand given day and date forsaid by

And Fletcher
to all Gentlemen and Inhabitants of Stirling Shire [2]

Walter Grossett received orders to acquire as many cannon as he could from Bo'ness and to transport them to Edinburgh immediately for its defence. That city had been left devoid of ordnance following the previous visit of the Jacobite army. Accordingly, Grossett took a vessel to Bo'ness and started to load her. In the meantime, the agitated citizens of the capital continued to fortify the place. Their morale was greatly raised by the arrival of the Scots Royals and Battereau's Regiment ahead of schedule. The men had been provided with mounts by the equally anxious gentlemen of Lothian.

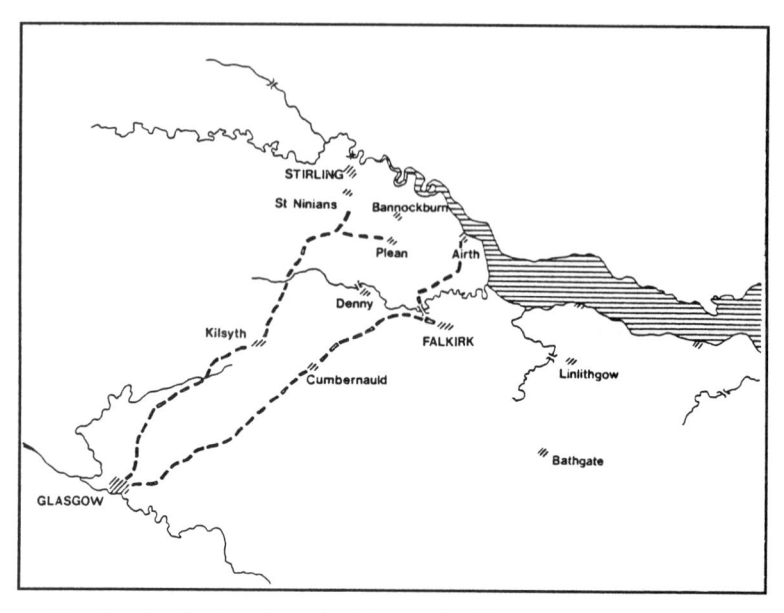

Map showing the line of march of the two Jacobite columns from Glasgow.

On 3rd January 1746, after a much needed rest of eight days, the replenished and refreshed Jacobite army marched out of Glasgow in high spirits. They headed east, towards Edinburgh, with the object of accelerating the junction of the two armies now in Scotland.[3] Lord George Murray had planned such a movement for some time and had written from Moffat to Lord John Drummond of the northern army to urge him to make his way south.[4] The northern army was slowly preparing for its descent.

The army leaving Glasgow divided into two columns. One, with Prince Charles, stopped that night at Kilsyth. The second, led by Lord George, made its way to Cumbernauld, not far to the south. With Lord George were most of the clan regiments, the fighting core of the army, and ahead of them was Lord Elcho with his cavalry. That night Lord Elcho pushed on as far as Falkirk.[5] Their arrival shocked the already apprehensive bairns. They realized that great events were afoot and looked upon the riders with consternation as they settled down for the night.

Sir Archibald Primrose of Dunipace had heard through the grapevine of the Jacobite army's approach. With government troops

Sir Archibald Primrose of Dunipace
(1693-1746)

mustering in Edinburgh, the way to England barred and the whole country up in arms he foresaw trouble ahead for himself. Like the Earl of Kilmarnock he found himself in dire financial straits. Five years before the rebellion had broken out his estate had been sequestered and a factor appointed to administer it. From these he was allowed £40 a year of aliment, the rent of the parks which were let at £25, and the customs, ie 14 capons, 82 hens and 126 chickens. He had also the use of the house, offices and garden. Unsure of his own future, Sir Archibald Primrose decided to secure his delayed aliment from the factor. This would leave him financially free to vacate his family from the area for the duration of the hostilities, or for him to throw his lot in with one side or the other. It was thus on the very day that the first Jacobite forces appeared in the district that Primrose received the outstanding amount of the aliment to Martinmas 1745, being the sum of £34 10s 7d. In addition he obtained an advance of £20 4s 2 3/4d.[6]

To the nervous government officials in Edinburgh the deployment of the Jacobite troops looked like the first step on the road to the capital. With no sizeable army to hand they were not in a position to interfere with the march of the enemy and the rebels went about unmolested. The next day Grossett arrived off Leith with the cannon from Bo'ness, but before he had time to unload them and to haul them to Edinburgh Major-General John Huske reached the panic stricken city with two more regiments of foot. The inhabitants and the civil servants now felt secure, and the cannon stayed at Leith.[7]

However, Prince Charles had not been intending to retake that prestigious target. He had already reaped all the propaganda benefit he was likely to get for so doing on the first occasion. Instead, he had decided upon the capture of Stirling Castle to secure the crossing of the Forth there. This location had now assumed considerable strategic importance. On 4th January Charles arrived at Bannockburn House, the home of the staunch Jacobite Sir Hugh Paterson. Whilst he took up residence at the house his column was dispersed amongst the surrounding villages, notably those of Bannockburn, St Ninian's and Denny. From here they could carry out the siege of the town and the castle.

Lord George's column left Cumbernauld with the Atholl brigade in the van, carrying the Royal Standard. Then came Ogilvy's, Perth's, John Roy Stewart's, Glenbucket's, Manchester, Glengarry's, Clanranald's, Keppoch's, Appin's and Lochiel's, with Cluny's bringing up the rear. Their march was covered by the cavalry; the Life Guards out in front, the Hussars on the flanks and Kilmarnock's troop as a rearguard together with Pitsligo's. The artillery and ammunition trundled along between Glenbucket's and the remnants of the Manchester Regiment.[8] Thus it was that they made their way to Falkirk to provide a forward guard so that the proposed siege could be conducted without fear of interference from the forces gathering at Edinburgh.

Elcho's cavalry were now forwarded to Elphinstone (modern Dunmore), where Lord Elcho took up residence with Mr Wright at Kersie House. Elcho had been briefly engaged to Miss Graham of Airth the year before and now his casual acquaintance with the area was to be put to the test. His task was to guard the Forth

Bannockburn House where the Prince spent many days during the campaign.

Lord George Murray
(1694-1760)
By Permission of the Duke of Atholl

David Wemys, Lord Elcho
(1721-1787)

crossings in the area which had been re-established with the departure of the government's representatives. Pitsligo's Horse were stationed at Airth itself. The Perthshire Horse were sent to protect the inland crossing at the Fords of Frew; and Kilmarnock's Horse naturally took up post on the Edinburgh road at his residence of Callendar House.[9]

Foraging parties were sent into the surrounding countryside to obtain food and intelligence reports. The presence of landed gentlemen in the area was to be made known so that their cooperation might be obtained, if necessary by holding them hostage. This would also ensure that none of them was likely to become spies for the government. Through his personal contacts Lord Kilmarnock knew which of these could or could not be trusted. Since July 1732 he had been an officer of the Royal Company of Archers, the monarch's personal bodyguard in Scotland, and it is tempting to think that he earmarked his comrades from that regiment for special treatment.[10] Sir Archibald Primrose had been in the Company for some 32 years and narrowly avoided a party sent to seek him out by hiding in a thicket of firs on his own estate.[11]

On Sunday 5th January the Jacobite army started the process of investing the town of Stirling. As this involved most of the men in the Prince's column Lochiel's brigade was ordered from Falkirk to provide him with a personal bodyguard. The proximity of the government forces at Edinburgh and of the Forth Estuary which connected them with Stirling may have made Charles a little overcautious. Certainly Lord George thought so and protested strongly about the weakening of the advanced party at Falkirk.[12]

To Lord George the priority was to get the northern army, and more particularly their cannon, across the Forth. The large cannon would be essential once the town of Stirling capitulated and attention was focussed on the castle itself. Most of the troops were to be sent by way of the Fords of Frew, having already learned at first hand the problems associated with the Alloa crossing caused by the activities of the Royal Navy. The lighter artillery, including two 12-pounders, were also directed by way of the Frew. This route was extremely difficult. The problems of generally poor roads and river crossings were exacerbated by the winter weather. The heavier guns, ammunition and the associated baggage, together with the bulk of the lighter guns were therefore making for Alloa with the intention of bringing them up the river and landing them on the south bank near to Stirling. The battering cannon, such as the 18-pounders, were proving hard to transport. It took 20 horses to draw one piece of this type, and a great deal of effort.

The government was well aware of the importance of the Alloa crossing and their agents informed them of the imminent arrival of the large calibre weapons which the French had sent and which were now on their way from Perth escorted by a contingent of the Earl of Cromarty's Regiment.[13] Such concise intelligence reports were to be essential in determining future manoeuvres. Grossett dutifully arranged for two reports a day from the Alloa area where his family still lived.[14]

Lord George Murray went to Alloa to make the arrangements for the big guns and for their forwarding to Stirling. He met Lord John Drummond who had just arrived there with an advance party and the two of them discussed the possibility of using floats.[15] Leaving a party of 100 of the Earl of Cromarty's Regiment behind, they proceeded to survey the river on horseback hoping to find a convenient passage. From Alloa they travelled to the Cambuskenneth ferry which they realized was too far from Alloa to be of use. It was late in the day by the time that they reached Dunblane for a rest. Here they met the young Lord John Macleod and directed him to join that part of his father's regiment stationed at Alloa.[16]

Lord Kilmarnock's local knowledge was very useful to the Jacobite command as they sought to prepare for a lengthy stay. The arduous trip down to Derby and back had left his own troop in need of fresh horses and recruits, both of which he sought from the neighbouring estates. As part of this routine he sent another party of horse under the command of Major James Brand to Dunipace. They reached the house in the dark at 9 o'clock in the evening and searched for arms and horses, but these had already been put out of the way. They turned abusive, threatening the Primrose family and property, and insisted that Sir Archibald go with them to see Lord Kilmarnock at Callendar House. They were even about to plunder the house when Major Brand stopped them. So it was that, after his first distressing face to face encounter with the Jacobite forces, Sir Archibald Primrose was taken back to Falkirk as a prisoner.[17]

On the same day Lord Lewis Gordon finally left Aberdeen on his way to the Stirling rendezvous. The government forces too were on the move. The urgency behind their original movements had been to save Edinburgh which now became their rallying point. Lieutenant-General Henry Hawley was appointed to command their forces gathering in Scotland for what they assumed would be the final phase of the campaign, and on the 6th January he arrived in Edinburgh with further troops.

In the town of Falkirk the clans were settling down. They commandeered houses for use as billets and set about obtaining provisions. Soldiers were deployed to detect any movement of government troops in the area at the earliest possible moment. An outpost was provided at Linlithgow Bridge, and probably another was placed at Polmont Hill to watch the crossings of the River Avon, with the main guard on the Edinburgh road near Laurieston. At the first sign of the enemy the guards were to use bagpipes to signal the alarm. This was to be transmitted back to the town by piping relays. The parish church bell and that in the Steeple would then sound out. On hearing this the clans were to muster in the field opposite to Callendar House, then known as the Dovecote Croft and now as the Pikes. Each clan was to take turn about at providing the men for the outposts.[18] Anyone passing through the district was to be closely examined and searched as it was well

The Cross on Falkirk's High Street, with the Steeple and Tolbooth at the end and the Cross Well on the right.

known that government spies were about. Raiding parties were sent across the river Avon to Linlithgow and Bo'ness. At Linlithgow they demanded 25 horses, or £250 as the value of them. At Bo'ness goods from the town and the shipping were seized.[19]

These raids were made in force and were officially sanctioned. Already there were reports of small bands of Highlanders plundering the neighbouring countryside without authority. Campaigning armies have to feed off the land, particularly when, as in this case, their supplies are cut off. The winter season further exacerbated the problem. Livestock, eggs, bread or meal were all prone to being uplifted. The Highland officers did their best to keep such pilfering within reason in the knowledge that a prolonged stay would require the cooperation of the local populace who had hidden much of their food at the first signs of their approach. The command issued orders for the men to stay in the town unless on official business. Any other soldier caught beyond the confines of the town would be punished. Likewise, complaints were received that some men were not paying for their billets and the regimental officers were made responsible for their conduct.[20]

Lord George, tired from his trip to Dunblane and back, requisitioned a large house on the High Street not far from the Steeple for use as the divisional headquarters. One of the rooms was assigned to purely administrative duties and here the intelligence reports were brought in throughout the day. Lord George himself had a small room on one of the upper floors. This acted as a bedroom and office where he was kept busy into the small hours of the morning writing orders, passes, requisition notes, letters to supporters and his family, assigning guard duty, choosing the daily password (on the 4th January the parole had been 'James' and 'London'; today, the 6th, it was 'Robert' and 'Bruce') - generally organizing the daily routine and pattern of life of the army of occupation. He had gathered around him an efficient and trustworthy general staff which included such men of proven courage and ability as Lieutenant Kerr. These were delegated duties of inspection and maintenance, but the main burden still fell upon Lord George. For four months he had had the additional stress of the rapid thrust into England, but the sedentary position that the army now found itself in gave him more chance to delegate responsibilities and to have more of a rest.

In the long march to Derby and back Lord George had earned the regard and admiration of the highland chiefs. He had always appeared to behave with tactical skill and bravery and had treated the highlanders with great respect and courtesy. Together they had taken most of the risks, and whilst there would always be clan rivalry they had developed considerable camaraderie. In the evenings the clan leaders met in a first floor room in the headquarters building to discuss how matters stood and to voice their opinions on future tactics and requirements. Seated around a long wooden table in the wood panelled room with a peat fire glowing in the hearth and wine in their glasses they spoke freely. That evening Lord George listened to their complaints. They had been greatly annoyed at the manner in which Prince Charles' haughty general staff had treated them and had continually issued insignificant and often irrelevant orders from the comfort of Bannockburn House. The irritation was increased by the lack of personal commitment displayed by the overbearing foreigners who exhibited this level of incompetence. Together they agreed to prepare a petition urging the Prince to reintroduce councils of war which had been abandoned by him after his bitter disappointment at Derby. They also asked to be given discretionary powers of action during emergencies. Both of these were reasonable requests, but unfortunately the document that they produced that evening was clumsily worded and ended up being framed as a series of demands and accusations.

As the commander of the division Lord George was honour bound to deliver the petition to Prince Charles himself, which he did the next morning. In his own words he explained why: "This proposall Ld Geo: Murray gave in to the Prince's own hands, for by this time all the Principal people in the Army were convinced that the litle people, who were the only persons that were consulted, and manag'd everything, had their own interest more in view then the good of the cause." The petition read:

PETITION OF 6TH JANUARY 1746

6th Janry 1746.

It is proposed that His Royal Highness should from time to time call a councile of War, to consist of all those who command Battalions or Squadrons; But, as severals of those may be on partys, and often absent, a Committee should be chosen, to consist of Five or Seven, and that all operations fo the carrying on of the War should be agre'd on by the Majority of those, in his Royal Highness' presence; and, once that a measure is taken, it is not to be changed except by the advice of those, or most of them, who were present when it was agree'd on.

That upon any sudden emergancy, such as in a Battle, Scirmish, or in a Sege, a Discrationary power must be allowed to those who command. This is the method of all armys, much [more] so should it be of this, which consists of Volunteers, and where so many gentlemen of fortune, not only venture their own and their family's all, But, if any misfortune happen, are sure of ending their Lives on a Scaffold, should they escape in the field.

If this plan is not followed, the most Dismall consequence cannot but ensue. Had not a Council Determined the Retreat from Derby, what a castrophy must have followed in two or three days!

Had a Council of War been held the evening the army came to Lancaster on their return, a day (which at that time was so precious) had not been lost.

Had a Council of War been consulted as to leaving a Garison at Carlisle, it would never have been agreed to, the place not being teneable, and so many brave men wou'd not have been sacrifized, besides the reputation of His Royal Highness's arms.

It is to be concidered that this army is an army of Volunteers, and not mercinarrys, many of them being resolved not to continue in the army were affars once settled.

GEORGE MURRAY [21]

Lord George did not have time to wait for the reply as it was evident that the document would require lengthy deliberation. Instead, he turned his attention back to the problems of the river crossing at Alloa. As luck would have it a detachment from the Duke of Perth's Regiment was able to seize a brig at Airth on the 7th January.[22] It was taken straight up the river to Alloa to be used in preference to any floats.[23] By then the 'Vulture', sloop of war, lay off Inverkeithing which it had reached the night before. Its pilot had refused to take responsibility for taking the warship further that day as it was already dark and he was unfamiliar with the narrows there.[24] The ship's cutter and some long boats were therefore sent up the river towards Alloa to gather intelligence. They arrived off Kincardine just in time to see the Jacobite brig come out of Airth and head up the Forth.[25]

The boats from the 'Vulture' were seen from the south bank of theestuary and Lord George, now back in Falkirk, sent a message to the Prince and his advisors informing them of the situation. He also dispatched Colonel Kerr and some more troops to Airth in anticipation of an attempt by the government to land forces in that vicinity.[26] In the evening a second sloop, the 'Pearl', moved up the Forth and passed the 'Vulture' which also took advantage of the tide and sailed.

Acting on intelligence that the Jacobite cannon would arrive at Alloa the next day it was decided to dispatch a large party of soldiers up the river to take that place by surprise. Late that night and early into the morning some 300 government soldiers were embarked on transports at Leith, commanded by Colonel Leighton to be conducted by Grossett.[27] Grossett had commandeered 200 bales of flax from a Dutch ship then at Leith and these were placed on the sides of the transports to protect the soldiers from musket shot. The wind being favourable they set sail to the west, full of confidence.[28] Lord George had clearly predicted correctly.

LIEUTENANT-COLONEL HAWLEY TO THE DUKE
OF NEWCASTLE

Edinburgh. 7 Janry 1745/6

... the intelligence ... varies so much every Hour, and afterwards proves so often false, that I can depend upon Nothing. The accounts to day are, that Ld Kilmarnock is Fortifying, by Pallisades, & Intrenchments a strong Camp, at his own House at Kallendar by Falkirk, to cover the Siege of Sterling Castle; It is nine miles on this side, (a new Way of Covering a Siege). The main Body of desperate men (as they still call them here) have left Glasgow, & are about Sterling; and they have a Post at Allowa, where they are trying to make Floats, to pass some cannon on this side.

I am getting the Foot into Repair, as fast as they come up, in order to go to Them. I will not go to have the King's Troops affronted. I am pushing on some Posts towards them; and when I can move I will; and hope to give your Grace a good account of them, if they stay; which I neither believe; nor expect.

As to Artillery; There is not a Gun here can move, for want of Gunners, the same at Berwick there is but one ... [29]

Lord George had other problems to consider. He received back the petition that he had signed on behalf of the clan chiefs the day before. Its return evidently indicated an outright rejection, but on the other side of the paper Charles had written a derisive note emphasizing his disgust and distaste at the manner and tone of the proposals as well as their abnoxious content. Relations between the two camps, for so long bottled in by the necessities of the rapid retreat from Derby, were becoming strained.

Janry ye 7th, 1745.

When I came to Scotland, I knew well enough what I was to expect from my Ennemies, but I Little foresaw what I meet with from my Friends. I came vested with all the Authority the King could give me, one chief part of which is the Command of his Armies, and now I am

required to give this up to fifteen persons, who may afterwards depute five or seven of their own number to exercise it, for fear, if they were six or eight, that I might myself pretend to ye casting vote.
By the majority of those all things are to be determined, and nothing left to me but the honour of being present at their debates. This, I am told, is the method of all Armies, and this I flatly deny, not do I believe it to be the method of any one Army in the world.

I am often hit in the teeth that this is an Army of Volontiers, consisting of Gentlemen of Rank and fortune, and who came into it meerly upon motives of Duty and Honour; what one wou'd expect from such an Army is more zeal, more resolution, and more good manners than in those that fight meerly for pay: but it can be no Army at all where there is no General, or, which is the same thing, no obedience or deference paid to him.

Every one knew before he engaged in the cause what he was to expect in case it miscarried, and shou'd have staid at home if he cou'd not face death in any shape. but can I myself hope for better usage? at least I am the only Person upon whose head a price has been already set, and therefore I cannot indeed threaten at every other word to throw down my arms and make my Peace with the Government.

I think I shew every day that I do not pretend to act without asking advice, and yours oftner than any body's else, which I shall still continue to do. You know that upon more occasions than one I have given up my own opinion to that of others.

I staid, indeed, a day at Lancaster, without calling a Councile; yet yrself proposed to stay another. but I wonder much to see myself reproched with the loss of Carlile. was there a possibility of carrying off the Cannon and Baggage, or was there time to destroy them? and wou'd not the doing it have been a greater dishonour to our Arms? After all, did not yrself, instead of proposing to abandon it, offer to stay with the Athol Brigade to defend it?

I have insensibly made this answer much longer than I intended, and might yet add much more, but I choose to cut it short, and shall only tell you that my Authority may be taken from me by
violence, but I shall never resign it Like an Ideot.

CHARLES, P:R [30]

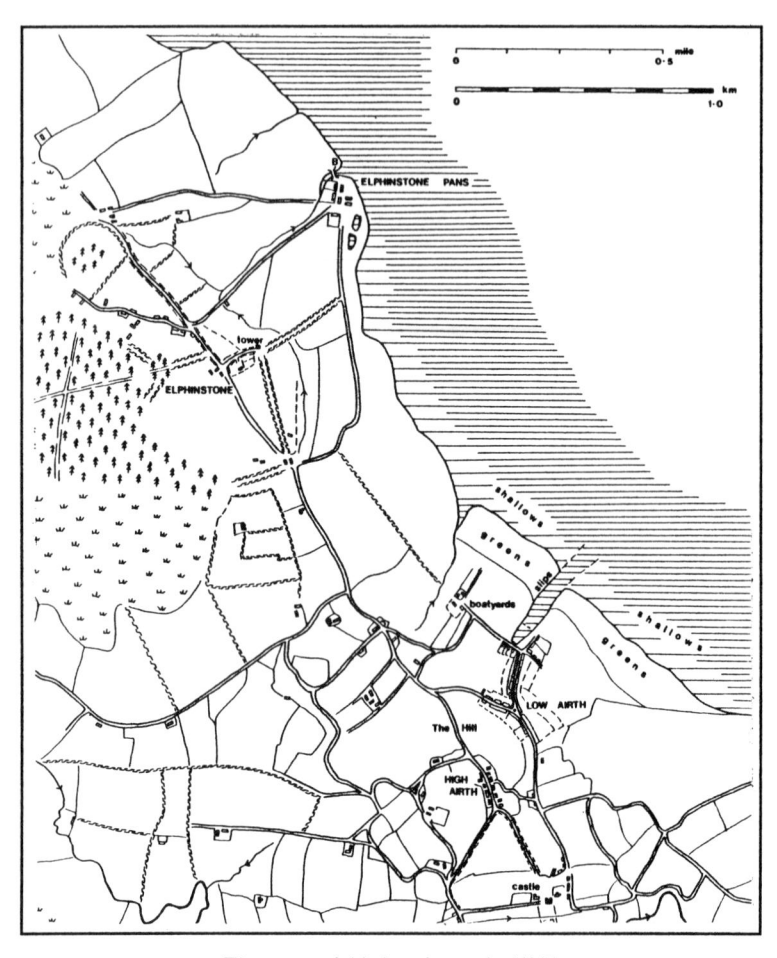

The town of Airth as it was in 1745

Events, however, now distracted them from such internal wrangles. The next morning the 'Vulture' caught up with the 'Pearl' off Kincardine. Its commander, Captain Faulkener, was informed of the brig's movements and that there were still two skiffs in Airth that might be used by the Jacobites to carry their cannon to the siege of Stirling. He immediately sent his heavily manned longboats into the harbour to burn them.[31] The two ships had been laid up for the winter and lay some distance along the Pow on their slipways away from the town. The water was only just lapping up to them and they were to have rested there until a spring tide which was needed to refloat them. Airth at this time had a shipbuilding trade and there can be little doubt that these ships were still awaiting repair on the stocks.[32] At any event, the government troops were not taking any risks and as there was sufficient water for the longboats they pulled up alongside the skiffs and torched them. The Jacobite infantry were unable to cross the water to save them and could only watch despondently from the wharfs. Some ineffectual volleys were fired by a Jacobite detachment in their frustration.[33] However, whilst the government troops were busily engaged in their task, covered by the cannon on board their sloop, the tide turned. By the time that the boats reached the 'Vulture' the tide had sunk so low that the ship was beached and unable to return to the deeper channel. In itself this presented no structural problem for the vessel as this was a common way of resting over, nor could any of the enemy reach them on foot across the mud flats and shallows. There was not even a small boat in the hands of the Jacobites which they could have used to approach the stranded ship for Grossett had very effectually removed all such vessels from the area earlier that month. Not that it would have posed much of a threat given the protective shield of the 'Vulture's' guns. Captain Faulkener posted a guard for the night confident in the knowledge that he would be on the move again the next day.

Whilst all this was happening the Jacobites were busy at Alloa. Their artillery had arrived early in the morning and Lord Macleod and his detachment hurriedly put the finishing touches to the battery that they were raising on the quay. They were supervised by Colonel Kerr who had performed much the same task the previous August. By the end of a tiring day they had mounted the six 6-pounders that had been captured from the 'Hazard' sloop[34] Macleod's men were placed on a status of high alert due to the proximity of the two enemy sloops of war. Extra guards were posted around the town and the new arrivals that had brought the artillery were lodged in three barns so that they could be kept together and more easily mustered in the event of an attack. Likewise, they were all ordered to sleep in their clothes.[35]

Up the river at Stirling things had gone well for the besiegers. After protracted negotiations the town had surrendered for a second time to the Jacobites. They entered it at 3 o'clock that afternoon and immediately sent off three 4-pounder cannon that they had been using in the siege to Airth.[36] These guns arrived there late that night together with an engineer, Colonel Grant. It had been dark for some time, but upon hearing of the stranded sloop Grant decided to mount the guns, without resting or delaying, on the Hill in order to play upon it at first light. It was long hard work.

For Colonel Leighton and his 300 men aboard the transports it had not been a good day. Full of confidence at their early morning departure from Leith they knew that they held the element of surprise. However, by the time that they had got one third of the way to Airth the wind had turned completely against them. So much so that it took them well nigh 36 hours to effect the voyage and it was 1 o'clock on the afternoon of the 9th January before they reached Higgins' Neuck where they encountered the ebbing tide.[37]

As light dawned the Jacobite battery on the Hill of Airth opened fire on the 'Vulture'. The sloop's crew were taken completely by surprise, but the low calibre of the guns and the poor gunnery of the Jacobites meant that the advantage was not pressed. Recovering from their initial shock the sailors on the 'Vulture' "return'd their Salutation with the Expence of one hundred and Ninety shott" from their larger guns and after some time put the hurriedly prepared battery out of operation by dismounting the guns.[38] A government agent put the Jacobite losses at four Highlanders killed and two wounded.[39]

Tension was growing in the rank and file of the Jacobite army. These first ineffective encounters were exasperating as they waited like sitting ducks whilst the enemy probed each part of their defences. Prince Charles, still the figure-head of the campaign, went to Falkirk to raise the clans' spirits and reviewed the regiments there, presumably on the Pikes, about 1,685 men in all.[40]

At Alloa, the Jacobites started loading the battering cannon that had just arrived on to the brig. The two 16-pounders were their first priority, together with the requisite ammunition and stores. In the meantime three of the smaller guns were added to the bristling battery. Reports soon arrived that the government transports under Colonel Leighton had been seen off Kincardine. Lord Macleod immediately sent spies to that village to see if they had received any contact from the fleet. At the same time patrols were forwarded in the same direction to gather further information. The reports that he received throughout the day satisfied Lord Macleod that the government forces intended a landing on his side of the Forth near Alloa. He addressed an urgent letter to the Duke of Perth, or in his absence to Lord John Drummond, outlining the situation and demanding reinforcement at the soonest possible moment. This was dispatched around midnight.

During the day the 'Vulture' had refloated on the tide and then joined Colonel Leighton's force and the 'Pearl'. Walter Grossett had spent much of his working life on this part of the river as a customs officer and together with the other officers decided upon a plan of action. Under cover of darkness 50 of Colonel Leighton's foot soldiers, in a large boat from Kinghorn which had been specially fitted out with a platform, joined up with two armed boats from the sloops each carrying the same number of sailors. The Kinghorn boat was then placed in tow and together they proceeded stealthily up the river past Airth. As they boldly approached Alloa their brave pilots, local men recruited by Grossett, must have known how vulnerable they were. Intelligence reports had been reaching the government task force regularly whilst they were at sea and they knew that the cannon had arrived at Alloa and that a formidable battery commanded the Forth passage from the quay. Silently they slipped passed the port unobserved.[41]

Sticking to the main channel of the river the raiding party moved away from the searching eyes at Alloa. As the danger from that source receded the men steeled themselves for the operation ahead. After three quarters of a mile the pilots guided them to a small wooden pier on the south bank. Here the soldiers quickly disembarked and moved towards a nearby house. The house was surrounded and entry forced. Intelligence reports had reliably informed them that this was the temporary residence of one of the leading Jacobite officers, Lord Elcho. It was very late at night and they felt sure that they would find their prey in Kersie House with the intention of snatching his person. The capture of this influential Jacobite lord and his return to Edinburgh would be quite a propaganda coup. A room to room search was conducted, but to no avail. The raiders returned to their boats empty handed and disappointed.[42] As chance would have it Lord Elcho had left the house about half an hour earlier. After snatching just a few hours

Kersie House drawn by J S Fleming in 1902

sleep he had returned to Elphinstone Pans to supervise the raising of another new battery there under the cover of darkness. His presence there was quite unpredictable to the government spies and foiled what would otherwise have been a daring and celebrated abduction. However, Colonel Grant had realized that the river was too wide at Airth for his guns and had decided to transfer them to Elphinstone where it was significantly narrower. The three guns from the Hill were still serviceable and a fourth was brought from Falkirk.[43] Over 150 foot soldiers helped in this work and they toiled throughout the night. By morning it too was ready.[44]

The three government boats at Kersie House now set off down the river on their return journey. Their intention was to approach the brig at Alloa from up river, a direction that would be totally unexpected, and to set fire to her. Reports had led them to believe that the brig might attempt a sailing that night, in which case they would be in a good position to intercept it. The operation of boarding her was made easier by the platform on the Kinghorn boat. On their way, however, this boat being heavily laden with men and equipment hit a mud bank and grounded. The soldiers on board panicked, and "one of the Sailors forgetting where he was; Caul'd out to his Comrades. Damm you pull away for we are aground;

The Storm Approaches 61

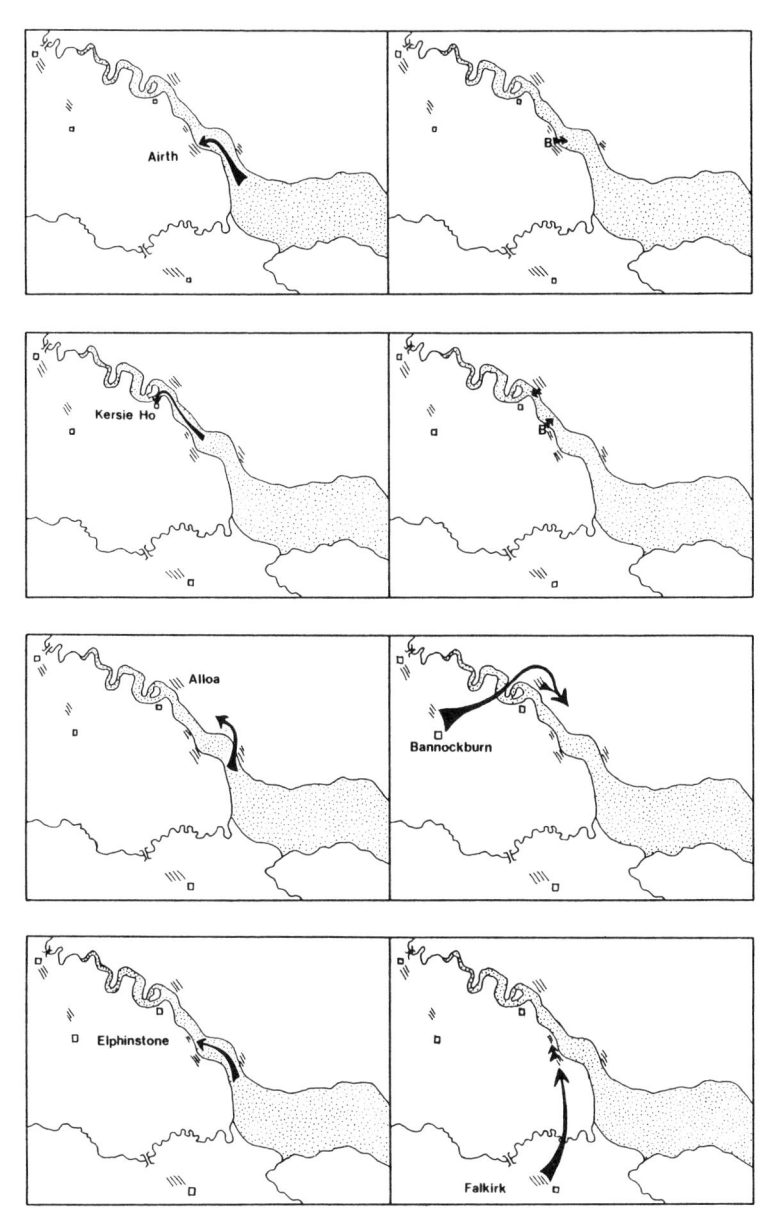

The Hanovarian probing of the Jacobite defences (left) and the counter (right).
(i) 8th / 9th January. (ii) 9th / 10th (iii) 10th pm. (iv) 11th.

which by the Calmness of the Night being over heard by the Sentrys on the Rebells Cannon on the opposite Shore at Alloa Quay, they were thereby alarmed".[45] Cromarty's Regiment beat to arms and lined the northern shore but were too far away to use their muskets effectively. This stand off lasted for some time and when the boat was eventually refloated it steered well away from Cromarty's men and the mission at Alloa had to be abandoned.[46] The tide carried the boats quickly passed the batteries at Alloa and Elphinstone, both of which opened fire on them. Their aim in the poor light against such a rapidly moving small target was not very good, and much of the shot and shrapnel that hit its target lay embedded in the flax mats tied to the sides of the boats. One man on the 'Pearl's' boat died straight away, and another lost a leg. How many others were wounded, and how many subsequently died we are not told. In the confusion the Jacobite brig failed to sail up the river as it had been intended.[47]

It was now the 10th January, and the Earl of Cromarty (Lord John Macleod's father) and Lord John Drummond arrived at Alloa with news that it was to be reinforced. Lochiel's Regiment moved from Bannockburn to South Alloa, about five miles by road, and started crossing the river. Only one boat was available and it must have seemed like an eternity before they were over in any significant numbers.

The government forces were busy too. They still held high hopes of stopping the cannon from crossing the river. Early in the morning they recovered their small boats from the previous night's escapade and returned to Kincardine. Grossett had received information that the Jacobite forces in Alloa were not even 200 strong and felt confident that these could be easily overpowered by the 300 soldiers at Colonel Leighton's disposal. These soldiers were therefore disembarked near Kincardine, formed up, and set off marching overland towards Alloa [48].

The Jacobite commanders had already surveyed the land to the east of Alloa and decided upon a field of battle. As soon as the Camerons under Lochiel had sufficient numbers over the river they went with Cromarty's Regiment under Lord Macleod to intercept the enemy landing party. Lord John Drummond, the Earl of Cromarty and some officers rode forward to observe Colonel Leighton's motions to ensure that he was marching into the trap.

COLONEL JAMES GRANT TO COLONEL JOHN O' SULLIVAN

Sir,
pray give Mr Barry Two Barrels of powder & one Barrell of Ball, and

I am
Sirs your humble servt
J.Drummond.
Alloa 10th January 1746

Sir,
having given you half a barrell of powder this day to the Camerons I sent to Lord John to send me some, but all being aboard the vesel for pomais he Coud send me none as you see by this billet directed to the superviso such of what powder might address to pmais.

Yesterday at 8 we arriv'd at airth, where the two men of was were aground in the middle of the Chanel. We fir'd about 29 shoots at em and probably pierc'd one for they were pomping for a Considerable time after, their firing was very hot but to no purpose.

Last night we had our Canon plac'd upon a good Batterie that we made viz in the old place at Elphingston and fir'd three shots at a boat going by, three men were kill'd and another had his thigh shoot off, as we learn'd this day from those that were at the burial at haigens nucke, it was very dark, still fortunedirected the willing hand to this executione. This day there appear'd about 10 ships in the Bay of airth, they landed a great number of men on the other side, but brought 'em aboard towards night, the Camerons marched from Alloa to meet 'em and we dont know yet the events. I've neither spades nor shovelles nor pick not since Carlisle. I've but one barrelle of powder and cany spare it, I sent to the Secretary for moneys but did not see the Messenger since, this place is very dear. I cant stay any longer without money for the men and me. I'm Sir your most obedient humble servant

Grant [49]

SECRETARY JOHN MURRAY TO COLONEL JOHN O'SULLIVAN

Sir,
My Lord Elcho came here above a quarter of an hour ago with accounts of number of troops being landed four milles below Alloa, probably with a view to attack Alloa. But his R.H. is of opinion it

may be a faint and that their principal design is to reimbark in the night and fall on the Port of Falkirk in the morning so has sent Mr Sheridan towards Down and Dunblain to hasten up the troops naw on their way so as to strenthen Lord George as much as possible. His H. desires you may make all possible dispatch and come here to concert wt further is to be done.
I am Sir
your most obedt humle Servt,
J.Murray.
Bannockburn, Jany 10th 1746 [50]

From his ship anchored off Kincardine Captain Faulkner realized the danger only too late "they are reinforced from the South, I saw my self by the help of my Glass, to the Number of two hundred pass over, their Conveyance is a Square Puntt they have built at Alloa".[51] He was unable to get a message to the troops now ashore to warn them. Fortunately for them Grossett was proceeding with caution "while they were Compleating in order to march I went to reconoitre the Rebels from an Eminence, when I luckily happen'd to observe a Reinforcmt of 300 Men to join the 300 we had design'd to attack".[52] The government troops quickly retraced their steps and hurriedly embarked on their transports again. That night they lay safely off Airth.[53]

Whilst all these events were unfolding the Jacobite brig sailed with the tide and reached Polmaise with the two 16-pounder cannon and the supplies. They were unloaded there, well beyond the reach of the Castle's guns.[54] That night ground in front of the Castle was broken for the entrenchments and the siege of the fortress began in earnest.

The delays incurred in using the brig and its inherent dangers persuaded the Jacobites to attempt to move some of the cannon around the north shore of the Forth by land so that a narrower crossing could be utilised with the aid of rafts. Two of the larger guns were taken from the Alloa battery and dragged along this route.

However, time was running out for the siege operations. On the 10th January Barrel's and Pulteney's Regiments of Foot arrived at Edinburgh and the build up of forces there was almost complete. At Falkirk, Lord George Murray began to worry about this concentration of government resources. He was well aware of the situa-

The Storm Approaches

tion as spies constantly brought news of events in Edinburgh. News was also travelling in the other direction and rumours were reaching the capital of the rough treatment that the people of East Stirlingshire were suffering at the hands of the Highlanders. The clans had been there now for six days and were finding supplies difficult to obtain. There was even talk about a tax of £600 levied on the quiescent town of Falkirk by its occupiers.[55]

At about 9 o'clock the following morning the nine government vessels proceeded to Elphinstone on the Spring tide.[56] The two sloops of war, the 'Vulture' and the 'Pearl', came within musket shot of the Jacobite battery at the upper end of the village, called Elphinstone Pans because of the salt pans on the foreshore. Here they anchored - a sure prelude to a bombardment as this enabled them to maintain their station. The small garrison in the battery watched solemnly as the boats manouvred into position. At about 1 o'clock in the afternoon the 'Vulture' commenced the bombardment with its twelve or so guns. Half an hour later the 'Pearl' joined in. Three of the smaller craft anchored opposite to the coastal lane linking the Jacobite battery to the small settlement, aiming their small-arms fire at the occupants of the houses. The remaining four boats contained the foot soldiers under Colonel Leighton. They hovered about seeking an opportunity to affect a landing.

The reinforcement of Alloa by Lochiel and the Camerons had left the forces on the south bank exposed. It had been for this reason that Lord George had opposed the sending of Lochiel, believing that troops should have been brought in from Dunblane for that task. There were only about 100 soldiers in the village when the attack began.[57] This depleted force had been on the alert for three whole days constantly responding to the aggressive tactics of their enemy. They had had little sleep and were short of supplies, but they knew that any sign of weakness would leave an opening for the sea-borne force. Directed by Colonel Grant they vigorously returned fire as best they could. Pitsligo could see the developing situation from Airth and rushed to support the battery there.[58] Lord George also sent reinforcements from Falkirk. He could spare few as he was well aware of the possibility that the engagement at Elphinstone might be a diversionary action to draw troops away from the forward guard at and about Falkirk so that the main spearhead of government soldiers could advance on him overland from Edinburgh. Already he had committed larger numbers of troops to these peripheral stations than he had wanted.[59]

The snipe-shooters alley to the battery was hazarded by some of the new arrivals from Airth, and it soon became clear to the assailants that the defenders were resolute in their intention of defending it. No landing was therefore attempted, the soldiers content with firing from behind the protective bales. Musket shots were exchanged with the Jacobite infantry and a constant banging noise like a fire cracker was added to the dull booms of the cannon.

The mutual pounding continued for hour after hour. Some time after 3 pm the tide began to ebb, and at about 3.30 pm a fortuitous shot severed one of the 'Pearl's' anchor cables, forcing her to leave her station. Captain Faulkener of the 'Vulture' prudently decided to follow suit having already received a considerable battering, and the whole fleet disengaged. Watched from afar by the garrison of Stirling Castle they slipped down river with the tide and anchored in the deeper water off Bo'ness.[60]

FROM STIRLING CASTLE

> Saturday 11 ..."About Noon we observed a fleet of nine sail coming up the River, at One the Commodore began to play upon a Batterie erected on this side the River, to secure a Pass near Elphingstone upon which we knew them to be friends, about half an hour thereafter another ship came to bear upon the same Batterie, and never ceased firing, till after three, when they were obliged to fall down the River, on Account of the Tide leaving them: By the other Vessels being small, and not falling into Line, we imagin'd they had some Forces on Board, but are doubtful of their landing any: They all ly now at Anchor within our view, and we expect to see them at the same work when the Tide answers tomorrow or Monday. [61]

While the foot soldiers on the boats had sustained no losses, the sloops had. Two of the pilots aboard the 'Vulture', Mr Adams a shipmaster at Elphinstone and Mr Morrison from Leith, each lost a leg. They both subsequently died of their injuries. Two sailors were killed outright, another lost an arm, and ten others sustained less serious injuries.[62] On the other side the battery was only partially disabled, but losses in men must have been greater. However, because the Jacobites had successfully repelled the naval onslaught their officers were able to claim victory and conceal the true numbers. Lieutenant-General Hawley put their losses at 20, dryly commenting that the action had been conducted "only to shew them wee are not asleep". [63] In this they succeeded, for the Jacobites were now so alarmed at the boldness of their enemy's actions that the cannon that had been removed from Alloa the day before were recalled lest the government boats sail further up the Forth and capture them - another day had been lost.

The rebel brig returned to Alloa by the same tide that had driven the government fleet away from Elphinstone.[64] All being quiet there, she was immediately reloaded with two 8-pounders and three other cannon taken from the Alloa battery, together with powder and supplies. Moving these cumbersome ordnance pieces was tortuous work but by strenuous effort the brig was fully loaded and ready to sail just in time to catch the evening tide. It set out at once for Polmaise again, but the loading operation had taken so long that it had barely travelled two miles along the river before the tide turned. She soon ran aground on a mudflat, possibly deliberately aided by an impressed sailor.[65] There was nothing to do but to wait for the next tide to float her off. Word of this predicament was sent back to Alloa. It was the end of the day before Lord Macleod arrived at the scene with his regiment to give the vessel as much cover as they could from the north bank. The river was much narrower here and so they were able to do this quite effectively. However, the ship was now in any case practically beyond the range of naval strikes by the government.

In fact, after their pounding of the day before, the government ships were quiet on the 12th January. They received orders to return to Leith so that the soldiers could rejoin the army at Edinburgh ready for the big landward advance which was imminent.[66] About 2 o'clock in the afternoon therefore they sailed east [67] much to the relief of the Jacobites defending the river. Their activities had been beneficial to the Hanoverian campaign. Not only had they delayed the arrival of the siege cannon at Stirling, but they had also softened up the enemy by keeping them on the edge of their nerves - as David Boswell of Pitsligo's Regiment admitted a few days later: "We had been masters of Stirling long ere now had not the badness of the road kept our Cannon back for some time ... we had a very dangerous & troublesom post for the first 10 days after our army came to Stirling for our Squadron was oblidged to be awake night & day Patroll & be upon guard all that time at the town of Airth which is 6 miles distant from Stirling & the main body of the Army.[68] Psycologically the government forces had gained the advantage because they were now calling the shots and dictating the pace and location of any encounters. Things were about to change as Lord George decided to seize the initiative. First, however, he wanted Lochiel's Regiment returned to his command.

LORD GEORGE MURRAY TO MR JOHN O'SULLIVAN, QUARTER MASTER GENERAL.

Falkirk 12th Jany 1746.
Sir
I received yours of last night, I wish from my heart that Locheall & his Men were at the posts I proposed, which is good Quarters, & upon any reall alarm could be here in two hours time. It weakens us here very much (& we are god knows few enough when togither) that I am obligd to send a Batalion at least evry day three or four miles to the River side, to hinder the enemy landing & taking possession of the carse of Falkirk, & Country so useful to us. I have sent two cartes for Amunition & Mr Symes along as, you will lett him know where to find it, & that he may get quick dispatch. I am Sir
your Most obedient Honoroble Servant
George Murray.

I hope the Troops about Dunblane can easely supply the place of the Camerons where the cannon are shiping so that this night they might be at the Quarters alloted for them, please see the Quarters for Locheall are Elphistonpans, Elphiston House, Town of Airth.[69]

With the departure of the fleet and the successful transfer of the cannon to Polmaise the Elphinstone battery became superfluous as the guns at Alloa could provide adequate cover for the upper reaches of the river. The cannon at Elphinstone were therefore dismounted and taken through to Bannockburn.[70] Here there was considerable activity as the troops marched and countermarched [71]. The Prince and his advisors were preparing a field of battle in the knowledge that the government army was about to leave Edinburgh. An order of battle was prepared and drills constantly held to ensure that each regiment knew where it was to stand and how to assemble quickly in answer to the call. The physical setting had also been determined; the site chosen as much for superstitious as for tactical reasons. It was to be Plean Muir, near where Bruce had beaten Edward II some four centuries earlier. On that occasion too an English army had marched to the relief of Stirling Castle. The highlanders in particular considered it to be an auspicious location for the impending collision. It also gave the Jacobites the opportunity to oppose the crossings of the rivers Avon and Carron, at which times they could badly maul the enemy. They would then harass them as they fell back through Torwood - good defensive terrain where guerilla like tactics could inflict heavy casualties on the government troops before the set battle was even entered into. Charles II had held the indomitable Cromwell at bay here almost a century before.

In the late afternoon Lord Elcho and his Horse Guards were moved to Westquarter to assist the forward patrols along the Edinburgh road.[72] The clans at Falkirk had been brought to a state of readiness to move at a moments notice by Lord George and were all on the alert. At 7 pm their officers waited on Lord George at his quarters in the town to receive their orders.[73] At last something was about to happen.

CHAPTER 4

The Storm Begins
12th January - 16th January 1746

Lieutenant-General Hawley had also been making plans which were well advanced. The government army was to march from Edinburgh to the relief of Stirling Castle. By January 12th preparations were made along the route to secure provisions for the troops, and particularly to obtain fodder for the dragoons' horses which could not graze at that time of the year. Over 3,000 blankets had been provided by the inhabitants of Edinburgh for the men that were to set off into hostile territory, uncertain about acquiring accommodation and expecting to be camping together in their cold tents for safety. The Earl of Hopetoun, relieved at their moving forward, and aware of the great shortage of food afflicting East Stirlingshire, arranged to give each regiment twelve guineas with which to buy beef.[1]

Hawley was also concerned about the battle tactics and drill of his men. A shrewd observer, he had analysed the enemy's mode of fighting and pinpointed its inherent weaknesses. That same day he issued the following directive in his orders:

> The manner of the Highlanders way of fighting which there is nothing so easy to resist If Officers & men are not preposess'd with the lyes & Accounts which are told of them. They Commonly form their Front rank of what they call their best men, or True Highlanders, the number of which being allways but few, when they form in Battallions they commonly form four deep, & these Highlanders form the front of the four, the rest being lowlanders & arrant scum. When these Battallions come within a large Musket shot, or three score yards, this front Rank gives their fire, & Immediately thro' down their firelocks & Come down in a Cluster with their Swords & Targets making a Noise & Endeavouring to pearce the Body, or Battallions before them becoming 12 or 14 deep by the time they come up to the people they attack. The sure way to demolish them is at 3 deep to fire by ranks diagonaly to the Centre where they come, the rear rank first, and even that rank not to fire till they are within 10 or 12 paces but If the fire

is given at a distance you probably will be broke for you never get time to load a second Cartridge, & if you give way you may give your foot for dead, for they being without a firelock or any load, no man with his arms, accoutrements & c. can escape them, and they give no Quarters, but if you will but observe the above directions, they are the most despicable Enimy that are.[2]

The Highland army had been in the district around Falkirk for a week and were finding food harder and harder to come by. They were now having to procure provisions from much further afield which exposed their forage parties to great danger. Intelligence reports from Edinburgh informed Lord George that the government army had prepared themselves ready for an advance and were to leave that city on either the 13th or the 14th. The spies bringing the reports noticed the activity at Linlithgow in connection with this. Whig supporters and a small body of militia in Linlithgow were busy laying in stores for their army. Lord George determined to risk a night march to that town, as he had done on 15th September last, in order to seize the provisions of bread, cheese, fodder and other consumables. At the same time the town would be scoured for further supplies and the annual taxes collected. For this purpose, all the wagons and carts in the neighbourhood of

Lieutenant General Henry Hawley (1679-1759)

Falkirk had been requisitioned the previous night, together with the necessary draught animals. This move had caused much speculation in the government camp where it was thought to presage a Jacobite withdrawal to Stirling.[3]

In the early hours of the next morning Lord George sat at his desk and wrote a short note to inform the unsuspecting Prince of his actions. He was about to commit around a fifth of the Jacobite army to an advance in the face of an approaching enemy without the commander in chief's prior knowledge! He was exercising the discretionary powers mentioned in the chiefs' petition of the 6th. This curt message was then handed over to a courier and at 4 am Lord George set out at the head of five clan regiments. These were Glengarry's, Clanranald's, Keppoch's, Appin and Cluny's, making about 1100 in all. The haulage train followed some way to the rear. On the road the foot regiments were joined by Lord Elcho's and Pitsligo's Horse. Kilmarnock's Horse remained at Falkirk to act as a rearguard. Lord George also requested that Kilmarnock should "appoint a Guard up towards ffalkirk Muir to prevent any Deserters going that way, as they were Droping off every Night".[4]

LORD GEORGE MURRAY TO MR JOHN O'SULLIVAN, QUARTER MASTER GENERAL.

Falkirk 13th Jany
1746.

Sir,
Being sure that all the Ships except two are faln down the River, & those two have no souldiers aboard, I design to go just now, with the five Batalions here, & two Squadrons, for Lithgow where they have prepared a Considerable quantity of Vivos for our enemys, which we propose to make free with. And as I can aprehend no danger I'm persauded it will give spirets to our men. I shall be back in good time this afternoon. You will let his Royall Highness know of this, we are all in great concern for the bad coald his Highness has got, & hope upon all our accounts he will take care of his Health.

I shall be glad that Locheall come this day to Elphiston, Elphistonpans, Carsey nook, & c. I am Sir,
your Most obedient Humble servant,
George Murray.
      Monday four in the morning.[5]

At Linlithgow Bridge a small group was detached towards Bo'ness. The main party reached Linlithgow at sunrise and by 9 o'clock had taken possession of it. The startled population, many of them Jacobite sympathizers, put up no resistance and a few of the country militia were taken prisoner. The stores were soon secured. The Jacobite cavalry were sent out in small parties to patrol a mile or so out of the town, with particular attention focussing on the road to Edinburgh. Lord George, mindful of the possible approach of the government army, gave orders that his regiments must be prepared to abandon their task and leave at a moment's notice in whatever direction was decided upon according to the circumstances.[6] The Highlanders then started a search of the town to procure additional supplies probably collecting some loot at the same time.

Lord George now had to wait for the wagons to make the last part of their journey from Falkirk, and to give time for the few remaining magistrates to raise the money that was demanded of them. About 11 o'clock four of Elcho's Guards were confronted by an officer and 12 dragoons about a mile from the town. Two of the Guards returned to inform Lord George, while the remaining two retired in front of the advancing dragoons.[7] When this news reached Linlithgow the Jacobite cavalry there were immediately dispatched to deal with the situation. They found that the advanced party of the dragoons had pushed forward to within a quarter of a mile of the town. Lord George sent 200 of his best men after his cavalry to give them support.[8] Upon seeing the Jacobite cavalry in larger numbers the small party of dragoons retired in their turn. They fell back upon another detachment of dragoons, some 60 or so in number. Here they remained until Lord Elcho formed his Horse and advanced towards them. The dragoons made off and were pursued for about a quarter of a mile, at which point Lord Elcho quitted the chase, not wanting to be drawn too far from the main body of the army. He remained there watching the enemy riding off into the distance, and sent a report of the events back to Lord George.

Upon the first alarm Lord George had taken his infantry out of the town to meet the oncoming forces. At around 12 o'clock they had formed into battle order upon a hill to the south-east of Linlithgow. When news came to him of the dragoons movements

General view of Linlithgow from the south-east c1680 by Captain John Slezer

and that they were now over two miles distant he ordered Elcho to return leaving only a small reconnaissance party. Rather than keep his forces in a state of alert on the hill for an unknown length of time he returned to his original enterprise at Linlithgow.

Carts had been acquired in the town, and now those from Falkirk were also loaded and sent off as soon as each was ready [9]. The Highlanders then dined at the expense of the inhabitants. About 3 o'clock the Jacobite reconnaissance party brought news that the dragoons were again approaching, this time in force and accompanied by at least four regiments of foot.[10] In fact it was Major-General Huske with the five foot regiments of Munro, Cholmondeley, Price, Ligonier and Battereau, with the Glasgow Militia under Lord Home. Together with Hamilton's and Ligonier's dragoons this made a force of some 4,000 men, far outnumbering the 1,250 of Lord George.

Hawley's plan of campaign had been for Huske to take the 4,000 troops to Linlithgow and for 1,000 militiamen from Argyll to proceed to Kilsyth. They would then proceed to drive the Jacobite advance guard out of Falkirk[11] and the remaining half of the army would follow from Edinburgh. This course of action, dividing the army into two and only using one half, was disapproved of by the more cautious commanders who believed that the army should be kept together in case the enemy should give battle.[12] Hawley, however, was supremely confident that the rabble would flee before him.[13] Hawley had been with the Hanoverian cavalry at the Battle of Sheriffmuir in 1715 when they had put the Jacobite army to flight and consequently entertained a very low opinion of them.

Lord George naturally assumed that no general would thus divide his forces and believed that Huske's regiments merely represented the vanguard. He called a council of war to review the predicament.[14] It was decided to remain at Linlithgow as long as possible. There were two reasons for this; firstly they could more effectually cover the passage of the supply train which was still wending its slow progress to Falkirk; and secondly, they needed to buy more time for the main army at Bannockburn to receive the reinforcements which were still arriving from the north. Lord George also held out hopes of tempting the government troops into a rapid pursuit on seeing the clans fleeing. This would take them across Linlithgow Bridge where, when half of the government army had crossed, he intended to turn and cut them off, leaving the remainder as mere spectators in the ensuing battle.[15] He greatly regretted the absence of Lochiel's Regiment, some of his best men, who were still in Alloa.

Meanwhile, the government officers were laying their own schemes. Grossett had been sent with Huske in order to acquaint him with the countryside and to keep him informed about the movements of the Jacobites. Active as ever, Grossett procured information from his spies that the Jacobites in Linlithgow were only 1,200 strong. Along with the report of the party of dragoons this allowed Huske to deploy his forces appropriately. Grossett, knowing that the town lay in a hollow upon the south side of a loch which debarred access from the north, advised that the government army should march well to the south where it would be out of sight. They could then not only get between the advance party of the Jacobites and their main body, but they could cut them off completely by holding the bridge over the river Avon. This plan of action was agreed upon and a small detachment was sent up the same hill which Lord George had earlier occupied in order to deceive the enemy into believing that the main body was approaching from that direction as they would have expected.[16]

The government scheme had considerable merit. It would have allowed them to form into battle line in open country against an enemy only a third their number. The only escape for the Highlanders would have been either to force the crossing at great risk, or to head down river to a crossing near to the mouth. In the latter case they would have been harried by the dragoons as they retreated in the dark. As planned, the detachment of government soldiers halted on the hill, observed by the Jacobites who were still in Linlithgow.

Huske's army had been shadowed all the way from Edinburgh by a very large number of civilians intent upon witnessing the imminent conflict. There were several hundreds of these people, driven by their curiosity to neglect the danger in which they were placing themselves, and looking forward to the forthcoming entertainment. Everyone seemed to realise that they were living through truly historic events. Unfortunately for the government army there were some Jacobite supporters within the horde of keen observers. It was probably one of these, an innkeeper, who gave their game away. Apprehending Huske's stratagem, he rode into Linlithgow and alerted Lord George.

Lord George knew that he had to react quickly but without revealing that he was aware of the enemy's plan. He therefore "ordered the bagpipes to play and to march slowly through the town to make a feint to meet General Hawley till our men were out of the houses. Making a front of our rear we retreated".[17] The race to Linlithgow Bridge was on. It was now almost 4 o'clock and the highlanders, being more than ready, wasted no further time. They were irregular troops, lightly armed, and capable of marching at twice the pace of the government's laden regular troops. They rapidly narrowed the distance between themselves and the bridge. They moved quietly, everyone aware of the urgency of their movement. Approaching the bridge they could hear the horses of the dragoons, they could almost feel the horses breathing down their necks. The bridge was gained and they smartly filed across it, the last of them exchanging angry words with the frustrated enemy [18]. Walter Grossett was with the dragoons and "being somewhat lighter mounted than the Dragoons, came up wth & took one of the rascally rable of Robers Prisoner".[19] The government force gave up on any chance of a hot pursuit over the narrow stone bridge. Huske

Linlithgow Bridge c1900, with the public house on the right.

left the dragoons there to ensure that his foot were not disturbed in the night. The dragoons were now in the same camp that they had occupied in the first descent of the Jacobite army in September and no doubt the irony was not lost on either side. The infantry quartered in the town of Linlithgow and received the claims for damage made by its citizens.[20]

The Highland clans returned to the relative safety of Falkirk that night, having left a guard at their side of Linlithgow Bridge. It was dark before they arrived and the hard won supplies had to be dealt with before they could turn in. Nonetheless it had been an exhilarating experience as yet again they had come off the better for an audacious raid in the face of a superior enemy. Lord George promptly dispatched messages to prince Charles informing him of the day's events, and requesting greater expediency in drawing the still dispersed army together.

Elphinstone and Alloa were quiet that day. After the frenetic activity of the previous days this was a welcome change. The Jacobite brig had been successfully refloated by the incoming tide and landed its second consignment of arms at Polmaise. Lord John Drummond arranged for its disposition and then crossed the river to congratulate Cromarty's regiment upon completing their task. With Lord John Macleod, who was exhausted by his night vigils, he retired for the night to the house of a gentleman in the vicinity [21], probably Tullibody House. They had only been asleep for two hours when they were awoken by Alexander Macleod of Muiravonside, now acting as an aide-de-camp to Prince Charles. He had news of Huske's advance to Linlithgow and consequently Cromarty's regiment, and Lochiel's, were immediately ordered over the river to join the main body of the army now daily expecting a battle.

Early the following morning Lochiel and the Camerons marched west from Alloa and joined Macleod with his regiment on the bank of the river somewhere opposite to Polmaise. This was one of the narrowest sections of the river and thus best suited to ferrying the men across. However, yet again there was only limited transport. Three boats were now available to perform this feat, new ones having been constructed at Alloa each capable of carrying about twenty men.[22] William Verly, a carpenter in Alloa, had overseen this work for them.[23] The brig was not suited, or entrusted, to the task. The Camerons took precedence in the ferry service and so the other regiment had to wait another day.

While these operations were in progress the rest of the Jacobite army was busy redeploying. Arrangements were made for certain units to remain in the cordon around Stirling Castle, and others were forwarded towards Skeoch Muir. The new deployment was to face the approaching enemy at Linlithgow. The garrison in the Castle observed this activity and guessed the cause of the disruption [24] and so too did some of the whigs still left in the town.[25]

The prying portion of the population of central Scotland began to hover around Falkirk like moths to a flame. Amongst them was an individual from Kilmarnock, commonly called Auld Soulis. He left his home town on the 14th January and headed for Falkirk to gratify his curiosity, as he said, by seeing Prince Charles and his army. He also wanted to arrive there in time to witness the action which all felt was inevitable.[26] People flocked in from all directions and from considerable distances. As the numbers of these strangers went up so too did the price of food in the area.

Lord George had been anxious to have his division in Falkirk reinforced. Early in the morning he had travelled to Bannockburn

House to find out for himself what was being done and to arrange future troop movements. Much to his vexation he saw the tardiness of the crucial response to his previous night's report. Lochiel's regiment was still in transit and Cromarty's unable to progress towards the main body. Lord Lewis Gordon's troops and others from the north were still at least a day's march away. Realizing the hopelessness of defending Falkirk, or of meeting the enemy to the south of the river Carron, he returned there and withdrew the clan regiments to the Bannockburn area.[27] They had great difficulty in obtaining billets there. Lord George made his own headquarters at Easter Greenyards Farm. Prince Charles was furious. He believed that the withdrawal gave the men the impression of a retreat in the face of an advancing enemy, and indeed that was the way that the government troops saw it. Lord Kilmarnock assured him that this was not the case, but the Prince was bitter in his condemnation.[28]

Major-General Huske with his five regiments of foot and two of dragoons did not leave the vicinity of Linlithgow that day. However, the foot regiments of Howard, Pulteney and Barrel left Edinburgh under the command of Brigadier Cholmondeley. They arrived at Bo'ness in the late afternoon where they provided support for Huske. Grossett made the short journey from Linlithgow to Bo'ness to help with the arrangements there. He also procured the service of ten sailors from the port to operate the ad hoc field artillery which was being assembled in Edinburgh to support the army's advance. The properly equipped train of artillery from England with its well trained crews was experiencing considerable delays due to its recent participation in the siege of Carlisle. This had already cost Hawley a day's delay with his plans and so he was doing his best to improvise. Ten brass cannon, ranging from a 6-pounder to a 1 1/2-pounder, had been pressed into use from Edinburgh Castle.[29] They were placed under the command of Captain Cunningham, an officer with 30 years of experience, 17 of which were in the artillery. He had travelled up from Newcastle at short notice and had only been in Edinburgh for two days.[30] An Irishman by birth, he had an affinity with the bottle. The Bo'ness sailors had all served on a man-of-war and were to act as the gunners. They shrewdly insisted on being paid in advance, which from the necessities of the occasion was done.[31]

EXTRACT OF LETTER, LIEUTENANT-GENERAL HAWLEY TO GENERAL WENTWORTH

Edinburgh. Jany 14th 1745-6.

Major Kelaid dos not come at all, & this Cunningham is so ignorant & such a beast, he is of no use; I should be very glad to see Mr Sawyer with the money he, here is no more to be had here. when you will see a convoy for the stores & c I do not know; two of ye small ships are disabled, in a little action we have had at Alloway.

We are in the greatest want of Gunns, those at Berwick I hope will be ready, those here never can; thes have no hands, and I can get none M.Gel Huske yesterday drove out 1400 of the Rascals like sheep, where he has taken post wth 4000 men; I send three Battallions more to him today.

We want but Gunns to go to Sterling and drive them from thence.[32]

Quite late on in the day Lord Kilmarnock discovered Huske's tardiness in advancing from Linlithgow and wrote to the Prince to inform him that Falkirk could still be re-occupied by the Jacobite army.[33]. Without Lord George's cooperation, however, it was clear that matters would remain as they were.

LORD KILMARNOCK TO PRINCE CHARLES

Sir,
Within this half hour the Bearer came to me with a little bit of Intelligence he pickt up from a messenger of Mr Huske's with whom he got acquainted at Falkirk. You may trust the fellow, at least that he will tell you what he hears without adding or parring. I am well acquainted with him of old and of late he has used me very well in the Prince's Service. The Truth of his Information must depend on his Informer for he is no Sorcerer: Yet by what you can gather from him I believe you'll think the Pass at Falkirk is not yet lost and may still be saved tomorrow. I beg Pardon for giving a hurt and am faithfully,
Sir Your most obedient humble servant,

KILMARNOCK   Stirling Jan 14th 1746

Want of health oblig'd me to leave my Corps and come here for good Quarters in place of waiting three hours for Billets as the Rest did.[34]

Next day three more regiments of foot under the command of Brigadier Mordaunt left Edinburgh with the artillery. These were Fleming's, Blakeney's and St Clair's. They joined Huske at Linlithgow in the afternoon. Meanwhile the Argyll Militia marched from Glasgow to Airdrie. Colonel John Campbell had chosen the less risky southern route towards the east in order to rendezvous with Hawley's army near Falkirk.[35]

MAJOR-GENERAL HUSKE TO LIEUTENANT-GENERAL HAWLEY

Sir
Between one and two o Clock this morning, I was favoured with yours of the 14th. Since which time I have had the Deputy Sherrif of the County with me, the post Master of Falkirk and Captain Cunningham with me: we have talked over all affairs necessary for preparing for our march, which can't be before to morrow as time must be given, at least 14 hours for Horses to carry their baggage, blankets and such or leave men: as the Rebels have destroyed in some degree the Forage about Falkirk, and plundered the inhabitants time must be given for making preparation for ye reception of troops at that place.

I will march to morrow from hence with the five Regiments now in this Town and if the other three that you intend should march from Edinborough to day, comes here, as Capt Cunningham has found cover for them in this Town. I intend to march as many of the Troops with me to morrow from this Town as I can find cover for at Falkirk which I hope will be between 4 and 5,000 men, According to the opinion of the postmaster of that town and others, but to be at a greater certainty I'm sending Captain Cunningham away this morning at 6 o' Clock with 100 Dragoons and the Post master of Falkirk along with him. upon Capt: Cunninghams return according to the report he makes of what cover can be got for the Troops I shall determine the number of Regiments I shall march with me to morrow from hence. I am undetermined what Dragoons to take with me from hence, one of the Regiments I must take. I have sent a Detachment of 100 Dragoons at the request of Brigadier Cholmondley to Borrowstouness in order to patrouile between that place and this Town. I could wish if you thought it proper that Cobham's Regiment had orders to joyn me, believing them to be Troops that may be depended upon. I have given all the orders that's in my power for providing forage and provision for the Troops at Falkirk and the places there abouts. I am glad you have given orders for Lord Murray's Cattle to be sent to Falkirk, which will be very acceptable to the Troops. I hope the Men are to pay no more than two pence a pound for it. I am sending away an Express to Colonel Campbell according to your directions, to march his 1000 Highlanders to morrow to Falkirk which I include in the number of men before mentioned that we believe quarters may be found for. if these Highlanders are to be provided with bread you'l be pleased to give your proper orders to the Commissary.

As I am not certain what cover there may be at Burrowstouness, the two Regiments being there I must submit it to you to give the orders for the march of the Glascow Regiment.

If the Train could arrive at this Town to day I should be very glad of it, being desirous to take it with me to morrow.

The Tumbroll is arrived here with the Cartridges. it's a poor shattered one but will be put in order to day.

The bread will be welcome as its scarce and dear in this Country to the Soldier. When Capt Cunningham returns I'll send you another express this evening I am
Dr Genl
with truth and esteem
your most humble servt.

John Huske.
Linlithgow Wednesday morning 4 o'Clock January 15 1745/6.[36]

The Jacobites, believing that all the government army must have been at Linlithgow that morning, had expected them to march forward to give them battle that day. Accordingly the troops had been assembling since before dawn on Plean Muir. Their battle line was to be protected on the flanks by some old coal mines and by Torwood.[37] The order of the battle line had been worked out and each detachment was slowly placed on the field. It was late afternoon, however, before these dispositions were finished. During this time a large body of cavalry had been sent to Falkirk to ascertain the deployment of the Government army. They returned in the afternoon reporting that only the dragoons were to be seen around that town.[38] It was already late in the day and so the army dispersed, taking precautions against a surprise attack. An officer and twelve Horse Grenadiers were detailed to patrol the roads

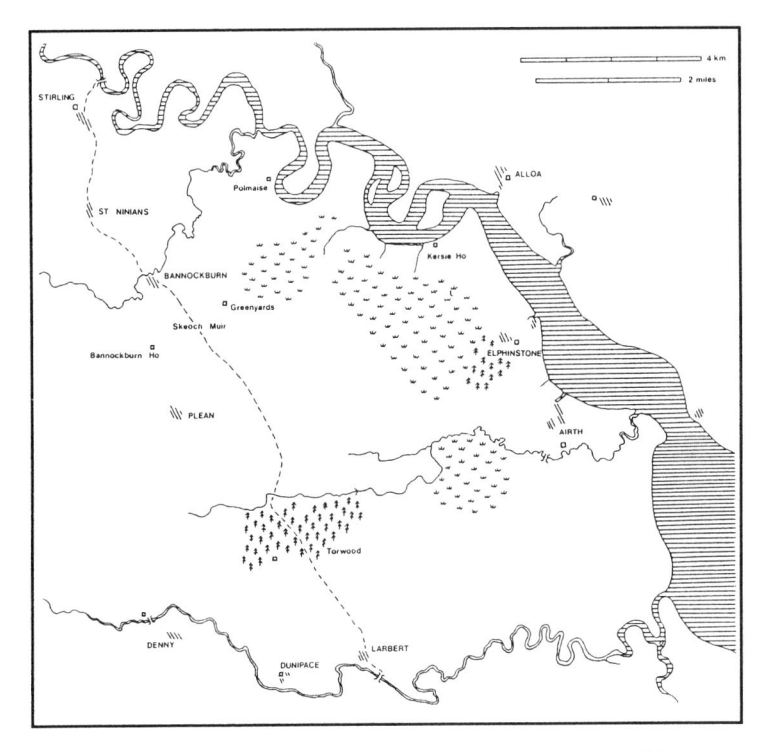

Map showing the main road from Stirling Bridge to Larbert Bridge.

from Glasgow and Falkirk, together with a matching number of Hussars. From 10 o'clock onwards they were replaced by like detachments from Balmerino's Life Guards and Pitsligo's Horse, supplemented by two officers and 30 infantry from Cluny's Regiment at Plean. The latter were to pay particular attention to the stone dykes beside the road at Torwood Pass. Thirty Frasers guarded the artillery.[39]

As the Jacobite army were widely dispersed in their cantonments it was essential to maintain good communications with the headquarters at Bannockburn House. This was ensured by having an orderly sergeant from each regiment stationed there at all times. The problem of how to tackle the shortage of food was harder to resolve. There were now more men due to the arrival of some of the northern reinforcements, and they were all confined to a smaller area than before having withdrawn from the land to the south of the river Carron. Two men out of every hundred were therefore seconded to the Commissary in order to hunt for provisions. They were only to return to their regiments when a battle was inevitable.[40]

Cromarty's Regiment finally crossed the river Forth, but arrived too late in the day to join the battle line when it had been formed up. Initially their orders had been to leave half of the regiment with the artillery at Polmaise and to take the remainder to the field of battle. However, as they were so long delayed, and no action was obviously to occur that day, they were all quartered in some farmhouses around Polmaise. Lord Macleod, not wanting to miss the battle, had borrowed a horse from Mr Murray of Polmaise, but arrived at Skeoch Muir just before the army dispersed.[41]

The 16th January witnessed a considerable movement of regiments as the two armies manoeuvred for position like pieces in a giant game of chess. Both government and Jacobite troops were in motion before the break of day. Lieutenant-General Hawley, having seen to as much of the administrative work connected with the general advance as he could, finally left Edinburgh in a carriage. He was accompanied by Wolfe's Regiment of foot and by a regiment of volunteers known as the 'Yorkshire Blues'. These men had been raised in Yorkshire by Captain Thornton who also paid for their maintenance and their blue uniforms. At their head was blind Jack Metcalf of Knaresborough, later to become famous as a road builder and a rival to MacAdam. He played the fiddle or the drum to encourage the men during the foot-slogging marches. Later that day Cobham's dragoons left Dalkeith, which they had reached after a long march, and passed straight through Edinburgh in Hawley's footsteps. Major-General Huske, knowing that there were no enemy forces between the rivers Avon and Carron, moved his eight regiments of foot from Linlithgow to Falkirk. These were immediately followed by Brigadier Cholmondeley and the three regiments from Bo'ness who had to wade through the Avon near the

Jinkabout Ford. For years the citizens of Linlithgow had opposed the efforts of the Bo'ness merchants to have a bridge constructed here as it would take away traffic from Linlithgow Bridge.[42] This campaign was highlighting the need for such a structure which would be a just reward for the part played in it by the little town of Bo'ness.

The Jacobite forces roused early and collected once more in battle formation upon Plean Muir. Lochiel's Regiment provided the personal guard for prince Charles for the day. It was once again mid-day before the army was completely formed, only a little better than the day before. The cavalry patrols brought word of the government's infantry arriving at Falkirk. Together they waited for news of a further advance, the day was still young. The Highlanders were now eager to get into action. The constant marching, counter-marching, lining up and so forth was not to their liking and they just wanted to get on with fighting the enemy. However, this was not to be. At 3 o'clock, hearing that the government army was entrenched in a camp to the north-west of Falkirk, the Jacobite army dispersed yet again.[43]

It was 1 o'clock when the government foot marched through the narrow streets of Falkirk and then halted only one hundred paces on the other side of the settlement, astride the road to Glasgow and Stirling.[44] Here they encamped on a well suited site. On the west side, the front facing the enemy, was a deep hollow morassy ground containing the Mungal Burn; the right flank, or north side, was covered by some inclosures with large wet ditches around them which included the west Burn; the same burn encompassed the south side at the foot of Arnothill; which left the town on the east side, though even this was separated by a stream.[45] Within the camp the regiments lay in two lines fronting the enemy towards the west with the hurriedly formed artillery train parked on the north side of the road. Within an hour the neat rows of over a thousand off-white canvas tents had been erected and camp fires sprung up between them. It was a cold day and the men were happy to gather around the hearths. Sentries were posted and the boundaries marked out. Beyond the confines of this strongly located camp three regiments had to be placed obliquely on the right flank due to lack of space. These lay between the West Burn and Graham's Road which led to the Stenhouse Ford on the river Carron.

Although reasonably strongly located the camp had been chosen from a belief that the Jacobites would not attack. Lord George's hasty retreat from Linlithgow, and then from Falkirk, without so much as a rearguard action had convinced the government commanders of that. It had also considerably boosted the morale of their troops. It was therefore partly for the comfort provided by the proximity of the town of Falkirk that the site was selected. Men on leave could enter the town and gain temporary warmth away from their freezing tents. Some of the junior officers even requisitioned accommodation in the town for themselves, though they found rents considerably inflated. The officers on Hawley's staff took over Callendar House[46] where they were greeted by the Countess of Kilmarnock. A location two miles to the west would certainly have been preferable for the camp on strategic grounds, covering the crossings of the river Carron. The area has the largest concentration of Roman camps in Britain, and was also used by Cromwell. To guard against a night attack the dragoons were sent to watch these crossings, especially that at Larbert Bridge where a large body of them were stationed.

The whig supporters in the Falkirk area had been dormant during the Jacobite occupation. They now came out of hiding to help the government forces. Notable amongst these was Reverend Bennet of Polmont. He not only provided intelligence of Jacobite sympathizers, but also procured accommodation for the troops and fodder for the horses.[47] It would seem that his fellow minister in Falkirk, John Adams - friend of the late Colonel Gardiner, had left the area on the first approach of the Jacobite army. In fact, there had been no sermons in the Falkirk Church for two weeks.[48] The presbyterian church as a whole was radically opposed to the Stuart cause and the Catholic religion which it represented to them. Many of them offered their active support to the government.

An example of this ecclesiastical zeal can be seen in the young pastor of the parish of Beith, between Irvine and Paisley. The Presbytery of Irvine had resolved "primo, to do all in their power for influencing such as are within their Bounds to exert themselves in support of the present Government; Secondo, That they will in conjunction with their own parishes contribute for raising some Volunteers for that purpose if it be found necessary". The Minister, Mr Witherspoon thereon drew up a subscription paper for the

The village of Larbert from the railway viaduct next to Larbert Bridge. The River Carron can be seen on the lower left.

purpose of defraying the expenses of a party of Beith Militia, at the head of which he proposed to march to Stirling to join the royal forces. The amount he collected was £88 15s. The militiamen, to the number of 150 were engaged to serve for 30 days from the date of their departure from Beith. On reaching Glasgow, however, this determined band were informed by the military authorities that they were not needed and were told to return the twenty miles to their homes. Disheartened, Witherspoon dismissed his party, and pushed on himself towards the scene of conflict, accompanied by his beadle bearing a trusty sword. They arrived in Falkirk, along with many other potential spectators, on the 16th January.

The carnival atmosphere that was developing in Falkirk was not to everyone's liking. Food prices continued to rocket as demand from the huge numbers of outsiders rose. Only the officers could afford to buy locally, as could the merchants from other towns. The optimism of the government army and the host of visitors was not shared by the inhabitants who had just endured almost two weeks of occupation. William Boutcher of Comely Garden sent one of his servants to bring home his cows that were in the Parks of Callendar and which he feared would be spirited away. The servant was arrested on his way there by the government troops and carried away to the Canongate Prison in Edinburgh under suspicion of being a Jacobite.[49] Or was the motive of the arresting soldiers to obtain the cattle for themselves? Perhaps a curfew had been invoked. Lord George was having trouble obtaining food as well.[50] He complained too about bad quarters, slow advances in the siege of Stirling Castle, "scandalous desertion", and poor discipline. However, the morale of the Jacobite army was generally high. As well as the earlier reinforcements they were joined that day by 800 men under Lord Lewis Gordon, 600 with Sir James Kinloch, and 350 of Lord John Drummond's Regiment.[51] Their army was now some 9,000 strong, over twice the number that had marched into England in October. They made similar security arrangements to those of the previous night.[52] It was obvious to all that a battle would occur within the next 36 hours, and the Jacobite army was ordered to carry provisions sufficient for three meals with them to cover any eventuality. In all probability they would have to stay under arms all the next night.

LORD JUSTICE CLERK TO DUKE OF CUMBERLAND.

Edinr 16th Jan 1746

On Monday Tuesday and Wednesday Twelve Regiments of foot and Two of Dragoons have marched west to Lithgow, the Artilery followed yesterday, as did this day Genl Hawley and Lord Cobhams Dragoons. All the people I employed to bring me intelligence, have orders to bring it to the first commanding officer they meet with, by which means I can write your Grace very little news. Only the Party of the Rebells that retired to Falkirk from Lithgow, on General Huskes comeing there, retired on Tuesday from Falkirk towards Stirling to their main body. The Rebells have certainly got over most of their friends to the southside of Forth; and the Chiefs of the Rebells, say they chuse rather to be killed in Battle than be hanged or starve, and therefore are for fighting, and endeavour to spirit up their men, with another Battle of Bannockburn, wch place is two miles on this side of Stirling; on the other hand the Common Men have got a great deal of money & Booty and are affraid to loose it in a battle, and therefore want to get it to their Severall homes.

ANDREW FLETCHER [53]

Both armies were now vulnerable to a rapid attack as they lay only four miles apart, separated only by the river Carron. The Jacobites had made several night marches already during the campaign which had allowed them to attack their enemy to their own advantage. Major-General Huske was only too aware of these previous engagements, and of General Cope's disgrace, and had posted the dragoons with the help of local people at all the river crossings up to Denny. More dragoons patrolled behind these outposts to provide a further screen. The command of the government army were confident in their security measures, and in the knowledge that the Jacobite army would not abandon their superior position at Plean Muir.

By contrast, the commanders of the Jacobite army were extremely nervous and agitated. With their troops widely dispersed it had taken them beyond noon that day, and the day before, to get into battle formation. This was quite a simple formation consisting of two lines and a corps de reserve. They knew that the government soldiers, encamped together in tents, could be placed in marching order within an hour, and could therefore reach them long before they were fully formed. In effect, the Jacobite regiments might easily be picked off piecemeal without so many as a thousand men gathering in any one place to oppose the enemy. The longer the government army stayed entrenched in Falkirk, the more sleep the Jacobites would lose; and the more exposed their reinforcements would be to the wintry weather; and the scarcer food would become.

The Jacobite cavalry was already suffering badly. They had been constantly on the alert for two weeks, carrying out the tasks of patrolling and providing outposts. On the night of the 16th they were described by the Frenchman Sir John Macdonald as being "composed of a large party of gentlemen without discipline or experience, and whose horses were very tired and extremely badly cared for, they were in an extremely bad state". [54] With their small numbers it was certain that they would play little part in any battle.

It was already dark when Lieutenant-General Hawley arrived at Falkirk at 7 o'clock at night.[55] The camp fires of the enemy could be seen glimmering in the distance on the hills to the north-west. With Hawley was the artillery train and the sailors from Bo'ness who had only just viewed the cannon that they were expected to use in the heat of battle within the next few days. Hawley checked the camp for himself and received the reports of his officers. A Mr Roger presented himself to the commander and gave his personal observations concerning the state of the Highland army. He vouched for their good spirits and their firm intention to march out the next day to meet him head on. Hawley was accustomed to such shows of bravado and remained unconcerned.[56] At 8 o'clock he went to his own quarters at Callendar House. Some of the Glasgow Militia officers who had arrived in Falkirk with the first division had already acquired some of the rooms, and indeed, were occupying the beds ready for an early start in the morning. They were unceremoniously displaced by Hawley and had to seek shelter elsewhere.[57] The Countess of Kilmarnock, Anne Livingston, who was keen to be seen as loyal must have exchanged a few words with Hawley before he retired for the night.

CHAPTER 5

The Tempest
17th January 1746

The next morning Hawley was up very early and at 5 o'clock visited the camp.[1] The night van and picket guards came in with no activity to report on the part of the enemy.[2] Between 8 and 9 o'clock the men in the camp, already awake with some of them under arms all the time, were further disturbed by the arrival of the Argyll Militia and Cobham's Dragoons. The militiamen caused quite a stir with their kilts and highland manners. Mostly Campbells, the corps consisted of 12 companies of men from Argyll, 3 companies of Lord Loudon's, and 1 of Lord John Murray's, making almost 1,000 in all. They had marched all the way from Bathgate by way of Linlithgow where they had met Cobham's Regiment. They were quite exhausted and sought some quarters. The camp being full, they were assigned to some farmhouses in front of it - that is to the west around Sunnyside and Dorrator. Not only were they spread out from one another, but they were also at a distance from the camp.[3] Their orders for the day were to be forwarded once the plan of attack had been confirmed.

The officers of the government army were wary of the next stage of their advance towards Stirling. It involved crossing the river by Larbert Bridge, which they now held and where they were vulnerable to an attack. The local topography provided sufficient cover for a Jacobite army to descend upon them very rapidly at that point with only part of their army across. From there they would have to march up hill to the top of Torwood. Here the enemy would have the cover not only of this ancient forest, but also of the stone dykes lining the highway for several miles. Then there was the small valley of the Tor Burn to negotiate. Intelligence reports had told them that the Jacobite army was entrenched at the Torwood Pass; certainly they had had the time to do so. History reminded them that King Charles II had created formidable defensive obstacles in this area only ninety-four years before. After consultation with local supporters it was decided to march very early the next day by a circuitous route and to surprise the enemy while they were still assembling. Local guides were to take them from the other side of Larbert Bridge west to Dunipace. From there they would begin the slow ascent to Torwood Head Muir by way of Kirkland.[4] This approach had the added advantage of keeping them out of sight of the Jacobite army until they had gained the hill. However, the cover of darkness was still considered essential for the commencement of the march in order to get across the river, and that is why they would have to wait for the another day. In the meantime they had taken all the necessary precautions for their own safety and ensured that the newly arrived troops could get some rest. The Jacobites, after a restless night, also had an early start. The Prince was wakened at 3 o'clock with the news that the government army had beaten the general assembly on their drums.[5] At about 4 o'clock the garrison of Stirling Castle heard the Jacobites themselves beat the general, and about an hour later this was followed by the assembly.[6] They were under arms and in motion at 7 o'clock. At 8 they had united with further detachments at St Ninians and proceeded towards Plean Muir. A body of horse was despatched towards Falkirk to ascertain the movements of the government army.[7] Whilst the main body of the army was thus engaged in its attempt to form into battle order, Cromarty's Regiment was sent from Polmaise to the head of Torwood where it met up with with a few other small detachments to provide temporary cover in the event of an early attack upon them.[8]

The Jacobite horse returned with the report that there was no motion in the government camp.[9] Upon hearing this the cavalry under the command of Lord Drummond were sent to Torwood and the advance guard ordered to rejoin the main body.[10] However,

A private soldier of Lord Louden's Foot c1742

Two highland officers of the period
(from The Antiquities of Scotland, 1797)

this last movement was seen from Falkirk by some Hanovarian officers using telescopes who observed the colours heading for Stirling.[11] These officers had taken up watch on a small hill about 500 yards away from their camp (probably on the Antonine Wall at Bantaskine). Hawley went out at 10 o'clock to verify the report for himself, but by that time there was nothing to be seen to the south of the Torwood horizon and consequently he perceived that there was no threat.[12] Alexander Grossett was there. His deep hatred of the enemy made him very wary of their actions. Using his own glass he had seen for himself the countermarching of the Jacobite army, and remained suspicious of their intent. Conveying this opinion to the General he promised in person to obtain further information on their movements. He then sent for his horses and servants and headed off in the direction of Denny where he knew he would be able to get a clearer view of the area around Torwood and the Bannockburn road.[13]

The government officers remained at their vantage point with their telescopes. It being a cold but dry and clear morning they could see at least four miles northwards towards the enemy. About 11 o'clock they espied another detachment of Jacobites at the Torwood. This time Major-General Huske and Brigadier-General Cholmondeley verified the observation.[14] They sent word to Hawley at the camp, and after a short deliberation the alarm was sounded and the men immediately went to arms. They were ordered to be ready to turn out at a moment's notice.[15] The artillery was put in harness ready to go and meet the enemy on the open field.

Again Hawley went out to check the sightings for himself, but seeing no Jacobites on the road from Torwood to Larbert he concluded that it was a false alarm. That road was the direct route between the two armies and gave the Jacobites the advantage of elevation and a bridge crossing of the Carron Water at Larbert and so it was the obvious line of approach. It was already half way through the day and it was unthinkable that they would try any other route. However, to be doubly sure Huske and a small party of officers and gentlemen rode out to their outposts for a better view. After about half an hour he returned saying that there was no hurry as there was nothing in the alarm.[16] The soldiers were stood down.[17] The men were quite jittery as a result of these events and in order to reassure them Hawley had them prepare a meal. He returned to his own quarters at Callendar House for his own refreshment about noon. It is said that, owing to the coldness of the day, Lady Kilmarnock made him a posset to warm him up.[18]

It would seem that both Huske and Hawley had seen Lord John Drummond's detachment at the head of Torwood and, observing that it was not in motion, correctly concluded that it merely represented their outpost against an attack. This detachment included a large part of the Jacobite horse, some 300 or so in number. Together with their colours they made quite a conspicuous appearance and were also seen by many of the civilians who had foregathered to witness the events.[19] Their mobility meant that they could rapidly respond to any tactical moves made by the government forces and rejoin the main body of the Jacobite army for a pitched battle. They were also able to keep Prince Charles and his commanders updated with their own observations.

The Jacobite foot had slowly formed into battle order according to plans modified by Lord George. The Earl of Cromarty's Regiment, and those which had formed the temporary screen earlier that day were incorporated into the left wing. There were two lines separated by about 200 yards. The front line, facing towards Falkirk, consisted largely of the clans. On the right wing the place of honour was given to the regiment of Keppoch Macdonalds under their clan chief, and included a small detachment of MacGregors. Next to them were the Clanranald Macdonalds under their chief's son. Then came two battalions of Glengarry Macdonalds under Angus Og of Glengarry and Macdonald of Lochgarry. These included the Grants from Glen Urquhart and Glenmoriston, and some Macleods under Raasa and Bernera. Then stood the Glencoe Macdonalds under their chief, and part of the Farquharsons under Farquharson of Balmoral. The remainder of the Farquharsons were with the cannon under Farquharson of Monaltrie. Then there were the MacKenzies under the Earl of Cromarty and his son Lord Macleod; the Mackintoshes under MacGillivray of Dunmaglass; the MacPhersons under MacPherson of Cluny; the Frasers and Chisholms under the Master of Lovat; the Stewarts of Appin under Stewart of Ardshiel; and on the left wing the Camerons under Lochiel. Over 4,500 in all, arranged in three ranks.

The second line consisted mainly of the lowland units. The Atholl brigade took the right, and with them were the Robertsons and the Menzies under their Chieftain Ian Menzies of Shian; next was Lord Ogilvy's; Lord Lewis Gordon's with whom were some of the Menzies of Pitfodels; Lord John Drummond's and the MacLachlans: making a line of about 3,000 men. The cavalry at

Torwood under Lord Drummond were to protect the flanks of the army. Lord George was in over-all command of the right wing, but he could not get a commitment from Prince Charles to name the other officers for the battle. It was clear that Charles and his own staff would take an over view of the battle from the rear at the centre, but who was to command the left wing?[20] Charles seems to have looked upon the appointment of a commander there in political rather than in military terms and left the decision for a later time, discussing it only with his closest advisors. Perhaps he thought that there would be quite enough central control from his own position! Consequently no aides-de-camp were yet assigned to that wing. These were the people whom the army would depend upon to coordinate the action by carrying the orders of the command to the regimental officers throughout the battlefield. For this duty they needed to be mounted on good horses to swiftly convey the messages. Lord George kept his own aide, Colonel Kerr, for this purpose. The two of them had acted together on numerous occasions and understood each other's meaning, a useful asset in the heat of battle.[21]

On hearing of the government army's continued inactivity the Jacobites called a council of war on the field. They had been more or less depending upon an encounter with the enemy that day. Their men had been primed to expect it and were growing restless, if not despondent at the anti-climax. They themselves had been living on the edge of their nerves all night long in fear of a dawn attack upon them. It was now about 12.15 pm and it had taken half the day to get into battle order. What little intelligence they were getting from Falkirk suggested that the anticipated raid would occur the following morning. The last of their own expected reinforcements had arrived that morning, making their force larger than it had ever been before, and putting all their men in high spirits. There were only two possible options, either to retreat to a safe distance or to advance and seize the initiative. The former was not even considered and without hesitation an advance was decided upon.

Lord George had the two lines wheel to their right to form two columns and placed himself at their head, this being the former right wing. The Royal Standard of the Stuarts was with Lord Ogilvy's Regiment.[22] Immediately they set off, heading across

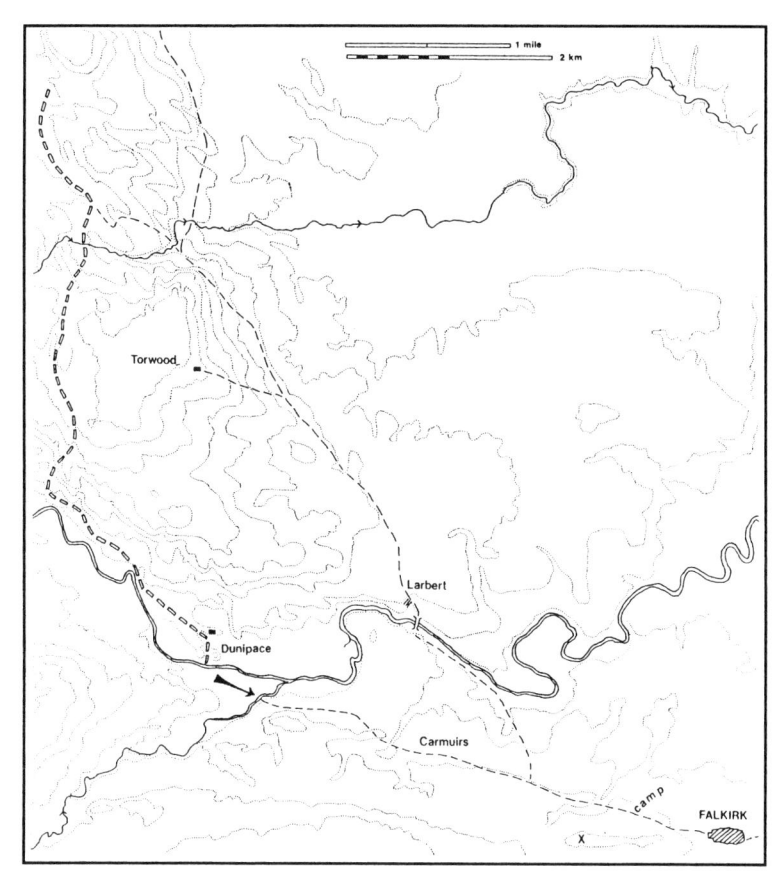

Map showing the route of the Jacobite Army from Plean Muir to the crossing of the River Carron at the steps of Dunipace. The main road through the Torwood to Larbert Bridge and Falkirk is also shown.

fields to the west of Torwood. The remainder of the cavalry were dispatched to Lord John Drummond. He now commanded about 740 horse, composed of his own piquets and hussars, and Lord Elcho's, Lord Balmerino's, Lord Pitsligo's and Lord Kilmarnock's squadrons. From the Head of Torwood he was able to observe the movements of the government army at Falkirk and would have been able to cover the march of his own foot had it been necessary.[23] The White Ensign was also given to this detachment so that the enemy might be deceived into thinking that it was their main body.

This urgent activity amongst the Jacobite army contrasted with that in the government camp. A little before 12 o'clock a messenger had left Falkirk for Edinburgh with the report that "there was no appearance of their moving to day. some by their prospects fancied they saw two flags a little beyond the Tor Wood belonging to the Highlanders as in motion, but this was doubtfull. Firing was heard, but they took it to be from Heggin's Nook".[24] The soldiers were preparing their meal from the supplies that they had brought with them. The Jacobites had already gleaned all the food that was to be had in the neighbourhood and the Glasgow Militia, being less well supplied, had difficulty in finding any.[25] The supply problems were exacerbated by the curious civilians who had arrived in the town to see the impending battle for themselves, and who were now numbered in thousands. The streets were crowded with these people and by merchants who had come to turn a quick profit at this unexpected market. The bustle on the High Street was even greater than it was on Tryst days! Not all the civilians were content to remain as passive bystanders and some were caught up with the excitment of the moment. Thus a small party of day-trippers from Kilsyth, consisting of the son of the innkeeper Alexander Forester and three other youths, had seized one of Pitsligo's Hussars on their way and carried him to Falkirk as a prisoner.[26]

The Jacobite army continued its march. They took the same course to Dunipace that the government army was going to take the next day. The two columns stayed about 200 paces apart with the field artillery in the rear.[27] Prince Charles and his entourage, which included the adjutant-general O'Sullivan and the French ambassador, marched between the lines giving the men encouragement.[28] They had not marched more than half a mile when O'Sullivan came up to Lord George at the head and informed him that upon due consideration the Prince and his advisors had formed the opinion that a crossing of the Carron Water in broad daylight, in the face of the enemy, was too dangerous.[29] Without stopping, or even slowing the march, Lord George retorted that it was impossible to do anything else - unless they meant to retreat! Relations between the two men were near to breaking point and O'Sullivan realized that he was wasting his time. Vexed at Lord George's tone he reported back to Prince Charles. Shortly afterwards, the Prince appeared with Brigadier Stapleton. Lord George again explained the problems involved in dispersing the men over night, exposing them to an early attack the next day, and making it difficult to reassemble them to cross the river in the dark. The point where he intended to cross the river was only about a mile away, but some three miles from the enemy camp where, at that time of day, the enemy would be dining. Nor could the government army have received any intelligence concerning their manoeuvre as they had themselves only just decided upon it. His arguments convinced Stapleton and Charles had to concede. The march continued uninterrupted.[30]

It had taken Alexander Grossett almost two hours to reach the head of Denny Muir from where he finally obtained an unobstructed view of the back of Torwood Hill. With the help of his glasses he was able to pick out two columns of infantry moving down the slope. Before setting out on his reconnaisance he had postulated that the enemy might be making such a move, yet the visual confirmation came as quite a shock. Without delay he dispatched one of his mounted servants to the camp with the news. Then he started to make his own way back, all the while keeping a wary eye on the rapidly moving mass of men on the hill opposite. It was important that he should endeavour to ascertain the destination of the enemy force. Their present location and direction still made it possible that they were heading for Glasgow again, on route for another advance into England with their reinforcements. If they were able to slip passed the government army encamped at Falkirk it would be difficult to keep track of them and they would leave a trail of havoc and uncertainty once more.[31]

The line of march adopted by the main Jacobite contingent kept them out of the sight of the main body of the enemy at Falkirk. Their pipers stayed silent as they trudged along over ploughed fields, ditches and broken roads. Soon they were tramping over the lands of Sir Archibald Primrose towards Dunipace House. Primrose himself, dressed in plain brown civilan clothes, was a captive observer with Kilmarnock's Horse at Torwood.[32] Dunipace House stood near to the Carron Water and a scouting party had been there earlier in the day and noted that the water in the river was quite low, making a crossing at the Steps of Dunipace possible. The government troops suspected none of this. They had been

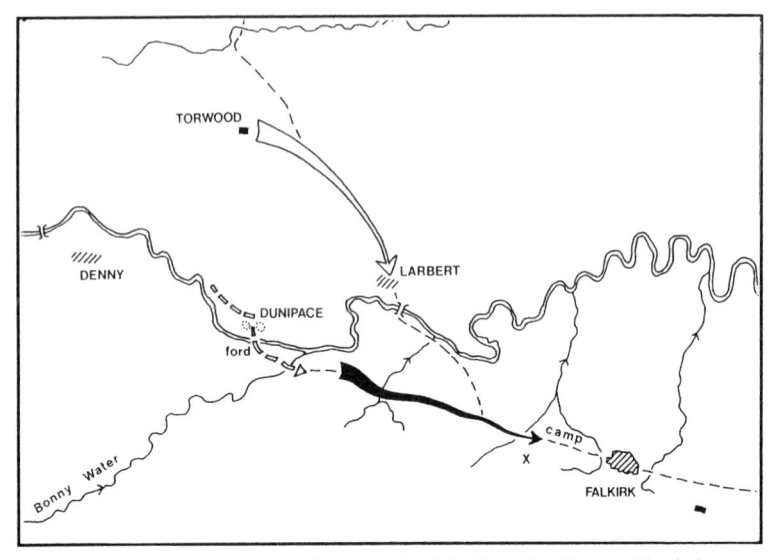

Map showing the two pronged approach of the Jacobite Army. The infantry (broken line) crossed at the Dunipace Steps while the cavalry (hollow arrow) approached Larbert Bridge. The Hanovarian Dragoons (black arrow) fled back to the camp in Falkirk where their infantry formed up.

convinced by Drummond's feint into believing that any approach would be by way of Larbert Bridge where a large contingent of dragoons was waiting. To add to the confusion the Jacobites also lit fires along the Torwood ridge as though they were still encamped there. One of the expectant spectators thought they had set the woodland itself on fire "The Rebells put the Whinns or wood on fire from Torwood to a Rock call'd Craig mad so that no body could know more about them".[33]

The course being followed by the Jacobite army took them in a more easterly direction than when they had set out and the change was noted by Alexander Grossett. They were no longer pointing towards Denny and it was evident that they were now heading for a collision with the government army. As soon as he felt confident of this conclusion Grossett sent off his second rider to Hawley with an urgent message, and made haste himself.[34]

As the Jacobite army descended from Kirklands onto the river plain they caught a momentary glimpse of the government army still in its camp at Falkirk. They proceeded to Dunipace, a small village huddled along the road from Larbert to Denny and overshadowed by the two Hills of Dunipace. The road to the ford lay between these hills, only a short distance away. On the south side of the river a small party of dragoons and some gentlemen volunteers watched in astonishment as the Jacobite army emerged from the hillside. There were numerous fords over the river and each had a scouting party at it to observe the enemy's movements, but none had expected the whole army to approach so directly without any advanced warning. It took but a moment for these startled witnesses to mount their horses and head off hurriedly towards their camp, the regular troops delaying just long enough to satisfy themselves that they were facing more than just a small raiding party.[35]

The first to reach the camp was Robin Sprewell[36], a gentleman volunteer. At about quarter past one he rode into the midst of the government soldiers exclaiming "Gentlemen, what are you about? The Highlanders will be upon you".[37] Robin was from Ormiston[38] and so was unknown to the soldiers and the local dignataries. He was immediately arrested for spreading a false alarm - a well known Jacobite ploy designed to spread confusion.

In the meantime Lord George and the main body of Jacobites crossed the Carron Water unopposed and made for a small ford across the Bonny Water, about 330 yards to the south-east across a flat plain. Once across they turned their march southward and started to ascend the ridge by way of a small valley. From the top of Torwood Lord John Drummond observed the successful crossing of the river and watched as the small government body of mounted scouts fled towards Falkirk. Things were warming up and it was time for him to move forward by the Larbert road as arranged. This movement was calculated to baffle the government command still further by making them believe that the two forces would reunite once the cavalry had crossed Larbert Bridge.

More volunteer scouts now arrived at Falkirk with the news that the main Jacobite force was heading for Dunipace. Upon these reports two officers of Howard's Regiment (one by the name of Teesdale) climbed a tree on their vantage point to get a clearer view in that direction. This time there was no doubt, the Jacobite army was advancing towards them. They immediately informed their commanding officer, Lieutenant-Colonel Howard[39]. Only too aware of the urgency of the situation Howard rushed over to Callendar House to report to Hawley and to collect instructions. Hawley, confident in the superiority of his own forces, was unperturbed. His well-placed spies had not informed him of any intention of the Jacobites to attack and he was sure that there would be plenty of time to dispute the bridge at Larbert. He ordered that the men be put under arms, but that they need not form up. More information was required before they knew from which direction the Jacobites would approach and this would determine his own battle order.

However, shortly thereafter the dragoons rode in from Dunipace. They had waited until they were sure that the Jacobite army intended to cross there and came with that confirmation. Major-General Huske, who was still in the camp, beat to arms and a pressing message was sent to Callendar House for Hawley. "I never was used to these things; but I was surpriz'd to see in how little time ye regular troops were form'd (I think in less than half an hour)".[40] The army was drawn up in front of their camp, facing west - the direction from which they expected the enemy. Their line thus stretched perpendicularly across the road to Glasgow, with the left flank by north Bantaskine House. The dragoons from Callendar House joined them on their flanks to give further protection, and from where they might try to turn the flanks of the advancing enemy. Some of the dragoons were still at Larbert Bridge with a detachment of the Argyll men, and other companies of the Argyll Militia were in their quarters between there and Camelon, unaware of the commotion. The men at Falkirk could all see Lord Drummond's force moving to Larbert Bridge. Their officers knew that the rest of the Jacobite army were crossing at the Steps of Dunipace, and so it seemed obvious to them that the two forces had designed to meet at Carmuirs. Huske and his officers were quietly confident as they waited upon events. They held a tactically strong position and were ready for the enemy. The weather, which had been cold, dry and calm all morning showed signs of deteriorating and a light wind was beginning to blow from the southwest, but did not threaten to hamper their efficiency much. Their cannon were planted ready for use and their camp and the town lay near by. Surely the enemy had made a mistake by doing all the hard work and bringing the battle to them!

The local population had been watching all these proceedings with great alarm and a growing sense of foreboding. They became very anxious as they slowly realized that they lay trapped in the war zone between the two armies now moving inexorably into conflict. They hastily left their homes, taking with them their few valuable possessions, and scurried off to the east in a dreadful fear of what might happen should they stay to protect their property. The young helped the old and the infirm and carried the youngest away from the scene of the forthcoming combat to seek refuge elsewhere. This sad stream of refugees included the family of farmer Muirhead who had friends in the town of Falkirk, one mile away. The route eastward took many of them through the lines of the waiting government army. As the soldiers opened their lines to let them through a hare started up and ran past them. "Halloo, the Duke of Perth's mother!" cried one soldier, it being a well known myth amongst them that she was a witch able to assume any such disguise in order to spy on them. Shouts, jeers and laughter issued from his comrades as they good humouredly joined in the jest.[41]

The Jacobite army continued its ascent, crossing the Glasgow road to the east of Bonnybridge heading towards Tamfourhill. As they crossed the road they could see the government forces standing by their camp. At about the same time, Lord Drummond and the cavalry turned off the Larbert road and headed for the ford at Dunipace.

The government officers saw these two events. Suddenly it dawned on them that the Jacobites were not going to approach them along the plain directly from the west and attack their strong position. Rather, they were taking a more southerly course to test them from the southwest. All the dragoons were ordered onto their left flank to prevent it from being rounded.[42] The two lines of infantry were faced left and marched for about half a mile along "hollow roads, and very uneven Ground".[43] The route took them along Maggie Wood's Loan to the present junction of Windsor Road. Here they spent some time reforming after the disruption caused by the poor terrain. They now faced south-west towards the enemy. Their left flank was protected by the enclosures of Gartcows, with Callendar beyond, and their right by those of Bantaskine, while the Argyll Militia was guarding the road through

104   *Falkirk or Paradise*

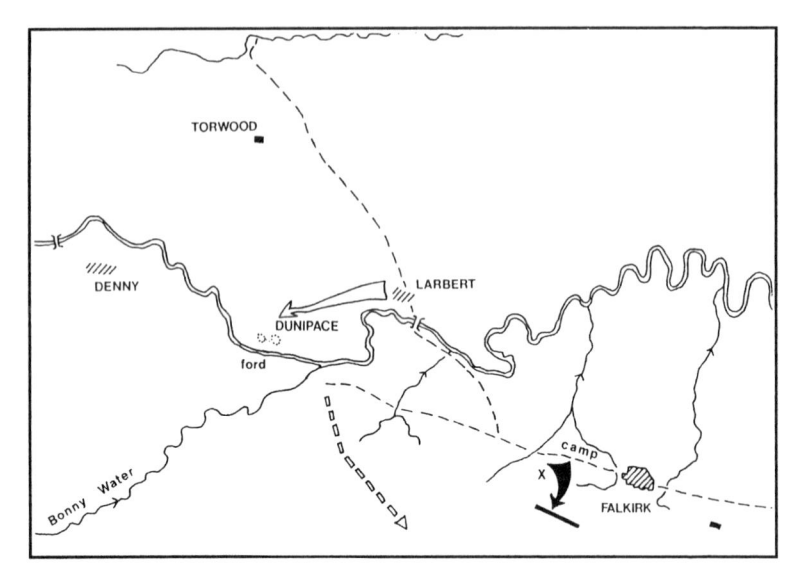

From Dunipace the Jacobite front went towards Falkirk Muir and the Hanovarian army formed into battle order to meet them from that direction.

Camelon. Brigadier-General Cholmondeley described the location as a "very good Situation".[44], but it had the disadvantage of lying below the hill to the south upon which lay the common muir of the town.

The Jacobite army pressed on, continuing to gain height. They had never intended to attack their opponents along the main road from the west, nor yet had they proposed to approach them that night from the south-west. Lord George had spent some time in and around the town and had become familiar with the terrain. His sole objective was to reach the summit of Falkirk Muir before the enemy [45]. Having taken possession of the hill he would then have a considerable advantage in the event of an attack from the government forces which he considered to be extremely unlikely so late in the afternoon. Rather, it was fully expected that the Jacobite army would lie that night in the open and attack the enemy at dawn. The proximity of the town, the numerous enclosures, and the government army's reliance upon further supplies from Edinburgh would all help his guerrilla warfare. By keeping the enemy awake all night he could further weaken their resolve. These were much the same tactics that he had employed at Prestonpans only four months earlier. There he had crossed the Esk at Musselburgh in daylight and had ascended the heights above Cope's army, attacking at first light the next day. Disregarding the government army's new position he pushed on to Howierigg.

Lieutenant-General Hawley had not gone straight to his camp from Callendar House. The regular soldiers were well drilled and he had left ample instructions concerning their battle order. He needed to ascertain what manoeuvres the enemy were contemplating and went to the vantage point to seek intelligence. On hearing that the Jacobite army were still ascending the hill two possibilities entered his mind. Was it possible that they intended to bypass his army, as they had Cope's in the Highlands, and to march on to Edinburgh and England? Had they raised the siege of Stirling Castle? Would he be cut off from his supplies? The second scenario caused him even greater consternation. Was this a repeat of the battle at Prestonpans where Cope's inaction had lost the day? The obvious solution to both dilemmas was to gain that hill before the enemy in the confident belief that any ensuing conflict would be to his advantage, especially as he had three regiments of dragoons with him and the enemy would be tired after their rapid march. All his energies were now bent to that course of action. He went to reconnoitre the high ground and sent his aides-de-camp, James Stuart Mackenzie and James Masterton, to order the cavalry to take possession of the summit without delay, the infantry and artillery to follow as fast as possible.[46] "we were no sooner form'd, but order'd a second time, to take Ground to the Left, and as we march'd, all the way up hill, and Over very uneven Ground, our men were greatly Blown".[47]

It had now begun to drizzle and the wind was picking up. As the sky darkened and the infantry marched forward they cursed under their breath. Their moans grew audibly as they slogged, ankle deep, through the mud which impeded their progress.[48] It had rained for much of the week and the ground was very soft underfoot. Before long the soldiers' feet were thoroughly soaked and they had to keep moving to keep the frost out. The gripping mud greatly fatigued them as they waded on laden with the impediments of war. As they ascended the escarpment they became more and more exposed to the stiff south-westerly wind blowing a cold, biting air full into their red raw faces. It started to sleet and they tramped doggedly on with their heads bowed to avoid the numbing effects of the wind. Their freezing hands tightly grasped their burdensome muskets with their bayonets already attached. Hawley at last appeared to encourage his brave lads on from the safety of his horse. His hat had been blown off by the wind and he looked not a little dishevelled. The intensity of the wind increased all the while in the dark gloom of a late January afternoon.

The artillery had to be harnessed to the numerous draught horses yet again. It was common practice for the army to hire carters and horses locally for their baggage and artillery train. The carters of Falkirk had gained a considerable reputation for their hard and skilful work and had been contracted to pull the cannon on this occasion.[49] Captain Cunningham received orders to bring the guns up behind the first line. To give him and the Bo'ness gunners some protection the Yorkshire Blues had been embodied into his command. They were also to help to manouvre the guns up the slippery hill along the deeply rutted roads. Together they all moved forward in good spirits, blind Jack Metcalf out in front playing music for them to work by. Their progress, however, was painfully slow. The gun carriages, lacking swivel joints and bearings, were totally inappropriate. In a short time they were falling well behind the first line of infantry, and were soon overtaken by the second line. Then the lead cannon sunk in the mire and try as they might they could not budge it. It was one of the larger cannon, probably the 6-pounder, in front because it had a larger range and would therefore be used first in a set piece battle.[50]

Captain Thornton dammed their luck. He had resented being placed under Cunningham's command and was eager to get up to the action. Leaving his men with instructions to extricate the stranded machine he rode off up the hill to join Hawley. Cunningham, knowing that time was of the essence, abandoned the first gun, only to find that the second gun was also held fast in the mud. After a struggle they managed to get two four-pounders and a one an a half-pounder past the larger guns, along with three covered wagons laden with powder, shot and some small mortars. With difficulty they moved on up the hill towards the field of battle, their excitement dulled by the amount of effort that they were having to expend. By now they had fallen a considerable way behind and soon encountered another patch of swampy ground. [51]

The Jacobite cannon were faring no better. They were escorted by half of the Farquharsons, about 150 men under the command of Farquharson of Monaltrie. They had reached the Carron Water but were unable to travel further until rafts had been prepared for them, the river bed here being too soft. Not being able to give assistance Lord John Drummond and his contingent of horse rode straight on over the ford to catch up with their vanguard. The cannon could be brought up later, ready for the dawn attack.

The Jacobite army had by this time reached the first ridge of the barren hill that they had been slowly climbing since crossing the Bonny Water. They then directed their path towards the east, along the backbone of the ridge. The slope here was relatively gentle and the temporary respite gave them the chance to recover their breath on the march and to take stock of their situation. Those at the head of the columns caught glimpses of the government army near the bottom of the hill further along the ridge. Their pace quickened. Having permitted the Jacobite army to cross the Carron Water unmolested, Lord George expected that the government army would have stayed within the relative security of their strong camp and in the town. As soon as he realized that they were also making for the hill top, and that the battle was to take place that day, it became a race to Falkirk Muir between the right wing of the Highlanders and the dragoons. The 2,000 men at the head of the first column, mostly Macdonalds, were sent on ahead. Breaking into a dog-trot they hastened eastward towards the collision. The dragoons, over 1,000 in number, approached from the opposite direction, occasionally galloping when the ground allowed.

The terrain between the two forces was relatively featureless. There were a few isolated trees, but no woods. Nor were there any hedges, only a few stone walls formed enclosures besides the sparsely spaced farmhouses. Most of the ground was covered by bleak heathland which had died back at that time of year. The ground was full of undulations and small pools sat in the hollows. As these were undrained the ground around them lay heavy and sodden. The eastern part of the hill contained the common muir of Falkirk from which the town's feuars obtained turf, clay and stone for their shelters by delving into the land. The clay was probably

One of the dry-stone walls at Seafield now tumbled down
but still showing the nature of the terrain.

also used by local potters who gouged out the material from deep pits leaving a lunar type landscape behind them. These holes were also full of water in the winter and presented an obstacle to man and beast. The common represented pasture for the town's herd and the cattle had churned up the surface creating stagnant pockets of water and mud. Lord George had seen this land before and knew that it suited his lightly armed, very mobile Highlanders well. The dragoons and their officers were taking their first view of it as their horses tried to keep their footings. It was not at all suitable for cavalry.[52]

The uneven ground on the plateau leaves no obvious summit in the area and so once the two advance parties had mounted the heights there was little advantage to be gained over an enemy. However, a large party of the dragoons reached the crown of the largest eminence first and now had a good view of the Jacobite foot rapidly closing in on them from along the ridge. The number of dragoons quickly increased before the eyes of the anxious Jacobites. Much depended on the opening manoeuvres and the next few minutes would be critical. The dragoons under the over all command of Colonel Ligonier had three targets; firstly to take possession of the hill and to hold it until the foot came up in support; secondly to gain the flank of the enemy; and thirdly, to turn the enemy's line so that their own army would not be facing directly into the dreadful wind when the battle began. They believed that the first of these had been achieved, the Highlanders would never attack so large a body of horse uphill. To effect the second a squadron was detached and sent down the southern side of the hill. Lord George had anticipated such a move. Intending to secure his right flank on the Glen Burn he directed the column towards the south-east and made a dash for it. A small band of MacGregors under Colonel John Roy Stewart, moving faster than the rest, reached the water first.[53] Their's was the honour of the right, standing knee deep in the bog that bordered the stream. Indeed, this was a considerable patch of swampy ground known as the Abbot's Moss. The dragoons, in moving further south to get around the flank, also encountered the mire and shortly after gave up the attempt. The right flank of the Highlanders was securely anchored. Their column then faced to their left to form their first line of battle, and as they did they gratefully turned their backs on the chill wind and the sleet which it bore.

The dragoons did not give up entirely. Not allowing the enemy time to arrange themselves they made several feints as though about to charge, at the same time cheering and waving their swords over their heads, in an attempt to draw the Highlanders' fire. The clans were reknowned for their rashness in such circumstances and the intimidating advances of the swaggering dragoons made a tempting target. Lord George, however, had issued strict instructions to his men that they were not to fire until the enemy were within pistol-shot, when a signal would be given. They were therefore honour-bound not to fire at the taunting figures who were still too distant. They were particularly obliged to follow this feat of courage by Lord George's own actions. He had paid them the great distinction of standing on foot a little ahead of the first line - putting himself to the same risk as they were under. Had they fired their muskets they would not have had time to reload them.

There was a brief pause while both sides weighed each other up. The Jacobite left wing was still to catch up with their right, and the cavalry were behind them again. Likewise the dragoons waited for their foot to ascend the hill behind them.

During this spell Lord George and his officers went along their line straightening it up and getting the clans organized. His first line was three men deep and now that Lord George knew that he was to face a large body of dragoons he was able to issue appropriate commands. As well as Colonel Kerr, who was on horse, John Roy Stewart and Oliphant of Gask acted as his aides-de-camp. They ensured that each man knew what was expected of them. O'Sullivan, the adjutant-general of the army, joined in this task. In the midst of this medley several priests wandered up and down the lines giving prayers, praising God and his chosen army, and preparing them for death should the need arise. Captain Reverend Allan McDonald of Clanranald's clan, and Aeneas MacGillies the chaplain of Glengarry's, both performed this duty in their native Highland dress sporting both sword and pistol. The Catholics received their blessing kneeling.[54]

The second line soon took up its position with the Atholl brigade right behind the Macdonalds. The cavalry too arrived to form the third line. Lord Elcho and Lord Balmerino had been assigned to protect the right flank and, being unaware of the earlier manouvres, they tried to take up their positions there. It was not long before the leading horses of Elcho's unit were up to their bellies in the bog and the attempt was abandoned.[55]

In the meantime Lord George had sent John Roy Stewart and Anderson of Whitburgh along the ridge, as far as it was possible, to determine where the government infantry lay.[56] From his post on the right wing all that he could see were the dragoons up the hill, about 660 yards distant.

Hawley had been urging his foot soldiers on and was unaware of the posturing that had taken place on his left wing. He sent his aide-de-camp, James Masterton, to order the dragoons to move more to their left to avoid any attempts that the rebels might make to outflank them and to make room for the foot. These instructions were taken straight to Lieutenant-Colonel Shugbrough Whitney of Ligonier's regiment. Whitney had distinguished himself at Prestonpans and had received promotion as a result of his actions there. His subsequent inclination to apply a rigid military discipline to his men had met with Hawley's approval and so he

Private infantry soldiers of Munro's and Barrel's regiments. The uniforms of the Hanovarian regiments were similar with their red coats, but their trimmings varied. Munro's had yellow lapels and turnbacks, Barrels had blue facings, waistcoat and breeches.

was acting as second in command of the cavalry wing. On this occasion, however, Whitney must have felt that his commander was losing touch with the situation on the ground for the proposed motion had already proved to be impracticable and the foot regiments were still at a considerable distance.[57]

His men were becoming restless and he advanced a little closer than the rest. Here he recognized his former friend John Roy Stewart in the front of the Jacobite line. "Ha! are you there?" he is said to have exclaimed, "we shall soon be up with you". Stewart retorted, "You shall be welcome when you come, and, by G--, you shall have a warm reception!"[58]

Lord George's scouting party returned with the report that the government infantry were still ascending the other side of the hill and were only partially formed into battle order. The dragoons consequently appeared to be unsupported. In fact, the Glasgow Militia together with the Paisley volunteers lay at some distance to the rear of the dragoons, but they were obscured from view by the lie of the land. They had been sent to secure some farmhouses in this area in order to protect the left flank of the regular infantry. Moving more rapidly than the rest, they were beginning to arrive at their designated station. This partially exposed task would have been allocated to the Argyll Militia had they arrived earlier, or if they had not been quartered in several places in front of the camp. Dispersed as they were from Dorrator to Glenfuir, the Argyll men now took on the job of guarding the right flank and the camp with the baggage. It was only to be expected that a Jacobite raiding party would head direct to Falkirk from Dunipace.

Lord George had the news he wanted, though he scarcely believed it. He took up his position with the Macdonalds of Keppoch. John Roy Stewart and Oliphant of Gask stood beside him. Calmly he put his wig in his pocket and scrogged his bonnet.[59] The Jacobite ranks had fallen eerily silent as each man laid his plaid down on the ground beside him, they would only prove cumbersome in what was to follow.[60] Slowly, doggedly, they moved forward, foot by cautious foot, their pieces presented to the enemy in front of them. The line stretched from the bog along the stream at the southeast to just over the top of the ridge where the left were still in the process of forming. At the bottom the right wing was amongst the stone enclosures of Seafield Farm. Over the first wall they went, up to the second, and then over it too. All the while the gap between them and the dragoons closed.

Colonel Ligonier and the 1,300 dragoons were massed upon the hill top. He was a brave officer. Suffering from pleurisy, he had been blooded in Edinburgh on the 14th January but still insisted upon riding to Falkirk on the 16th at the head of his regiment. He had been observing the motions of the enemy for some time although the wind and rain blowing directly into his face obscured much. He was aware of the failed endeavours to outflank or turn the enemy, and that it had proved impossible to draw their fire. His adjutant, Colonel Ker, was sent to find out where the foot

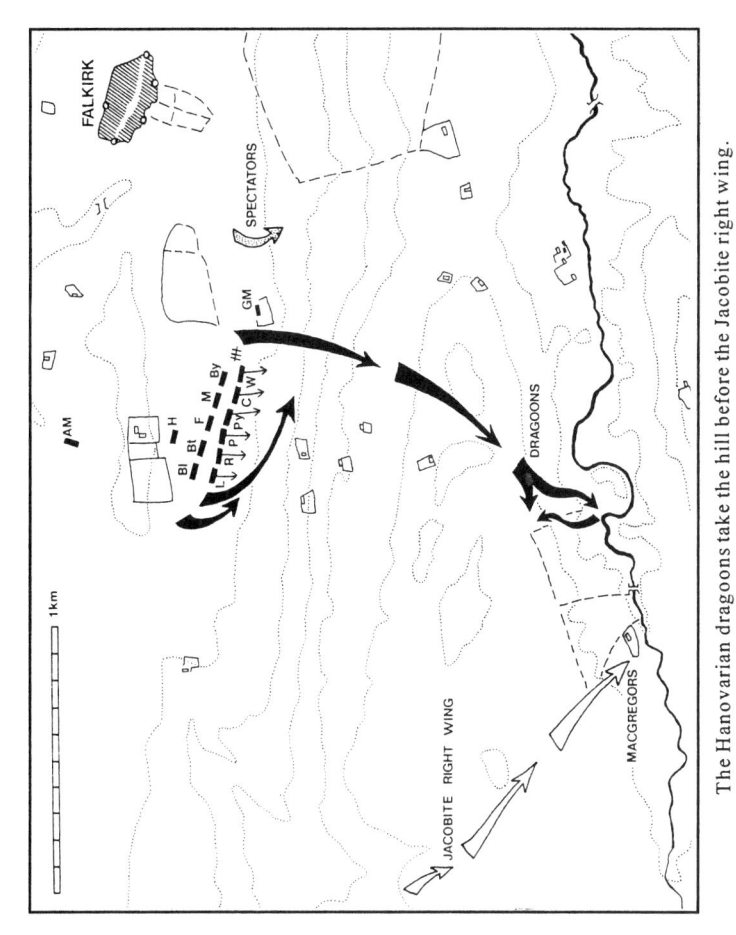

The Tempest 113

The Hanovarian dragoons take the hill before the Jacobite right wing.
AM Argyll Militia; H Howards; Bl Barrels; Bt Battereaus; F Flemings; By Blakeneys; L Ligoniers Foot; R Royals; P Prices; Py Pulteneys; C Cholmondeleys; W Wolfes; GM Glasgow

regiments were that would be supporting the cavalry, and to report events to Hawley. The adjutant had brought the unwelcome news that the infantry were still struggling up the hill as fast as they could. Now that the Jacobite right wing was audaciously approaching the dragoons Ligonier needed to respond, or risk being pushed off the hill top and losing this advantage to the enemy. He quickly dispatched Colonel Ker again to Hawley seeking instructions. Hawley was still urging on his first regiments of foot on the left wing and was soon located. However, he was unable to see the dragoons' predicament being yet some way down the hill. Nor did he return with Colonel Ker to view the field for himself. His orders were therefore somewhat ambiguous and took the form of a request that the dragoons do all that was necessary to retain possession of the hill.[61] He had no doubt that the cavalry were capable of beating the rebel mob on their own.[62]

Ligonier looked puzzled when he received his instructions from Hawley's aide-de-camp. His principal officers questioned the wisdom of such an attack unsupported by infantry.[63] However, they were determined to eradicate the shame and ignominy of their behaviour at Prestonpans.[64] They had been formed into a long line of battle stretching along the crest of the hill and made an awesome sight. Their well disciplined closed ranks made a solid wall only punctuated by the gaps between the regiments. Cobham's Regiment lay on the right. They had seen duty on the continent and had been brought back to quell the troublesome rebels who stood below them. Their horses had been subjected to enemy fire at Fontenoy and were battle hardened. For the horses of the two other regiments this was to be their baptism of fire.

Slowly they were set in motion, their harness rattling in unison and the hollow thud of hooves echoing down to where the Jacobites stood waiting. Their pistols were drawn, their swords still sheathed. John Daniel looked on in dread "Here I Must acknowledge, that when I saw this moving cloud of horse, regularly disciplined, in full trot upon us down the summit, I doubted not but that they would have ridden over us without opposition and bear us down without difficulty in their impetuous progress".[65]

A Highland officer stepped out of the ranks of the Jacobite first line, took off his bonnet and saluted, "Colonel Whitney, your most humble servant!" "You bare-breeched rascal, we'll be your humble servants presently" came the reply, and Whitney urged his men on. Their pace quickened with Whitney slightly forward from his troop.

The Jacobite foot calmly watched as the seething mass of animal flesh got closer and closer, their silhouetted forms slowly merging into the hillside. At just over 20 paces the dragoons discharged their pistols and unsheathed their swords, bracing themselves for the enemy's reply. Their shot, however, was largely wasted as it passed over the heads of the Jacobites who were standing down the hillslope.[66] The Jacobite first rank returned the fire with their muskets, but to little effect at that range. Throwing their muskets away they then drew their pistols for use close up.

And now the range was very close indeed. The dragoons had kept their composure, closed their ranks and pressed on more eager than before in the sure knowledge that the enemy had expended their shot and did not have time to reload. Propelled ever faster by the slope of the hill and the urging of their riders there was no doubting but that the sheer mass and inertia of the first shock of impact would steamroller over the first line of Jacobites and hurl the dragoons into the second, scattering the foe.

The noise of the approaching cavalry was deafening. The Macdonalds could almost feel the warm breath from the horses' nostrils as they stared into their wild eyes. Almost every Jacobite eye was transfixed on Lord George as he stood slightly ahead of them. Twenty yards, fifteen yards, thirteen yards - the passage of time and distance rushed quickly away. Then at just ten yards, Lord George levelled his own musket.[67] The crack of the lone shot rang out giving a hollow peal in the cold winter's air. That was the signal. A devastating volley now echoed along the Jacobite line. It started on the right, by Lord George, and ran up the hill like a rolling wave crashing on the rocks. The second and third ranks of the first line had reserved their fire for this instant, and almost 2,000 guns were aimed at the dragoons at that one brief moment. At least 80 dragoons were instantly killed, many more wounded. Their horses' flesh was ripped and torn. More horses fell, dislodging their riders. A cloud of sulphurous smoke descended over the carnage from the discharge, carried as luck would have it by a sudden ferocious storm blast of wind and hail. It was as though the very elements themselves had declared for the Jacobites.

The dragoons were totally disordered, their horses uncontrollable and the men in panic and shock. Daniel was elated: "The brave front-line of McDonells suffered the enemy to come within ten or twelve paces of them before firing. Nobly together presented, and sent their benediction upon them, so that in the third part of a minute that rapid and impetuous torrent, which seemed in rolling to lay all waste before it, was now checked and stemmed in such a manner, that it was made to retake its course faster than it had proceeded. Upon seeing this, we immediately seconded our work with a hearty huzza, victory now declaring for us".[68]

Huge gaps opened up in the ranks of the dragoons and William Cross, standing behind them, saw daylight through them in several places.[69] Graham, the Glasgow bellman out on a day trip, tells in his colourful language that "Many in their saddles swang".[70] Amongst these was Colonel Whitney. [71]

Hamilton's Regiment gave way first.[72] They veered off to the sides, further confusing the other two regiments. Their horses, not being accustomed to battle conditions, had been spooked by the general volley, but more particularly by the smoke and by the first rank who had fired their pistols at the horses' faces.[73] They bolted in all directions. Some fled to the left, straight into the bog. Up to their saddle-laps in the mire they were cut to pieces by the Highlanders who found it "as easy as cutting bacon".[74]

Near the centre of the Jacobite line was a small regiment of Farquharsons under the command of Lieutenant-Colonel James Farquharson of Balmoral. They found themselves opposite to the right flank of the three regiments of dragoons. So, while the first line had been getting ready to receive the enemy cavalry, Balmoral had drawn his own men up in the form of a wedge. It was arranged with him at the head, two men in the second rank, three in the third and so on to the rear. They had marched forward with the rest of the line in silence with the order "Fire not a shot till you can discern the colour of the horses' eyes, then give one volley altogether; throw down your guns and rush upon them, cut the horses' bridles, and we will deal with the men." As they advanced a bullet hit Balmoral in the shoulder. "Four men," cried his henchman, "to carry our wounded chief to the rear." "Never," cried Balmoral, "four men to carry your chief at the head of his children into the thickest of the fight".[75]

Likewise, the other Highlanders threw down their muskets and giving their blood curdling war cries, unique to each clan, they fiercely advanced sword in hand on the dragoons giving them no chance to recover their senses. Already shocked, the remaining dragoons were startled to see themselves now attacked by infantry. Only in the centre did the momentum of the charge carry thedragoons up to and through the Jacobite first line and on to the second. The first line opened up to let them through and then closed again behind them. As they broke upon the second line it brought them to a halt with a volley.[76]

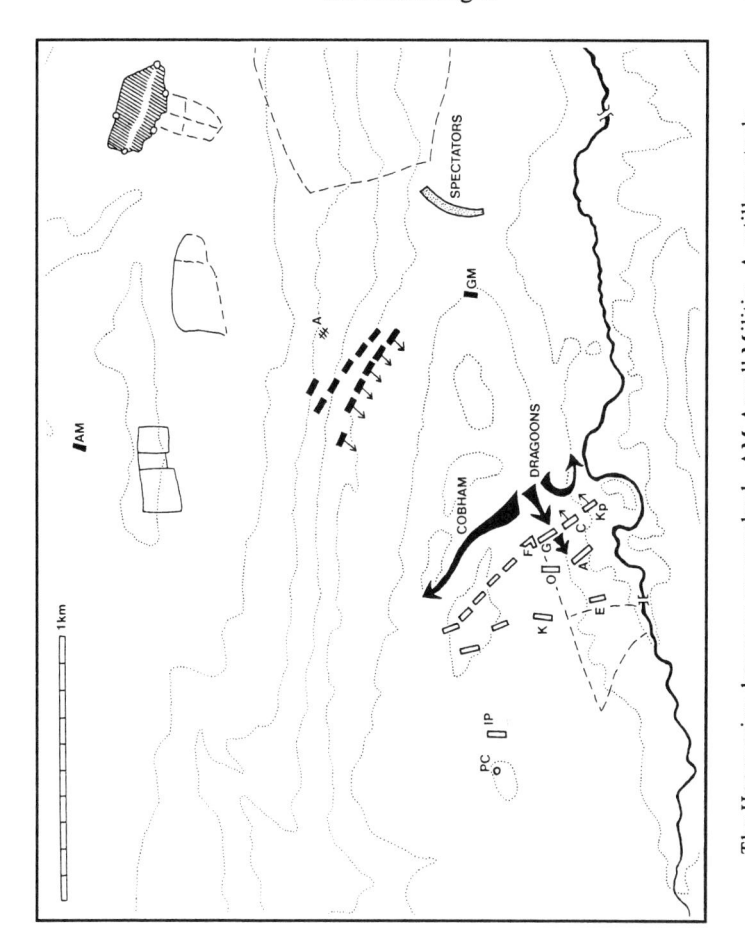

The Storm Rages

The Hanovarian dragoons are repulsed. AM Argyll Militia; A artillery stuck; GM Glasgow Militia; PC Prince Charles; IP Irish Picquets; K Kilmarnocks; E Elcho; O Ogilvy's; A Atholl Brigade; F Farquharsons; C Clanranald; Kp Keppoch.

The first line now struggled with the enemy in their midst. The dragoons "throwing down every thing before them, and trampling the Highlanders under the feet of their horses. The most singular and extraordinary combat immediately followed. The Highlanders, stretched on the ground, thrust their dirks into the bellies of the horses. Some seized the riders by their clothes, dragged them down, and stabbed them with their dirks; several again, used their pistols; but few of them had sufficient space to handle their swords. Macdonald of Clanranald, chief of one of the clans of Macdonalds, assured me, that whilst he was lying upon the ground, under a dead horse, which had fallen upon him, without the power of extricating himself, he saw a dismounted horseman struggling with a Highlander: fortunately for him, the Highlander, being the strongest, threw his antagonist, and having killed him with his dirk, he came to his assistance, and drew him with difficulty from under the horse".[77] Lord George too was caught up in the hand to hand combat and fought "like a lion".[78]

In the second line the fighting was also fierce. Alistair Shaw the captain of the 1st division of Lord Ogilvy's Regiment was wounded by a dragoon but still managed to slay his assailant.[79] That regiment's ensign was not made of such stern stuff. His name was James Stormonth, younger of Kinclune, and during the heat of the fight he allowed the Colours to drop from his hands - or else he threw them away and fled. Lord Ogilvy, happening at that moment to look round, and not seeing the flag, called out "My Colours are gone!" whereupon Major Glasgoe, a French officer attached to the Angus Regiment, who was close by, immediately picked them up. The ensign rejoined his regiment a week later![80] Another ensign of the regiment, James Carnegie, was wounded.[81]

For a moment it looked as though the dragoons had broken the Jacobite brigades in this part of the line and some were in the process of retreating. Colonel Ian Menzies of Shian observing the dogged retreat of the men ordered the Menzies to charge into the thickest of the fighting and turned the tide.[82]

In Ligonier's Dragoons was Lieutenant George Cumming. He was fortunate enough to be taken prisoner in this melee and later related that "in less than five minutes your ffriend, with about fifty broadswords and daggers at his breast, ready to cutt him in pieces, was stripped of his cavalry arms, furniture, baggage of every sort, and field-equipage, to above three hundred and fifty guineas value; nay, of the very things and cloaths about himself, down to his hatt, perwigg, and spurs".[83] He was then passed back to Lord Kilmarnock's Horse for detention. Colonel Jordain was badly wounded in the stomach by a pistol shot during this time.[84]

Not allowing the fleeing dragoons a moment to recover from their flight the Macdonalds and MacGregors keenly pursued them, running as fast as their horses.[85] Cobham's Regiment wheeled to the right, passing between the two armies. In doing so they ran along the length of the first line of the Jacobite left wing which was now almost formed. They thus presented themselves like moving targets at a shooting gallery to fire from that quarter. Their depleted ranks were further decimated. However, having expended their shot in this way the Jacobite left now had to resort to their trusty swords during the imminent encounter with the government foot. The other regiments of dragoons scattered and fled in incontrollable haste. A large body of Hamilton's headed direct for the farm buildings where the Glasgow Militia were almost formed into battle order. Seeing them thundering up, and anticipating a collision, the Earl of Home gave orders to shoot at them "and brought down some of these Rascalls", [86] thinning their ranks still further. Some militiamen fled before the dragoons came upon them, - one noted that he "would then have given my life for a shilling".[87] About 60 of the dragoons broke through the ranks of those that remained, totally disordering them. The Glasgow Militia was now too fragmented to form a fighting unit, though they tried to regroup. The officers and men that had fled in the face of the stampeding dragoons were rid of them after 500 or 600 yards. They turned back to return to their companies up the hill. The Earl of Home, who was on horseback, did not. He followed the dragoons down the hill towards Falkirk and continued his course to Linlithgow without stopping all the way. Such was his sense of self-preservation that he is said to have arrived there before 6 o'clock, long before anyone else.[88] The dragoons knew whom to blame for their predicament:

> I am alive and well at present though it is more by God's blessed will than our general's conduct. For he drew only 400 dragoons, sword in hand, up against 10,000 of our enemy and we had orders not to draw a pistol nor fire a gun; and as soon as he had given these orders to the rest of the officers he rid away from us and we never saw him more till next morning. We lost the day for we were all sold to our enemies by treacherous General Hawley, for we could have got the day if he had done us justice or let us fight like Englishmen as we are. I wish the Duke had been with us. They was 10,000 we 8,000 and enough to have beat them, but our officers would not let the foot come up, so the dragoons was forced to suffer. Regiment was cut all to pieces except 30 men, and we lost but 12 out of my troop".[89]

The battle had started well for Lord George and a Jacobite victory now seemed assured.

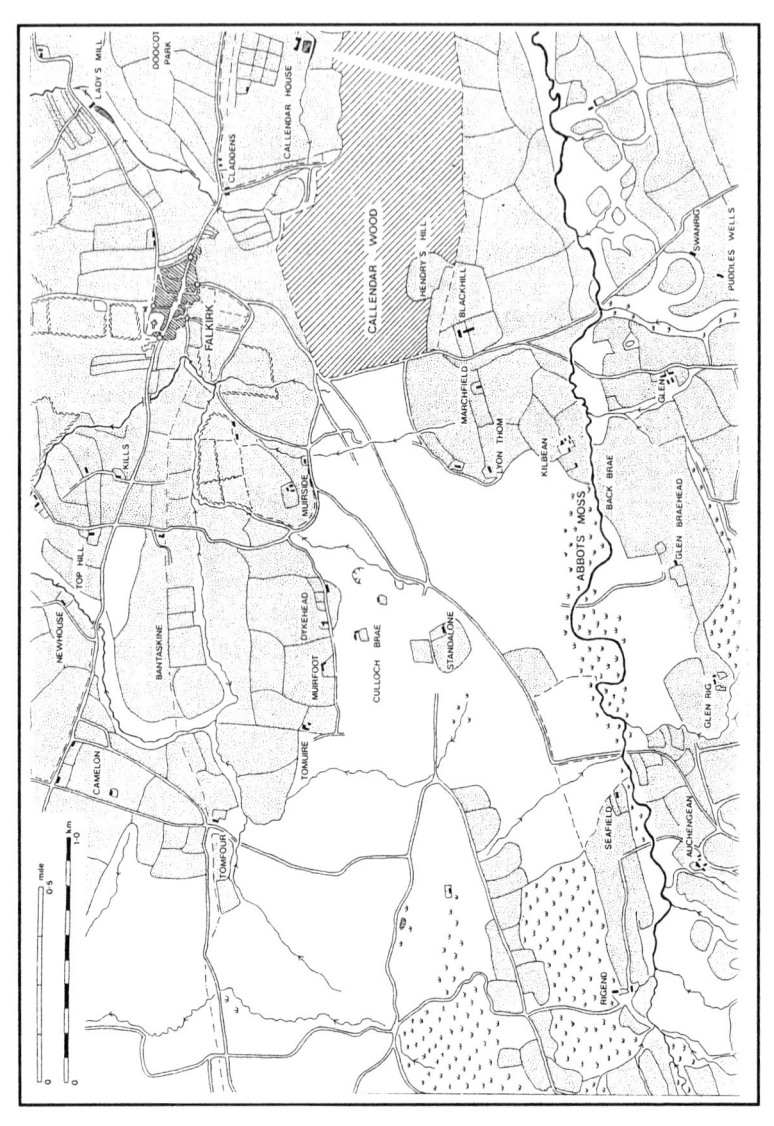

Map of the Falkirk area c1746 showing the town, areas of woodland (hatched) and cultivated land (stippled). The battlefield site is quite clearly shown on the moor (blank) to the south-west.

CHAPTER 6

The Storm Rages
17th January 1746

Having repulsed the bold attack by the dragoons Lord George set about organizing the Jacobite ranks to recover their composure. He ordered them to reload their muskets so that they could all advance in line sweeping the enemy before them. However, elated by their success in the heat of the battle the Macdonalds continued their pursuit and broke rank. Keeping the dragoons on the run they stampeded them like cattle. Close on the heels of the dragoons, about seventy Macdonalds came across the disordered rump of the Glasgow Militia just over the crest of the hill. They poured some shot into the militia and received some very irregular fire back. The Macdonalds momentarily retired over the hill, only to return a few minutes later, their numbers augmented by about two hundred of their clan. They gave the nervous militia another fire and started forward, intending to rush upon them sword in hand. The already intimidated volunteers were not prepared to wait for them. After returning a few scattered shots they turned tail and took to their heels.[1] During their panic-stricken flight, however, they were sorely exposed and suffered many casualties. "No Highlander pity'd their case - 'Ye curs'd Militia,' they did swear, 'What a devil did bring you here?'".[2]

The swift departure of the impulsive Macdonalds, despite Lord George's pleas, had been followed by most of the first line. Only a small part of Keppoch's Regiment where Lord George had stood remained, Alexander Macdonald explains why: "As the enemy's dragoons rode off to their right betwixt the lines, our men ran eagerly in pursuit of them, but were much surprised to find themselves stopt by our generalls and officers who with difficulty restrained them with their drawn swords and cocked pistols conjuring them to return to their ground or they would be undone".[3] A group of MacGregors also rallied to his command.[4] The cavalry of the third line would have also have followed up the pursuit had not Lord George's aide-de-camp, John Roy Stewart, halted the Life Guards.[5] Lord George's problem lay in knowing where the enemy foot were as they still could not be seen from the right wing where he was. Nor did he want to charge them in small groups which might easily be repulsed, or outflanked if they got too far ahead of the rest of the line. He therefore went back to the second line where the Atholl Brigade had kept their battle order, and brought them up to what little remained of the first. The Menzies too returned from their earlier foray. Together, they slowly advanced up the hill, Lord George still on foot, the cavalry bringing up the rear.

Meanwhile, the Jacobite left wing, having been more or less formed, could not be held back either. Lochiel and the Camerons saw the Macdonalds charge forward and wanted their share of the glory and action. The Stewarts of Appin, the Mackenzies, Frasers and the rest were of a like mind. Some of them pursued Cobham's dragoons as they went past, most ran on sword in hand towards the government front which those on the left could now see coming towards the hill top.

The government's infantry had, up until this point, been arduously advancing in formation up the steep broken ground on the north facing slope of the hill. Keeping formation had proven rather difficult with the result that the two lines that they were supposed to make were rather haphazard. Some regiments had fallen behind giving the Jacobite officers such as O'Sullivan and Eguilles, observing from slightly ahead of their left flank, the false impression that they were forming hollow squares as an insurance against flanking movements. In fact, the distance between the two lines increased markedly towards the north. Hawley was with the left wing of the first line, egging the regiments of Wolfe and Cholmondeley on. Huske was likewise on the right, further down the hill. These foot soldiers had been unable to reach the summit in time to support their cavalry and to take advantage of the disruption caused by the dragoon charge on the Jacobite right wing. Indeed, they had been unable to witness that encounter because it had taken place on the other side of the hill. They had only heard the brief exchange of gun fire and the harrowing screams of horses and men. They also heard the thundering hooves of the dragoons' horses as they made their escape. All the while the chill wind blew full into their faces. Those regiments upon the left

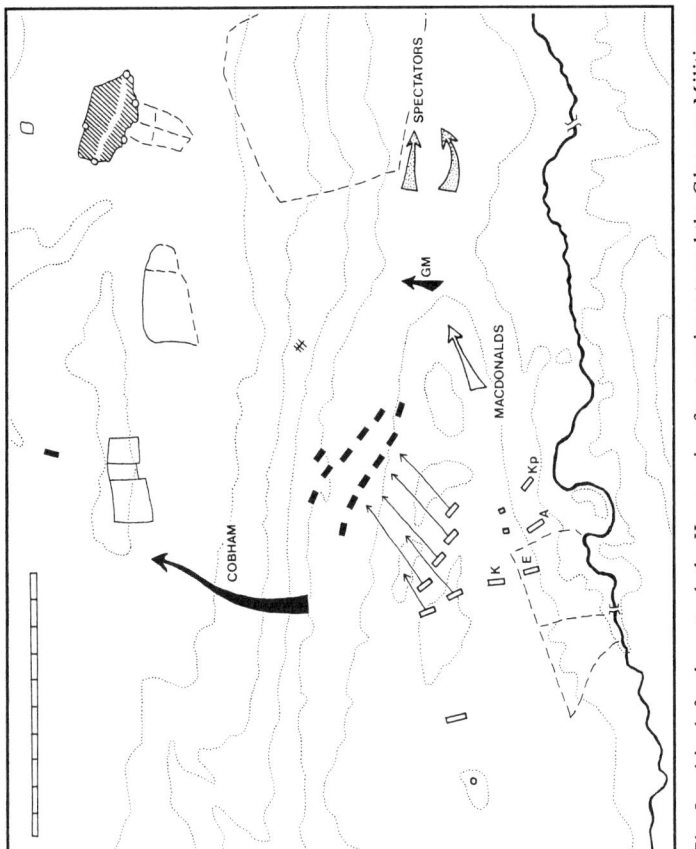

The Jacobite left wing attack the Hanoverian front regiments and the Glasgow Militia are routed. K Kilmarnock; E Elcho; A Atholl Brigade; Kp Keppoch; GM Glasgow Militia.

peered through the driving rain with a growing sense of unease. They watched as the Glasgow Militia were carried away by the panic stricken dragoon horses. Riderless horses appeared everywhere, bolting in all directions - including that in which the infantry stood. Beyond where the militia had once halted another large body of men could be seen in flight. Their muffled shouts of excitement and terror communicated a dreadful sense of foreboding to the government's left wing. These were just some of the thousands of spectators who had taken up their ring side positions on the hill to get a better view of the battle which, like the government soldiers, they believed would be fought on the lower ground around Falkirk. They now found themselves uncomfortably close to the Jacobite army in its frenzied charge and in the path of some of the fleeing dragoons. Amongst this crowd was the minister from Beith and his trusty beadle who made the rash mistake of waving his sword about in his animated enthusiasm caused by the turn of events. The Macdonalds soon put a stop to his posturing and before long the minister found himself a captive.[6]

Unaware of their true identity, many of the government soldiers mistook the spectators for a detachment of their own army in retreat. They did not, however, have long to contemplate all these signs as they slowly trudged, cold, wet and anxious, towards an unseen enemy. Bursting upon their left wing, helter-skelter down the slope, came yet more of the dragoons and their horses.

Pulteney's Regiment in the centre of the first line, already tense, fired upon them before reeling under their impact.[7] Once again the horses played havoc amongst the ranks of the left wing "and ye Dragoons had very near rode down Genl. Hawley, he Drew his pistol and endeavoured to Rally them but threats and fair words would not do".[8] The right escaped this demoralizing episode as Cobham's dragoons rode beyond their flank and through the quarters occupied by the Argyleshire Militia.

The vociferous Hawley commanded the infantry to reform as he rode up and down between the lines of the left wing. As the junior officers tirelessly tried to regain their composure the rain turned to sleet. Through it they could see no more horses, but dimly on the summit they could make out the darkened forms of the Highlanders. Their numbers grew before their eyes. Not only were these strange and noisy Highlanders descending rapidly upon them from the hill in front of them, but they now also emerged from the spot where the Glasgow Militia had stood. They had been outflanked!

The Highlanders, having already expended their shot, had thrown down their muskets and were charging down the hill with the appearance of all the momentum formerly possessed by the dragoons. This was the moment that the government infantry had been trained to expect, though it hardly led them to accept this awesome spectacle calmly. Their officers, wild with excitement, started the drill. At fifty or so yards the back ranks of the individual regiments fired their volleys. And then another horror emerged to terrify the redcoats. The rain, driving so heavily onto their front, had dampened their musket pans and cartridges so that only four out of every five muskets presented to the quickly advancing enemy actually fired. This was one area were they should have been able to gain an advantage. The Jacobites did not use cartridges and so were usually unable to reload during a battle, and most of them never even tried to do so. But the regular forces of the government did use them, and had the training to make it possible to use them several times in this kind of battle. With the cartridges damp and the failure rate likely to increase, their advantage was lost. In such atrocious weather the claymore sat more comfortably in the hand than the unwieldy musket with its bayonet stuck out at one end.

Frozen hands fumbled for their next cartridge, but for many the gun's failure had been the last straw. Throwing them away they turned their backs to the weather and the enemy and let their legs carry them away. A broken fire followed as the government troops of the front ranks fired, but seeing their neighbours absent they too followed flight. Brigadier-General Cholmondeley, who was commanding his own regiment on the left wing of the first line, tried to halt the desertion. Four days later he wrote despairingly: "our Foot gave a feint Fire, and then faced to the right about, as regularly as if they had had the word of Command, and cou'd not be rallied, 'till they got a Considerable distance, altho' I do not think they were pursued by two hundred men".[9] Wolfe's and Blakeney's Regiments on the extreme left broke first, then those of the first line between them and the centre, and then the rest of the front line except Ligonier's.[10] Hawley too attempted to stem the haemorrhage of troops from their positions, "Rally, rally, my brave boys!".[11] His attempts to staunch the flow were to no avail. He soon became engulfed in a stream of bodies which carried him down the hill with them. After a short distance he broke free of them and was approached by Lieutenent Home of the Edinburgh Company of Volunteers. Home was acting as the commanding officer of the Volunteers who had not yet begun to fly. He knew Hawley from previous meetings, desperately he "asked if there were any regiments standing? where they were? The General made no answer to his questions, but pointing to a fold for cattle which was close by, called to him to get in there with his men. The disorder and confusion increased, and General Hawley rode down the hill".[12]

O'Sullivan, watching from a safe distance behind Lochiel's Regiment, saw them as they "rished in upon them sword in hand, immediately after the enemys discharge, & cut them to pieces. This was perhaps one of the boldest and finest actions, yt any troops of the world cou'd be capable of".[13]

Back in the town of Falkirk the people were anxious for news. Some of the burghers and the prominent citizens had taken up positions on the battlemented crown of the church's steeple and in the upper floors of the tolbooth steeple in order to gain a better view. From these vantage points they saw the government army enter the misty and storm-covered moor at the top of the hill; then they saw the dull atmosphere thickened by a fast-rolling smoke, and heard the pealing sounds of the discharge; immediately after they beheld the discomforted troops burst wildly from the cloud in which they had been involved, and rush, in far-spread disorder, over the face of the hill. From the commencement till what they styled "the break of the battle". they later said was only an interval of about ten minutes.[14]

Behind the government lines Captain Cunningham was still labouring with the artillery when he heard the first discharge of smallarms. Looking up the hill he and his men saw the regular units of the foot, upon whom they depended for protection, rushing away from the field of battle. Some were heading straight for the town by way of his position. Seeing his perilous situation he gave orders for the larger cannon to be abandoned, and for the horses to be set free to help to convey the remainder back to the camp.[15] Upon being detached from their burden the horses and the Falkirk carters took flight, the Bo'ness gunners and the Yorkshire Blues followed. Someone, however, seems to have had the presence of mind to spike the abandoned cannon with iron nails driven into their touch holes, rendering them useless.[16]

Seeing the wonderful success of their first line the left wing of the second line rushed in behind them. Together they hotly pursued the enemy in their disorderly retreat. The officers of the government's foot regiments behaved exceptionally well. They tried in vain to rally their men by shouts of encouragement and by setting an example. Many of them held their ground while all about

The Old Kirk and the town Tolbooth whose steeples offered
people handy vantage points as the battle developed.

them fled. They were thus exposed to the Highland onslaught. Amongst these was Sir Robert Munro, one of the heroes of the Battle of Fontenoy fought the year before against the French and their allies.[17] He had been brought back from the continent with his clan regiment in order to help to quell the rebellion. As most of his regiment had relatives fighting for the Jacobite cause it had been humanely decided to station them in Kent in readiness for an anticipated French invasion there. For the same reason the Duke of Cumberland was also in the south of England. The staunchly anti-Jacobite Munro was rewarded with a command in Scotland. He succeeded General Ponsonby in command of the 37th Foot, which then took his own name. However, the dastards of this newly assigned regiment now deserted him. "Ochain! Ochain! had his own folk been there!" exclaimed one of his loyal clan with sincere regret at the news[18]. They would never have left their clan chief on his own. "My father, after being deserted, was attacked" wrote his son five days later, "by six of Locheal's Regt, & for some time defended himself wt his half Pike. Two of the six, I'm inform'd, he kill'd; a seventh, coming up, fired a Pistol into my father's Groin; upon wch falling, the Highlander wh his sword gave him two strokes in the face, one over the Eyes & another on the mouth, wch instantly ended a brave Man".[19] The blow across his mouth whilst he was uttering profanities seemed providential to the Jacobites.[20] The assailant was Callum na Biobhaig - that is, Malcolm of the Small Lock of Hair - whose real name was Malcolm Macgregor, one of Glengyle's men.[21] Munro's brother, an unarmed physician, together with the regimental surgeon and a servant made their way to where his body lay. It was then the custom in battle to allow medical aid to the senior ranks of the stricken enemy. But this was not a regular army. In the heat of the battle, unarmed as they were, they too were all despatched by the wheeling broadswords, and their butchers moved on.

Cholmondeley's Regiment had also turned tail, leaving Major Alexander Lockhart and some brother officers to fend for themselves. The Jacobites here gave quarter and Lockhart was fortunate enough to find himself a prisoner. Straight away he lost his fine red major's uniform to Ninian Dunbar.[22]

At the beginning of the battle the Jacobite right wing had moved down to the Glen Burn to secure its flank. Their first line had subsequently stretched to cover a frontage a over half a mile long over very uneven ground, and consequently as they advanced their left wing passed close by a small valley formed by a burn. The result of this disposition was that the Jacobites extended beyond the left wing of the government forces and had thus been able to outflank the government's infantry after defeating the dragoons. It had also meant that the Jacobite left wing had been able to move round the ravine, jumping the small stream in a slight hollow instead of climbing in and out of the valley that it soon becomes on descending the hill which would have exposed them to shot. Once passed the little valley, however, the Jacobite left flank was exposed to the government right which outlined it. The Jacobite first line had charged so quickly that the government soldiers had been incapable of seizing this advantage as it first presented itself. On the almost instantaneous success of the Jacobite first line here, most of the second line had rushed in to the general foray after them. This left their left flank even more fully exposed to danger as there were no further fresh troops here to plug the gap. It provided a slim chance for the government forces to recover from the near rout that was happening in almost every part of the battlefield. Could the government regiments on their extreme right keep their nerve when all about them had abandoned hope?

The panic amongst the government infantry had spread like wild fire. The whole of the first line was sheering away taking the second with them. The Royal Scots were standing next to Ligonier's Foot on the extreme right. They had not been engaged but they had seen enough. They smartly wheeled about to take their leave, only to find some 400 muskets of Barrel's Regiment pointing directly at them! Refusing to stand their ground as the Lieutenant-Colonel Rich the commander of Barrel's demanded, they were forced to open ranks to go round that regiment [23] to make their exit. Despite the firmness of purpose exhibited by Barrel's Regiment only Captain Ramsay and Sergeant Henson joined them from the Royals to fight alongside them. Already in their ranks for the duration of the battle was a junior officer from Hawley's staff, Brigadier-Major Wolfe, later to become famous for the capture of Quebec.[24] Barrel's had gained a reputation for their drills and now they acted as coolly as though they were on exercise. Marching forward in order they replaced the Royals in the front line. The rot was to go no further.

While this was happening Lieutenant-Colonel George Stanhope had held the 300 men of Ligonier's Regiment in place. At the comparatively youthful age of 29 years he had been given temporary command of the regiment so that Ligonier himself could be with the dragoons. He therefore had something to prove. For almost five minutes they had stood alone, quietly facing the enemy, until joined by Barrel's.[25] Now Stanhope was joined by Brigadier-General Cholmondeley who had suffered the indignity of watching his own regiment melt away. He assumed command of the two regiments and placed Barrel's with its left flank against a small farmhouse. Ligonier's, to the right of Barrel's, had on its own right the steep sided valley running down the hill. The junior officers calmly executed these manoeuvres giving their men instructions and maintaining discipline.[26]

Meanwhile, Lord George Murray was marching diagonally up the back of the hill with the Atholl Brigade and some Keppoch Macdonalds, Menzies and MacGregors. Keeping rank, they mopped up the few pockets of resistance left and organized the detention of those taken as prisoners. A few government officers were brought to Lord George by the runaway Macdonalds on the rare occasions when they gave quarter. Lord MacLeod brought one of them whom "some Highlanders were threatening to kill after he had been taken prisoner".[27]

As Lord George proceeded his ranks were joined by some of the highlanders who had broken ranks during that first impetuous charge. Many of them had fallen to plundering the dead, whilst others had simply lost their sense of direction and purpose. Indeed, many of the Macdonalds had run along the crest of the hill instead of over it to where the government infantry lay. In doing so they went well beyond the left flank of the enemy. Some of them met up with the crowd of spectators and finding a small group of presbyterian ministers amongst them started another slaughter. "Spare my life" said one of the ministers to the Highlander as he was about to take it, "for I am a Minister of My Master Jesus Christ!" To which the Highlander is said to have indifferently replied "If you are a good one, your Master has need of you; if not, it's fitting that you go and take your punishment elsewhere!" The dilemma was quickly solved by the highlander's sword.[28] The highlander's reply was doubtless apocryphal. Another minister, seeing the situation his brother was in, and knowing he was next, begged his life of another highlander for Prince Charles' sake. By that means he preserved his.

A good number of the Macdonalds found no one to fight and fell into some confusion.[29] "They then stop'd their pursuit, and walk'd about, talking with each other and telling what merveils they had perform'd, with the same unconcern as if no enemy had been near".[30] Those of the right wing who had retained a true direction fell in upon the Glasgow Militia. These were soon routed and fled with the Macdonalds on their heels. Amongst the latter was Major Donald Macdonald of Tiendrish. However, the government troops left the field with such precipitation that he too soon found himself alone and wandered over the scene of confusion not knowing where his own regiment lay or what had become of the enemy. Eventually, after some wandering, he found himself amongst the deserted enemy cannon.[31] Lord George sent out his aides to rally the dispersed highlanders, bitterly regretting that they like him were mostly on foot. He desperately needed a piper to draw the men to his standard amidst all the confusion.[32] No piper was to be found at that instant for they, being good fighters themselves, had given their pipes to boys at the beginning of the action and had charged with sword in hand along with the rest. The boys looked after themselves.

Likewise, the left wing of the Jacobite army had become directionless following the initial onslaught. Despite Lord George's earlier request Charles Edward had failed to appoint a commander there. Lord John Drummond had arrived on the scene rather belatedly from his diversionary excursion to Torwood and Larbert Bridge. O'Sullivan who should have taken the initiative here preferred the company of Charles Edward towards the rear once the battle had begun. Before the action proper had started he had reconnoitred the area and seen the danger presented by the outflanking government troops to the north, but had been too intimidated to act.[33] Consequently there was no over all command in this vital arena. Instead of following up their success in the centre of the line by harrying the fleeing regiments, some 400 of the Jacobite left wing moved down the line in order to dismay the remaining government troops. Doubtless they themselves had grown concerned about the prospects of being outflanked - their victory had been too easy and they were worried that this might be a trap. For them this was an unfortunate decision, for whilst they had been engaged in hand to hand combat with government soldiers it had not been possible for the flanking regiments on the right of the government army to shoot at them because of the risk to their own men. Had they then given chase to the government's left wing they would have left Barrel's and Ligonier's Regiments without a target and so isolated from the main action. However, they now approached these two regiments consisting of some 700 men. Some of the highland force had just moved up from the second line and at a distance of about 50 yards a few of them fired what muskets they still possessed, ineffectually, at the government troops. Then they all charged together, sword in hand. Out came the blood curdling war cries as this terrifying mass of strong limbed men descended as a unified body with a single purpose. As they rapidly got closer and closer the realization grew that these opponents were of a different mettle from their comrades. Instead of taking fright the government troops patiently waited as the highlanders drew ever nearer. Both regiments had been drawn into a single line, three ranks deep, with the front rank kneeling.[34] The front rank had orders not to fire until the enemy were practically at bayonet length from them, if they could hold their nerve that long. Then, at almost 20 yards the second and third ranks started to fire by platoons. When the soldiers of a platoon had fired they instantly reached for another cartridge, primed the pan, rammed home the ball, and then fired again as their turn came round indicated by the beat of a drum. A series of devestating rolling volleys brought the charge to a shuddering halt. The highlanders were outnumbered and outgunned. The government infantry were delighted with the results of their work and shouted three loud huzzas to give themselves encouragement before firing yet again. Completely intimidated, the Jacobite detachment turned about and hastily retraced their steps.[35] The first rank of the two steadfast regiments never fired.

These government troops now moved cautiously forward, maintaining their rate of fire. By this move they were able more effectively to cover the retreat of their left wing. They met with no serious opposition and after about 50 yards made a temporary halt. The Jacobites were rich with the proceeds of their earlier looting during the campaign and Ligonier's Foot in particular made a good deal of money out of plundering those they had just shot dead. "a Serjeant I saw had about 30L. Value in 3L.12s Pieces" as a consequence of this incident.[36] One highlander that had been shot through the head by Brigadier Cholmondeley was rifled by one of Barrel's men who, to his astonishment, found 16 guineas in his sporran.[37] This last incident, probably embellished, is also told by Michael Hughes who left us with a vivid account of Culloden:

> while one of the Rebels was pursuing a Soldier belonging to the old Buffs down the Hill, the Soldier turn'd and attemted to fire, but it was so wet that his Piece would not discharge: He then fronted the Rebel, and was instantly going to attack him with his Sword, but the Rogue seeing his Courage, turned tail and run from him: The Soldier was going to pursue him, but Brigadier Cholmondley, observing the Adventure, rides after the rebel and fires a Pistol at him, which happened to miss; he then discharged a second, which finished his Course. Upon this, he bids the Soldier go and search the Man's Pockets, where accordingly the happy Soldier found a Purse of sixteen Guineas.[38]

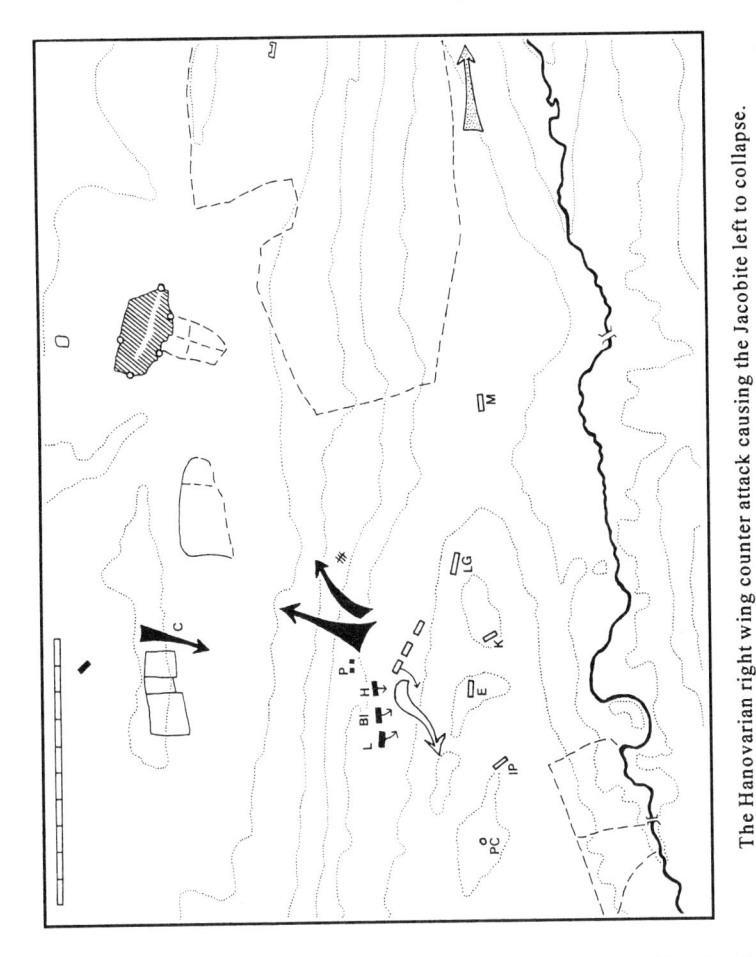

The Storm Rages 133

The Hanovarian right wing counter attack causing the Jacobite left to collapse. L Ligonier's Foot; Bl Barrels; H Howards; P remnants of Prices; C Cobhams Dragoons; PC Prince; IP Irish Picquets; E Elcho; K Kilmarnock; LG Lord George's unit; M Macdonalds

The attack on the two regiments had probably been led by Lochiel at the head of his Camerons. He was wounded by a musket ball in the leg. His brother, Dr Archibald Cameron, was with him in anticipation of just such an occasion. Observing his brother's plight he went to assist him and urged him to retire to have his wound dressed. Lochiel consented and while his brother was thus assisting him he too was shot.[39] The lead lodged in his chest, its velocity retarded by his targe,[40] and it proved not to be fatal.

Those of the Jacobite left wing who were still engaged in close combat with the enemy's centre heard the sounds of gun shot coming from behind them, followed by the loud cheers of the government infantry. Realizing that things had not gone well for their colleagues on this flank they suspected a trap. Lord John Drummond was now on the scene. He had fought against many of the government regiments then present at Fontenoy where they had acted with great courage. He could not conceive that they would now run away faced with such slight numbers of foe. Upon hearing the government right advancing he too believed that it had been a ploy to lead him into an ambuscade. He called a halt to the slaughter in the centre. The government troops there were extremely relieved and gratefully seized the opportunity to disengage and rapidly put as much distance between themselves and the enemy as they could.

The whole Jacobite left wing was now gripped with the same sense of panic as had earlier overwhelmed the government's left wing. The few remaining lowland companies in their second line departed entirely from the field and made their way back towards Stirling. Amongst these was Lord Lewis Gordon.[41] The rest drifted around the field in scattered groups looking for their reserve or any body that still remained formed. Alexander Macdonald and O'Sullivan tried to rally them.[42] However, the former had trouble in making his broken French understood, and the latter lacked the personal authority despite his official rank.

Coming over the crest of the hill Lord George now had a commanding view of the field of battle. In the dark evening light he saw the dilemma that the left wing was facing. As the Marquis d'Eguilles said of this stage of the battle, it was only Lord George who "had the requisite energy, authority, and good fortune to rally them in time".[43] He immediately sent Colonel Kerr to Brigadier Stapleton with instructions to move the Irish Picquets up from the reserve to confront the government right. He was to take with him the cavalry from the third line, all of whom were still in position. At the same time he directed John Roy Stewart to regroup all those he could from the centre.

Barrel's and Ligonier's Regiments had come to a temporary halt to allow time for further consolidation in their army. They had bought themselves, and their colleagues, a breathing space. Howard's Regiment of Old Buffs had been in the reserve behind Barrel's and had stayed in formation. They now moved forward and to their left to give Barrel's flank further protection. Major-General Huske had been active. He rallied parts of Price's and Battereau's Regiments and came to join Howard's flank. Together these formed a considerable body of men presenting a wedge-shaped line projecting towards the enemy. They no longer looked directly into the wind and the sleet had eased a little, though the chill of the evening was beginning to freeze the little puddles of water on the ground. Some distance behind these men, almost at the camp, a large number of runaways had been gathered and formed into another defensive line by Brigadier-General Mordaunt.

Some way to the left of Mordaunt the drums of the dragoons had been frantically beating to signal the recall. Colonel Ligonier had exerted himself with such amazing energy and purpose that he had been able to regroup a small detachment of his own regiment of dragoons, and they now guarded one of the crossroads leading to the town.[44] Groups of foot soldiers, forty to fifty in each, passed by them at intervals.[45]

Lieutenant-General Hawley was in the camp rallying those troops that had sought it out for refuge. He deployed some as guards intending to make a stand there. All the tents were still standing and he went to check his supplies, looking at the same time for horses to retrieve the cannon. Many of the fleeing soldiers had given the camp a wide berth and made straight for the highway to Edinburgh. Chief amongst these were the dragoons that had been so heavily mauled in the initial assault. Even as the government forces had started to rally, riderless horses had scampered through the lanes of Falkirk. Some of them had their saddles turned below their bellies, and others trailed their intestines on the ground.[46] A few horses were secured by the inhabitants of the town, but many followed the headstrong dragoons to the east. Flyers were sent along the road towards Linlithgow to recall the soldiers who had fled without hearing of the counter-attack made by Cholmondeley. Few could be persuaded to return. At Westquarter their fears had been re-awakened by a stream of terrified civilians hurtling headlong towards the same destination. They had fled from the hill by the back of Callendar Wood.

Cholmondeley himself did not rest on his laurels. With the temporary respite that his two regiments had earned he left them with instructions to hold their ground and rode off to where Cobham's

Dragoons had reformed. Having ridden along the front of the Jacobite left wing these dragoons had travelled down the hill to Camelon. There they had run straight through the quarters of several of the companies of the Argyleshire Militia. Whilst they did not tread any of them under foot, as their fellow dragoons had with the Glasgow Militia, the poor wretched volunteers were so intimidated that many of them ran off. [47] Cobham's regiment had been severely depleted and of those that remained many were injured. One of them, Carleton by name, had received two bad wounds.[48] Despite this, about 100 of the dragoons had regrouped and Cholmondeley now put himself at their head. They greeted his news of the turn in events with good spirit and agreed to return with him to the fray. He got them as far as Ligonier's Regiment of foot, but had difficulty in persuading them to advance any further. This he only achieved by firing a pistol amongst them and they very reluctantly followed about 100 paces behind him. Cholmondeley recognized that the Jacobites were in considerable disarray and found none to oppose his ascent to the hill top. On reaching the ridge he was able to discern part of the Jacobite reserve formed up behind some barns and houses. He now believed that so few of the enemy remained in a fighting condition that he would be able to clear them from the hill that night. Leaving the recalcitrant dragoons on the hill top he returned to the foot intending to march them up as well.[49]

Cholmondeley's observations were right. The Jacobite left wing had completely collapsed and many of those in the centre had gone to join Lord George on the right. James Johnstone wandered about the area noting that:

> The Highlanders were in complete disorder, dispersed here and there, and the different clans mingled pell-mell together: whilst the obscurity of the night added greatly to the confusion. Many of them had even retired from the field of battle, either thinking it lost, or intending to seek a shelter from the dreadful weather. It is often more dangerous to stop the fire and impetuosity of soldiers, of whom the best are but machines, and still more of undisciplined men, who do not listen to any orders, that to let them run all risks in order to carry every thing before them.
>
> I met, by accident, Colonel Brown, an Irishman, to whom I proposed

that we should keep together, and share the same fate. He consented, but observed, at the same time, that the Prince having made him the bearer of an order, he wished to find him, with the view of communicating an answer. After having sought the Prince for a long time to no purpose, and without finding any one who could give us the least information respecting him, we fell in with his life-guards, in order of battle, near a cottage on the edge of the hill, with their commander, Lord Elcho, who knew as little of what had become of Charles as we did ourselves. As the night was very dark, and the rain incessant, we resolved to withdraw to the mansion of Mr. Primrose, of Dunipace, about a quarter of a league from Falkirk, having a crowd of Highlanders as guides, who took the same road. On our arrival at the castle, we found Lord Lewis Gordon, brother of the Duke of Gordon, Mr Frazer, son of Lord Lovat, and six or seven other chiefs of clans; but none of them knew what had become of their regiments. Other officers arrived every instant, all equally ignorant of the fate of the battle, and equally in doubt whether we had gained or lost it.[50]

One fugitive with a dreadful wound to his head crossed the Carron Water at Dunipace Steps where he was asked which side had won. "I don't know," he replied, with a bitter groan, "but, och on, I know that I have lost!".[51]

Farquharson of Monaltrie had been with the detachment of his regiment tending to the Jacobite cannon at the crossing of the Carron Water when the battle had begun. When he heard the first fire he abandoned his vain task. He left a small party with the artillery and proceeded with the rest as fast as they could to join the main body. On his way he met 200 to 300 men flying towards the place that he had just left. He made them turn back and return to the field with him. However, instead of proceeding up the hill he made straight towards the government camp. The Argyll Militia moved to intercept, but the small Jacobite force pulled up short to survey the situation.[52]

Back on the top of the hill Lord George had largely succeeded in rallying the right wing which now consisted of a mere 700 or so soldiers.[53] His officers had slowly formed a line with those that they had gathered, but were forced by necessity to do so regardless of clan.[54] For some time Lord George had been worried by a large detachment, barely discernible in the evening light, on his right. This body posed a considerable threat to him if he moved down the hill to aid his troubled left wing. That movement was therefore delayed until he could deal with this perceived threat. Before long his scouts brought news that the huge muddle of people further along the ridge were in fact civilians, scared out of their wits and heading to the passages by the top of Callendar Wood. The right wing started the cautious march down the hill.

Colonel Kerr was moving forward too. He had found Brigadier Stapleton agreeable to this suggestion and, together with Lord John Drummond's Regiment and some of the cavalry, the Irish Picquets made towards the dragoons of Cobham's Regiment. There was thus a considerable gap between the two Jacobite wings occupied only by small confused groups of men. These slowly gravitated to the formations on the extremities. Some were so far ahead of these two groups that they had to wait some time before they caught up.

Isolated fighting was still occurring in some of these pockets of men. One such combat took place between an Irish dragoon and a highlander. Samuel Johnson takes up the story:

> They were both skilful swordsmen, and the contest was not easily decided: the dragoon at last had the advantage, and the Highlander called for quarter; but quarter was refused him, and the fight continued till he was reduced to defend himself upon his knee. At that instant one of the Macleods came to his rescue; who, as it is said, offered quarter to the dragoon, but he thought himself obliged to reject what he had before refused, and, as battle gives little time to deliberate, was immediately killed.[55]

Major Macdonald of Tiendrish had spent almost a quarter of an hour at the government's abandoned cannon by this stage, undecided upon what course of action to take next and uncertain where his comrades stood. Nor was he sure of the enemy's dispositions. He was lost in a sort of no-man's land. The turbulent storm was bringing a premature end to that bleak winter's evening when a stranger passed him by bidding him "to take care of yourself, for the Campbells and others are rallying at the back of Falkirk to return to the battle." He therefore started to make his way obliquely up the hill to rejoin his unit. Shortly thereafter he saw Lord Drummond's Regiment and the Irish Picquets ahead of him. He briskly made up to them with his sword still drawn exclaiming "Gentlemen, what are ye doing standing here? Why don't ye follow after the dogs and persue them?" Scarce had he spoke these words when he discovered his mistake and saw that the body of men was actually Barrel's Regiment!

> When the Major, through the fatal mistake, had rushed in among them a cry was soon raised, 'Here is a rebel! The Major having advanced so far that he could not retreat, endeavoured to screen himself by saying he was one of their own Campbells, his white cockade being so dirty with the heavy rain that had fallen and with the smoke of the firing in time of the action that there was no discovering the colour of it. However the Major did not succeed in the stratagem of passing for a Campbell, for General Husk (being in Barrel's regiment) swore it was easy to discover what he was by his sword - the blade of which happened to be covered over with blood and hair. Husk immediately cried out to shoot the dog instantly; upon which seven or eight musketeers presented their pieces to the major's breast to dispatch him. But Lord Robert Ker generously interposed and saved his life by beating down the muskets, of which the Major entertained a most grateful sense. At last the Major, being obliged to surrender his arms, said as he himself was an officer, he would chuse to deliver up his arms to General Husk, because he appeared to be an officer of dignity; but Husk swore he would not do the Major that honour. Upon which Lord Robert Ker politely stept forwards ro receive the Major's arms. When the Major was pulling off his pistol from his belt he happened to do it with such an air that Husk swore the dog was going to shoot him. To which the Major replied, 'I am more of a gentleman, Sir, than to do any such thing, I am only pulling off my pistol to deliver it up'.[56]

Brigadier-General Cholmondeley had returned to Barrel's and Ligonier's Regiments to march them up the hill to where he had left the small detachment of Cobham's dragoons. He seems to have become involved in the incident concerning Tiendrish, for he noted that "Major McDonald ... has great Obligations to me".[57] Cholmondeley was met by Major-General Huske who had taken over the command of all of the right wing in his absence. As it was rapidly growing dark and Lord George and the Jacobite right wing had been seen descending the hill Huske decided upon an orderly withdrawal to the camp. Muskets gave little advantage over swords in open country in the dark and the two fighting regiments were in any case running short of dry gunpowder that would burn. Cobham's dragoons reached this conclusion on their own. On seeing the Irish Picquets advancing towards them they descended the hill again. With drums beating and colours flying the right wing of the government army marched off the field of battle unopposed in an orderly retreat, covered by these dragoons. The regiments of Howard, Ligonier and Barrel continued firing off volleys at straggling Jacobites as they went.[58] In all it was calculated that the men of these regiments fired some fifteen times each during the entire action.[59] They were soaked by the continuous rain and it "hail'd so hard that the Water ran out of our Soldiers Shoes".[60] On their way to the camp they came across the stranded cannon. A young officer of the train had returned to them when he saw that the right wing of his army was approaching.[61] He helped as some of Barrel's grenadiers attached a rope to one, and yoking themselves to it pulled it down the hill. A second was rolled down, and a third dragged along behind towards the camp where fires had been lit to provide warmth for the troops - a welcome sight. Kettles had also been placed over the camp fires to provide for internal warmth.[62] Brigadier Mordaunt had been ordered to hold the camp.[63]

The Jacobite army was now in a dilemma. They had been forced to disengage and their enemy had reformed, retreating in reasonable order to the town and their camp. They were loath to attack an armed enemy entrenched in a strongly defended camp or a town which provided good cover for musketeers against swordsmen, for few Jacobites had retained their own muskets. It was now quite dark and the appearance of camp fires in the government's base made the chevalier Johnstone think "that we had not obtained a complete and substantial victory. The honour of remaining masters of the field was of little avail to us. We had no reason for believing that we had lost the battle, as the English army had retreated; but as we supposed them still in their camp, we considered it, at most, as undecided, and expected a renewal of the combat next morning".[64]

Elements of the government army had long since fled the area, but many had rallied behind their right wing. There were therefore several thousand soldiers, infantry and cavalry, together as a single fighting unit. By contrast, the Jacobite army was in confusion and widely dispersed. Groups of 200 or so were clumped here and there over the hill. Many had returned to pick up their muskets

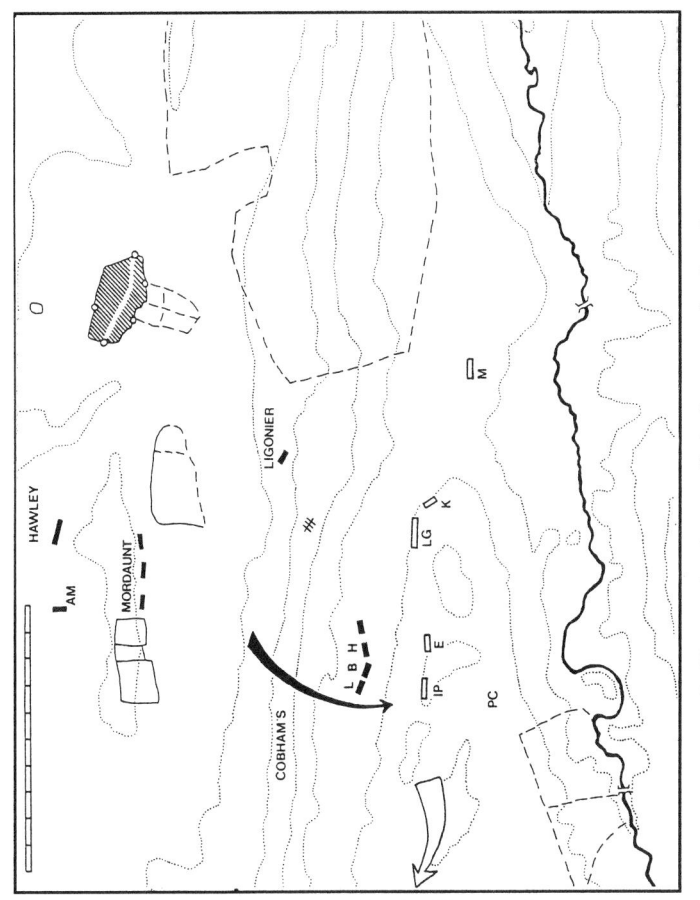

The Hanovarian forces rally before retreating in order.

AM Argyll Militia; L Ligoniers Foot; B Barrels; H Howards; PC Prince Charles; IP Irish Picquets; E Elcho; LG Lord George's unit; K Kilmarnock; M Macdonalds.

and not a few to plunder the dead. Few understood where they were relative to the overall dispositions. "They continued where the night had overtaken them very alert, uncertain whether they were in the neighbourhood of friends or enemies, but sending on all sides to reconnoitre. By degrees the army got together".[65]

Lord George passed the enemy cannon and arrived at the foot of the hill with almost 700 men, not enough to be effective against the government rearguard. He was only just over a musket shot from the town but his military options were few. In the darkness of the evening his first priority was to seek intelligence concerning the movements and disposition of the enemy. Mr Drummond (Lord

Sections from an official map of the battlefield drawn by 'an officer in Batteraus' and published by order of Parliament in 1746

Strathallan) and Oliphant of Gask disguised themselves as local people and went boldly into the town to reconnoitre.[66] At the same time Lord Kilmarnock with his cavalry skirted to the south of the Edinburgh Road by going along the private ways through his own estate of Callendar.

After some time the Irish Picquets arrived along with various fragmented corps that had rallied around them. There were then around 1,500 Jacobites in that location, barely a fighting force. It did, however, include many of the best officers and their immediate entourage such as Keppoch, young Glengarry, Lochiel with his ankle wound, Arshiel, Lord Ogilvy and Colonel Roy Stewart:

> We did not know what to do. We had neither bread nor tents. It was raining, a cold wind swept around us that would have caused the army to perish had we attempted to pass the night there. To return to our quarters was to abandon the battlefield and renounce the fruit of our victory.[67]

> The men had been under arms and in motion from seven o'clock in the morning, were all wet to the skin, and nothing but wet ground to lay upon. It was to be apprehended they would not be prevailed upon to remain there, but would straggle away on all sides to shelter themselves in villages. This might make the victory appear doubtful, and encourage the enemy to retake their artillery next day, and even attempt something further.[68]

> We decided, therefore, in spite of the danger of the undertaking, to go without cannon, without guides, in the profoundest obscurity and attack the enemy in their camp, that we knew to be strongly entrenched from the nature of the locality, and provided them all the defences of art.[69]

The government forces had anticipated such a move. Unaware of the problems afflicting their enemy's organization, they still perceived them to be very dangerous and a night attack seemed probable. Hawley still had the nightmare of repeating Cope's errors, and a dawn attack like that at Prestonpans could be anticipated. He therefore reversed the earlier orders and decided to abandon the camp in favour of the town.[70] At this time the town still had its ports, some of which had been erected towards the end of the sixteenth century. These were simple structures consisting of "arched gateways of stone, battlemented at top, and with arrow or hagbut loopholes in the side-walls".[71] They were thus typical of Scottish town gates like those of St Andrews, or the precinct gate at Linlithgow. They could, nevertheless, be effective against bandits and marauders, and even poorly equipped armies. There were five gates in all. The west gate faced the government's camp (on West Bridge Street near to the present West Church); the Bantaskine or water gate looked south-west along the Howgate; another guarded the main route to the south, commonly used by the common herd and known as Cow Loan; the fourth overlooked the East Burn (at the head of East Bridge Street); and the last opening was on the north at Vicar's Loan (near Manse Place). The approach to each of these was up a hill, except for that on the Cow Wynd, which imparted further advantages to the defenders. Superficially, the town looked very strong. However, the curtain wall connecting the gates together and enclosing the town's properties was in a poor condition. It consisted simply of property dykes at the backs of the houses. Much of it would have been constructed with clay bonding material which had not been properly maintained and it had long since lost its original function of keeping unwelcome visitors at bay.

Before leaving the camp the government army tried to salvage what they could. The horses which had pulled Hawley's coach the day before were found and used to remove three out of the four cannons that had been rescued from the hillside. Some of the baggage was also brought along. Much had to be left. The tents, in particular, were seen as expendable as the men would be lying in the town. In any case they were absolutely sodden with rain and were too heavy to be conveniently moved. Rather than have them provide shelter for the enemy that night Hawley ordered them to be torched and rode into Falkirk. "We observed many fires in Hawley's camp, and his men at the same time marching, with great hurry, between the camp and town of Falkirk. We immediately conjectured that they were burning their camp and were to take possession of the town of Falkirk ... a few men properly posted could have hindered the highlanders from entering that night".[72]

> most were of oppinion to retreat towards Dunipace, & the places adjacent, where the men might be cover'd, it being a prodigious rain,

but Ld George Murray was absolutely for marching in to the town, for he said that if the enemy had the least time they might line the houses, and clean their guns, so as to make it impossible for them to get in, did they give them time, and that therefore there was not one moment to be lost, for he was certain the enemy were in the utmost confusion, & concluded with Count Mercy's expression at the Battle of Parma, "that he would either ly in town or in Paradice." H.R.H. came up at that very time, & aprov'd much of the resolution of attempting the town, & was advised himself to stay at some hutts in the face of the hill till Ld Geo: Murray should send him word of the success.[73]

Prince Charles retired to the hut and awaited the outcome of this risky strategy. There he was found by Lord Macleod warming himself in front of a fire. With him were Sir Thomas Sheridan and O'Sullivan, amongst others.[74]

It was still raining heavily and the tents which had been set on fire were soon extinguished. Lord George sent a detachment to reconnoitre the lanes between him and Falkirk in case of an ambuscade,[75,] and a second party went to the camp where a few prisoners were taken along with a considerable quantity of equipment,[76] including a large weight of gunpowder. Hawley had inspected the powder before abandoning it and found it to be too damp to be of use that night. Indeed, so short of supplies was he now that he took the drastic decision to retreat to the distant safety of Linlithgow. In his rage at the turn of events he smashed his sword against the Cross Well which then stood in the centre of the High Street.[77] He took with him only three covered wagons and the three cannon.[78] The Argyll Militia were drawn up behind the Callendar estate wall at the foot of East Bridge Street, a small distance from the East Port, in order to cover the withdrawal. They remained there for a considerable time while the regular foot filed past.[79]

Strathallan and Gask returned to Lord George with the amazing news that the enemy were withdrawing from the town.[80] The Jacobite force was divided into three columns to enter the town in unison with the greatest numbers that they could muster. Lochiel took his contingent, composed chiefly of Camerons, towards the West Port; Lord George had the Atholl brigade and the remnants of the Macdonalds with Lochgarry, Glengarry and Keppoch, they made for the Bantaskine Port; and Lord John Drummond headed

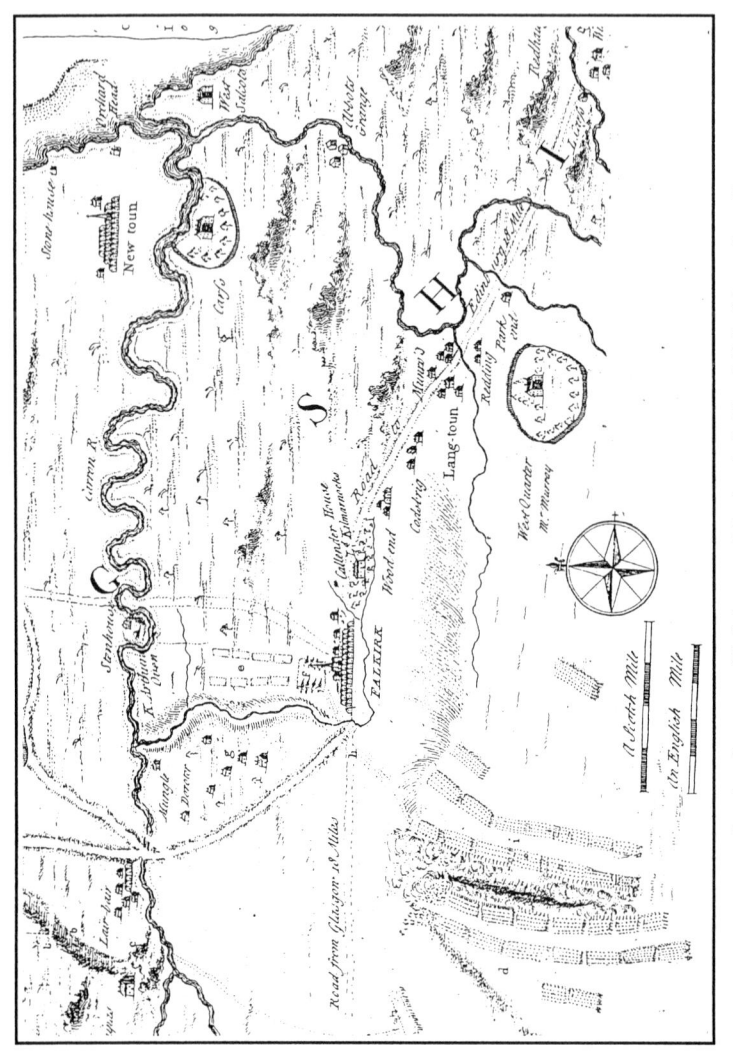

Section from an official map of the battlefield published by order of Parliament in 1746 after Culloden.

for the Cow Wynd with his own regiment and the Irish Picquets to what promised to be the most lively reception of the three as it lay furthest east and thus nearest to the retreating enemy.

It was about 6 o'clock as the Jacobite columns approached the the houses of the hilltop settlement. Finding that the rearguard were putting up a stiff fire they held back. The Earl of Kilmarnock returned with vivid confirmation of the plight of their enemy. He had seen the government army hurriedly making along the road to Linlithgow in considerable disarray and suggested that he should take a large detachment by the byways with which he was intimately familiar in order to intercept them before they got to the bridge over the river Avon.[81] Given the state of their own army, and the fierce resistance that they were encountering this was considered an impracticable proposition. The search for shelter was the paramount short-term goal.

The delaying tactics of the government army were successful, and almost an hour went by before the Jacobites gained an entry into the town. [82] Lochiel passed through the West Port with two battalions[83] encountering stragglers as they went. He quickly made his way along the High Street, pipers playing, to meet up with Lord George at the head of Robert's Wynd. As he was approaching this junction a small party of government soldiers issued from it, running from Lord George's men. Its commander was reeling from the loss of blood, but had still strength to wave his sword, and call upon his men to rally. The first highlander who approached cut down the unfortunate officer, upon which another highlander rushed up and slew the first one in his turn with a battle-axe -"..he ought to respect a teean [dying] prave man, whether ...he'll wear ta red coat or ta kilt" he exclaimed.[84] The speed of the final entry into the town took many more government soldiers by surprise. Some were fortunate enough to get away with a fright, like this member of the Argyll Militia:

> I must tell you the Collonells Volunteer Kilgroat made a narrow Escape, it seems when the Corps were going to join General Husk on his retreat, he found himself so faint with Cold & hunger and fatigued with marching in his Kilt & that at unseasonable hours that he Coud support it no longer but went in to Falkirk to take a little refreshment, but before he had finishd it his friends were gone, and the Philistines were upon him, however he plucked up heart & took to his Heels & without Drawing bridle ran twelve good miles, ... he had just stript of his regimentals & borrowed a Coat [85]

Not a few of the government soldiers had entered the dwellings in the town to take shelter from the weather and to dry their wet clothes in the belief that their army was to occupy the town all

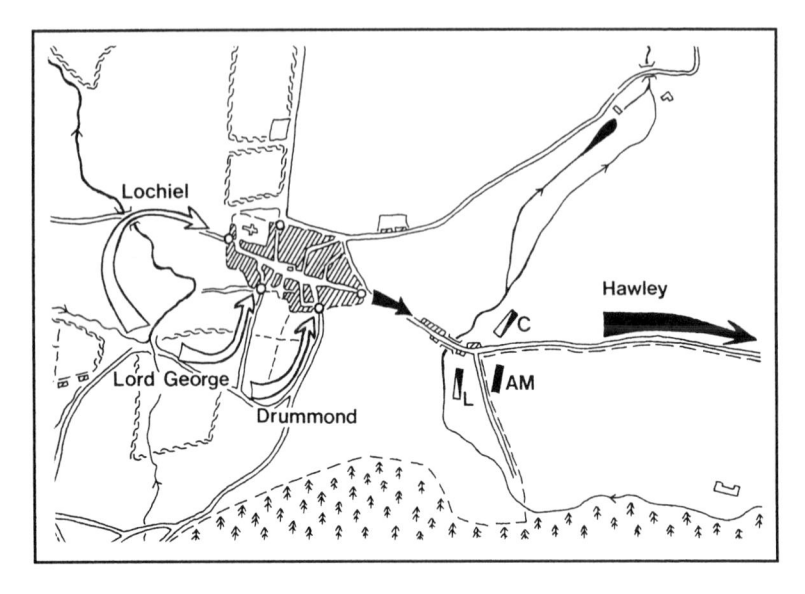

The investment of the town by the Jacobite army.

night. In the confusion and rush of the withdrawal these men were not apprised of the change in orders. Consequently, as the Jacobites immediately commenced a rapid door to door search, many prisoners were taken. These included twenty of the Yorkshire Blues. Mr Crofts, their lieutenant, had acted as their paymaster and had 80 guineas in his possession at the time. Lord George generously gave him a receipt for them, and indeed, eventually returned 6 of them.[86] Captain Thornton was also in one of the houses. "being alarmed by the bagpipes at the door, he retreated up stairs: in a few minutes several of the rebels rushed up, in search of fugitives; when one of them came to the very room door behind which he had taken refuge, and overlooking him, said, "Here are none of the rascals here." They left and continued their search along the street.".[87]

The eastern end of the town was still held by the government rearguard. It was said that Lochiel, upon hearing that this was composed of the Argyll men, hesitated. Many of the Cameron clan were related to the Campbells and he was unsure of their performance in such circumstances.[88] Lord John Drummond encountered stubborn resistance as he forced his way up the Cow

Wynd. He had his horse shot from under him, and was himself shot in the upper fleshy part of the arm by a musket.[89]

By about 7.20 pm the town had been secured and messengers were sent to Prince Charles with word that it was safe for him to enter. Men were also dispatched to gather in those groups of Jacobites that were still to be found on the hillside and had received no knowledge of the latest events. As many as 1,200 men entered the town at this time, but they quickly melted away from their units to take shelter.[90] So few remained at their posts that it was only with the greatest difficulty that enough were found to mount a guard that night.[91] Captain Thornton was trapped in the town. Fortunately for him,

> The woman of the house having seen the Captain go up stairs, went to him soon after, and opening a closet door, entreated him to enter, which he did - She then brought a dresser, and placed dishes, & c. upon it, which prevented all appearance of a door in that place; and fortunately there was no bed in the room. About ten minutes after he had been fixed in his quarters, a great number of people, consisting chiefly of Highland officers, amongst whom was Secretary Murray took possession of the apartment, which being large, they proposed making use of for their business during their stay.[92]

At half past seven Prince Charles entered the town with his entourage carrying torches which flickered in the wind. He was conducted to a substantial dwelling on the south side of the High Street opposite to the tolbooth Steeple (in 1995 this site is occupied by Dixon's Shop). It was the property of a well-known Jacobite sympathizer, Mrs Graham, the widow of a surgeon. Her mother had been one of the Livingstons of Bedlormie, a family with long Jacobite connections. It was therefore natural that her son Walter should be acting as a physician with the present Jacobite army. The house had once been the Great Lodging of the Livingstons of Westquarter, and whilst it had become slightly run down since it had been acquired by the Grahams in 1721, it was still well appointed.[93] The building had been divided up among various tenants and the room chosen for Charles was that of George Menzies of Grahamsfield, bailie and clerk of the town. He had made himself scarce on this occasion. The apartment measured only twelve feet square, and was lighted by one window overlooking the street. A

The Great Lodging in the High Street where the Prince and later the Duke of Cumberland rested during their time in Falkirk. The doors on the right concealed a box-bed. The drawings were done in 1900 shortly before the building was demolished.

roaring fire in the fireplace welcomed the tired leader into the room. Above it, the overmantle was a reminder of the former grandeur of the building. Carved in oak was a depiction of Solomon giving judgement.[94] The room also housed a concealed bed behind folding doors, as was the custom of the time.[95] This was removed around 1860, but the chair in which Prince Charles sat was kept as a memento.

Lochgarry was sent back to Dunipace to find that part of the army that had retreated there and to tell them that it was safe to come to Falkirk. When he got there, at about 8 o'clock he found the officers in the house unaware of the eventual outcome of the night's venture. "It is impossible" wrote Johnstone later, "without having been in our situation, to form an idea of the extreme joy which we derived from this agreeable surprise".[96] They resolved to go to Falkirk early the next day.

At Falkirk the Jacobite command decided to send a detachment of foot, 1,000 strong, to harry the enemy whilst they were vulnerable. However, much to their dismay they were unable to gather a force of any size to pursue the fleeing soldiers on account of the atrocious weather and the arduous and exhausting day. Only their horse brigades, which had played no significant role in the battle, were still in a condition to fulfill a military function. These regiments were more accustomed to the concepts of formation and had kept their order. Kilmarnock's horse went after the government army to pick off any stragglers. On his way Kilmarnock called at the house of a retainer, probably James Leishman of Claddens, to enquire after the welfare of his wife and to send her news of his own condition.[97] The government army had been marching hurriedly towards Linlithgow with the dragoons commanded by Ligonier forming the rearguard. Unused to such rapid movement many of the militiamen slowly fell behind and became easy prey for the Jacobite cavalry. Of the Edinburgh Volunteers, for example, William Macghie their captain, Lieutenant John Home, privates Thomas Barrow, Robert Douglas, Robert Alexander and Neil MacVicar, were all taken during this phase of the retreat.[98] They were taken that night to the cellars at Callendar House. All in all the number of prisoners taken during this critical period was much lower than it should have been. Even the Jacobite press admitted this: "They had the start of us by an hour and half, and some troops, which they left at Falkirk, disputing our entrance, gained them another hour; so that our cavalry, being poorly mounted, could not come up with them; hence it was that in a flight, in which 5 or 6000 prisoners might have been taken, we did not make above 600, only 250 of which were regular troops''.[99]

The bulk of the government army arrived at Linlithgow at just after 8 o'clock that night. The weather that had caused them so many problems during the battle had effectively sheltered them during their withdrawal so that they escaped very lightly. The Campbells were posted at Linlithgow Bridge to secure their sanctuary for the night. Ligonier and the dragoons continued to provide a screen for those troops still on the road towards the bridge. Indeed, they continued their exposed patrols until all hope of further survivors using that route was lost. Cold, wet and exhausted Ligonier finally turned in at one o'clock in the morning.[100] Kilmarnock was similarly employed on the Jacobite side until the early hours when he too gave up, having ensured that the enemy would not return to Falkirk that day. He made his way back to Callendar House where his wife was anxiously waiting for him. He had been in the saddle for over 16 hours.

Upon the initial rout the government army had splintered off in numerous directions. Some had run blindly to the east and eventually reached the banks of the river Avon. Unwilling to risk staying a moment longer on that side they rushed headlong across the water rather than search for a ford. The river was deep with the day's rain and some were swept away and drowned.[101] The riderless horses also went off without any care to their direction. As they grew tired and their panic eased they were secured by soldiers making their escape; or more often by the local population who gladly seized them for themselves. A brewer in Falkirk obtained such a prize for use in his business.[102] One of the horses passed through Redding where one of the locals was able to pluck a drum from its side, a souvenir of the historic day![103]

Part of the army, including Melford's and Achnabar's Companies of the Argyll Militia, made straight for the town of Bo'ness. The storm had been so violent during the day that many of the boats anchored off the port broke free from their moorings and were dashed against the shore.[104] Not feeling safe even there the runaways continued on for Queensferry with no idea where their main force lay.[105] William Campbell of Succoth had been travelling with them and decided to remain at Bo'ness where he booked into an inn. However, two hours later "we were alarmed with a report of the Highlanders having entered the town on the pursuit, tho this was false it was too strongly asserted, & imported me too much to be neglected. So Bailie John Sommervill, John Hall & I mounted & went on to Queensferry, but in the Hurliburly my servant lost his horse, so I was oblidged to leave both him & my baggage behind, & have not heard of either since".[106]

The first of the dragoons and the spectators to flee the field were in Edinburgh by 9 o'clock spreading dire news of the disaster that had befallen their army. The citizens of the city were amazed and shocked at such an outcome. The Lord Justice Clerk and the government officials were extremely alarmed, fearing a rapid advance on the city by the rebel army. The terror communicated by these early arrivals, particularly the bedraggled soldiers, caused widespread consternation and panic. This deepened during the following hours as some of the foot soldiers made their arrival and told their own stories of doom and gloom. Amongst these was the ensign of Munro's Regiment, the first man of his unit to reach the capital.[107] For those with Jacobite leanings it was a joyous moment, a repeat of Prestonpans.

Hawley was very mindful of the propaganda effect which his distant withdrawal might create and was anxious to counteract it - not least, in order to hide his own defeat. He met Walter Grossett in Linlithgow and instructed him to return straight away to Edinburgh with news of a government victory at a skirmish, followed by a tactical withdrawal.[108] For Hawley personally the battle had been a total disaster. "He seems to be sensible of his misconduct; for when I saw him on Saturday morning at Linlithgow, he looked most wretchedly; even worse than C[ope] did a few hours after his scuffle, when I saw him at Fala".[109] Hawley was alone and dejected; isolated by his command and hated by most of his fellow officers, he was blamed by them for their defeat. Dutifully he sat down at his writing table to pen a report to the Duke of Cumberland:

Lithgow, Jan 17,1746.

Sir,

My heart is broke. I can't say we are quite beat today, but our left is beat, and their left is beat. We had enough to beat them, for we had 2000 men more than they, But such a scandalous cowardice I never saw before ... I must say one thing, that every officer did their duty, and what was in the power of man, in trying to stop and rally the men, and they led them on with as good a countenance, till a Halloo began, before a single shot was fired, and at 500 yards distance: Then I own I began to give it over. I only beg leave to acquaint your R.H. that we were neither surprised nor attack'd. We met them half way, and rather attack'd them, tho' they were still in motion.

Pardon me, Sir, that you have no more this time from the most unhappy, but most faithfull and most dutifull your R:H: has,

H.HAWLEY

He continued at his table for some time, writing to the supporters of the government to pre-empt news reaching them from other sources. At a period of slow communications it was possible to steady the boat by deception - the campaign of disinformation ran hand in glove with that of intelligence gathering throughout the uprising.

Walter Grossett's arrival in Edinburgh brought welcome relief to the administration there. It ended a period of turmoil in the city during which panic had reigned as people prepared to leave. His message was reinforced by later arrivals of spectators who had lingered long enough to witness Huske and Cholmondeley make their counter-attack.

On his way to Edinburgh Grossett had come across the army's supply train which had been carrying provisions to Falkirk. When the first soldiers flying from the battle had come up with them they too turned about and headed back to Edinburgh. Now Grossett, with official backing, forced them to retrace their path to Linlithgow to supply the remnants of the army there which would otherwise have had no food other than what little was to be found in that town. Late as the hour was by then, he had another meeting with Lieutenant-General Hawley. Hawley had been taking stock of his situation and had concluded that his powder and ammunition supplies were so far depleted as to make his stay at Linlithgow untenable. The untiring messenger yet again set out for Edinburgh to arrange quarters there for the army.[110]

Prince Charles's position was far more confortable than Hawley's. He was elated by the success of his army and issued various orders to his commanders before sitting down to a victory meal in his room. In all, only just over 1500 Jacobites stayed in Falkirk that night. Lord Cromarty's Regiment, with some of the Mackintoshes and Farquharsons, only came in at 10 o'clock, having wandered around unconscious of their predicament.[111] Balmerino's Life Guards were also alerted to the situation at a late stage. "And now after four or five hours halt, we heard we might go, if we pleased [sarcasm at having been held back earlier], and take possession of the town".[112] As soon as they arrived a detachment from them, consisting of John Daniel and 17 men, was sent to a house where they were informed that some of the enemy were still lurking. The house lay near Dorrator and on their arrival they discovered that a whole company of the Argyll Militia, some 54 or so in number, were held up there with the doors and windows barracaded. They were commanded by Captain McNeil, who was determined to fight.[113] The building was surrounded, and after a few volleys from the Jacobites the occupants were persuaded to change their minds and surrender.[114] One of the prisoners was only a young boy who said that he lived within 14 miles of the place. Daniel mercifully allowed him to slip away. By the time that the remainder had been rounded up, disarmed, and marched to Falkirk, the town was full. The prisoners were placed in the church and the churchyard under guard, but Daniel and his comrades had no option but to lie, wet and cold, in the open fields near by, catching only a few hours sleep before dawn.

Meanwhile, up on the high moor and the hillside the dead and injured were being stripped naked by the some of the highlanders and the local population.

The Battle of Falkirk from a painting by Lionel Edwards

CHAPTER 7

Storm Damage
18th January - 22nd January

The confusion and uncertainty that closed the day of the battle continued on the Saturday. As morning broke it was clear that much hard work was required to create some order from the chaos. However, in this everyone was severely hampered by the dreadful weather. "The tempest raged with such violence, during the whole of the next day, the 18th, and the rain poured down in such torrents, that none of us quitted our lodgings".[1] Whilst Johnstone and some of the commanders stayed in the shelter of Dunipace House many of the other Jacobites returned to Falkirk from the fields and farmhouses around.[2]

The young Lord Macleod had been separated from his father during the battle and had searched for him in vain that night in the town. Overcome by fatigue he had finally spent an uneasy night in one of the houses, unaware of his father's fate. "When I awoke next morning, my servant, whom I had order'd to enquire, told me that my father was lodg'd not far from where I was, and that he was very well. I immediately gote up and went to him. Our mutual joy was very great to meet again, and to find that neither of us had receiv'd any hurt".[3] Not all friends could look forward to such a fortunate reunion.

The most urgent task facing the Jacobites was to secure their position. Accordingly the Irish Brigade, almost the only unit available for active duty, was sent to Linlithgow Bridge to block any renewed activity in the area from the government army.[4] Elcho's and Pitsligo's Horse performed the task of patrolling the road between there and Falkirk. The rest of the army, or at least that part of it that could be found, were kept on their arms ready for any action.[5] This might take the form of a retreat if necessary.

Having thus secured the area between the town and the river Avon from outside intervention a net was thrown over it. This mopping up operation involved numerous small parties roving around the country in search of hiding and concealed redcoats.

Indeed there were many to be found. Five or six men would bring in the prisoners and their arms in groups of thirty or so. The prisoners were scared and dared not even look the Highlanders in the face.[6] Many of the government foot had taken refuge in the farmhouses about the area and were gradually hunted down.[7] Some had got the length of the Avon but were unable to cross its swollen waters.[8] A large number of spectators were also sheltering in these dwellings,[9] and not a few were taken captive and marched into Falkirk.

Early in the morning Lord Kilmarnock came in with the prisoners that he had held over night in Callendar House. He had only managed a few hours sleep and was beginning to suffer from the severe exposure of the previous night. Leaving the prisoners with their guard on the High Street in front of the Steeple he went to Prince Charles's room. Charles was still upstairs and received the list of the prisoners. Charles took it over to the window, which he opened, and looked down on the captives, all the time talking to Kilmarnock. John Home was amongst the prisoners and describes what happened next:

> a soldier in the uniform of one of the King's regiments, made his appearance in the street of Falkirk, which was full of Highlanders: he was armed with a musket and bayonet, and had a black cockade in his hat. When the volunteers saw a soldier with his firelock in his hand coming towards Charles, they were amazed, and fancied a thousand things; they expected every moment to hear a shot. Charles observing that the volunteers (who were within a few yards of him) looked all one way, turned his head that way too: he seemed surprised; and calling Lord Kilmarnock, pointed to the soldier. Lord Kilmarnock came downstairs immediately: when he got to the street, the soldier was just opposite to the window where Charles stood. Kilmarnock came up to the fellow, struck his hat off his head, and set his foot on the black cockade. At that instant a Highlander came running from the other side of the street, laid hands on Lord Kilmarnock, and pushed him back. Kilmarnock pulled out a pistol, and presented it at the Highlander's head; the Highlander drew his dirk, and held it close to Kilmarnock's breast. In this posture they stood about half a minute, when a crowd of Highlander's rushed in, and drove away Lord Kilmarnock. The man with the dirk in his hand took up the hat, put it upon the soldier's head, and the Highlanders marched off with him in triumph.

This piece of dumb shew, in which they understood nothing, perplexed the volunteers. They expressed their astonishment to a Highland officer who stood near them; and entreated him to explain the meaning of what they had seen. He told them that the soldier in the uniform of the Royal was a Cameron: "Yesterday," he said, "when your army was defeated, he joined his clan; the Camerons received him with great joy,and told him that he should wear his arms, his clothes, and every thing else, till he was provided with other clothes and other arms. The Highlander who first interposed, and drew his dirk on Lord Kilmarnock, is the soldier's brother; the crowd who rushed in are the Camerons, many of them his near relations; and, in my opinion," continued the officer, "no Colonel nor General in the Prince's army can take that cockade out of his hat, except Lochiel himself.[10]

This Cameron was not the only Hanoverian soldier to see the light as a result of the battle. One of John Homes's fellow militiamen went over to the rebels after a few frightening days in their prison.[11] Sergeant John Christy of the Royal Artillery also changed his allegiance and joined the Duke of Perth's Regiment. Should any of these deserters in the future fall foul of the government they would receive the severest punishment of all.[12]

Soon there was an embarrassingly large number of prisoners for the Jacobites to cope with. "we had neither fort or other secure place to keep our prisoners in, so that, if it were not merely out of mercy, it was to no purpose to take prisoners, being without the means of keeping them".[13] The tolbooth could hold few men, so the parish church was pressed into service,[14] as was probably the three year old Erskine Church in Silver Row. The desperate shortage of accommodation meant that the cellars of Callendar House continued in use as well as the attics of some town houses.[15]

It was now time to take stock of the previous day's work and to view the battlefield again, the scene of so much carnage. One of the inhabitants of Falkirk surveying the field from a distance noted how the naked bodies of the slain and injured, having laid in the cold and rain, now resembled a large flock of white sheep at rest on the face of the hill.[16] Pools of water formed around the lifeless lumps.

The scavengers had been busy during the night and at first light. One highlander was seen stripping a richly dressed government officer. He had got one foot inserted between the legs of the deceased, and was endeavouring with all his strength to pull off the boots. At every interval between the succesive pulls he muttered to himself "Praw proichin! praw prochain!" (Fine brogues, fine brogues).[17] One Jacobite officer noted glibly that "there were a great many officers killed, for Goold watcheses were at a chape reat".[18]

Not all the plundering of the dead was done by the Highlanders. The local people took this unique opportunity to enrich their own lives and to make up for their own recent deprivations. Nor were all the victims dead when they were treacherously picked bare of their possessions and clothes and left to endure a lingering death in the freezing night air. Some were 'mercifully' murdered on the spot, though there was a constant moaning sound in the air.

> But on the morn, both great and small,
> Unto Falkirk assembled all,
> To view the field and bury the slain;
> But which was which, was ill to ken,
> For by their clothes no men could tell,
> They stripped were as fast's they fell.
> The plundering wives, and savage boy
> Did many wounded men destroy!
> With dirks and skians they fell a sticking,
> for which they well deserv'd a kicking;
> Some of the Brutish commons too,
> I saw them run the wounded thro'! [19]

Soon after daybreak the Hussars returned to the scene and, finding the country people still engaged in this gruesome task and collecting abandoned equipment, they fired shots to clear them away.[20] An award was offered for any arms brought in.[21]

Some attempt must have been made to ascertain the numbers of the dead on each side, but this was hindered by the continuing bad weather and the disparate groups involved in disposing of the bodies. There were problems also in identifying to which side the naked corpses belonged. By and large, it was noted that the government soldiers were to be recognized by the deep gashes which seamed their shoulders and breasts - the dreadful work of the broadsword. It was also remarked that the Highlanders had bannocks or other articles of provision concealed under their left

The Munro tombstone in Falkirk Parish Churchyard with its
decorative tablet displaying weapons or trophies.

armpits.[22] However, even with these distinguishing signs the mortality figures cannot have been very accurate. Nor was there any chance of having them independently verified and so for propaganda reasons the numbers of the government casualties were exaggerated and those of the Jacobites correspondingly diminished. The official Jacobite numbers gave the government losses as 600, and their own as a mere 40. No account was taken of the large number of spectators who forfeited their lives as a consequence of having become engulfed in the action.

Looking over the corpses that littered the field it was quickly decided that only the officers would be taken down to Falkirk for burial in the churchyard, the remainder would be dealt with on the spot thereafter. Several officers were recognised. Robert Munro's body, stripped and defaced as it was in its 62nd year, was easily found because of his corpulency. The right hand still clenched the pommel of his sword from which the whole blade had been broken off.[23] Beside him, in a pool of water, lay his faithful brother, aged 59 years. The Earl of Cromarty and the Macdonalds saw that their bodies were taken down to the town for internment.[24] Colonel Whitney was also well known to the Jacobites, particularly to John Roy Stewart. Captain-Lieutenant William Edmondstone of Cambuswallace of Blakeney's Foot was recognized because of his local connections. On the Jacobite side few officers had been killed, but these included two captains of the Stewarts. "They were searching among the dead all Saturday and Sunday for Some Person of distinction but could not find him, which they lamented very much.....they found his Sword and his Horse, but not himself".[25]

The common soldiers of both sides were alike buried in a large trench dug on the hill where they had fallen. The digging wasundertaken by the local people, after much coercion, in order to leave the Jacobite army free to deploy their few forces against a potential counterattack and to collect in the prisoners. It must have been a depressing duty to excavate a large pit into the wet slippery clay in the heavy rain on the exposed hilltop -and with several hundred bodies a large pit it was. The obvious method to employ would have been to place the corpses into the charnel pit at one end and then to cover them with the earth dug out at the other end as it was extended again and again. The dead and the dying of either side were consigned to the trench without distinction. A wounded highlander, probably from Skye, was dragged to the edge where he beseeched his murderers to be spared. "Just gang in wi' quiet, for maybe ta prince may be angry" he was told, and then hurled in among the dead.[26] The earth was then filled in on top of him. The lesser officers were placed into the same trench, but these were wrapped in flannel and laid down.[27] The number of the slain inhumed in the pit was such that some years after the surface sank several feet, and there was still a considerable hollow in 1827.[28]

Specific orders were given by Prince Charles not to bury the six or eight presbyterian ministers that had been butchered. Before they would be interred he wished to know their names and the places from whence they had come.[29] This action soon gave rise to the rumour that "if true, under pretence of knowing to what places they belong, their naked bodies will be exposed to dogs, the fashion in France with the dead Protestants".[30]

At Stirling the church bells were rung in the town by the Jacobites to celebrate their victory and to put on a show for the loyal garrison still holding out in the castle.[31] These scenes of jubilation contrasted strongly with the sombre mood at Falkirk where the bells were muted so that they might be used to warn of

The little copse of trees in Dumyat Drive is traditionally
known as the "English graves"

the enemy's return. General Blakeney at Stirling Castle decided to raise his own men's morale by drowning out the sound of the merriment with the noise of cannon fire, and the Jacobite party took the hint and retired. At about one o' clock the castle received its own version of the "skirmish" in which Hawley had been obliged to retire "by reason of the violence of the weather" having first done considerable "execution" on the rebel side.[32] Almost two hours later the castle was formally told by the Duke of Perth that their relief force had been obliterated and that the castle should now surrender as it had after Bannockburn. The reply was not very polite and left no room to doubt the resolve of the garrison commander.[33]

By the mid afternoon the bodies of the six officers, four of which were from the government army, had been brought down to the town ready for burial in the consecrated churchyard. A local joiner was ordered to hastily prepare coffins for them.[34] Wood being very scarce at that season he was given the stock that had been purchased for the building of the new manse and which had been stored in the church when the work there had been temporarily halted.[35] Holes were dug as the rain continued, and the funerals were held in the presence of most of the Jacobite commanders. Captain Robert Stewart of the Appin Regiment was given the use of the best mortcloth, whilst his comrade in arms, Lieutenant John Stewart, received the second best. The best mortcloth was also used for Edmondstone who had been killed in the battle exactly thirty-two years after his baptism at Kilmadock Church.[36] Their graves, and those of the Munro brothers and Whitney were given temporary wooden markers.

As well as the plunder gleaned from the field of battle there were also rich pickings to be had at the abandoned government camp. Lord George did his best to secure the material here from the individual pilfering of his men so that he could make use of it for the whole army. The most conspicuous item was the large number of tents which had been left standing. Although some had been set on fire by the retreating redcoats, there were still in excess of 1,000 left. These could be a valuable asset in a mobile campaign as they could provide shelter in any location and permit the whole army to be quartered together, if only the highlanders could be persuaded to use them. More important was the vast quantity of gunpowder and ammunition. There was 4,000 lb of powder in the 28 open wagons and 8 covered ones, and plenty of shot.[37] Along with these were the hand-grenades and some 600 muskets, enough to maintain the Jacobite army throughout its winter campaign. On the symbolic side there were three standards, two stands of colours and a kettledrum.[38] One of these standards, from Gardiner's Dragoons which had been renamed Ligonier's, bore the motto "Britons, strike home!".[39] Hawley's coach made an interesting spectacle.

Of immediate importance was the bread store. The bread was soon distributed amongst the Jacobite soldiers.[40] However, it did not go far and many of the men were left to fend for themselves, finding nourishment where they could. Patrick Lindsay had been quartered along with Major Macdonald at Torbrex with the episcopalian minister there. "We were agreeably surprised on his return from the battle of F_____k to find a great hoarseness of his quite gone. He told us that the only part of the booty he touched was a large lump of sugar candy 4 or 5 lb. wt., that he ate it till he loathed & that had cured him".[41]

The only money reported to have been recovered was the sum of 500 Sterling found in the Tolbooth left by the retreating army.[42] There was also a great deal of personal baggage belonging to the officer class. This included clothes, toiletries, wine and family items. Most of this had been left in the town where the men had sought the comfort of the open fires. Now it was commandeered by the residents, and only a fraction of it fell into Jacobite hands. O'Sullivan noted with delight the presence of hampers and good wine.[43] Colonel Campbell of the Argyll Militia had taken the precaution of having his baggage buried in the yard of the building where he had been settled, probably during the lull in the battle before the Jacobites entered the town. However, he made the mistake of leaving his French valet to look after it. The suspicious highlanders immediately seized him and soon forcefully persuaded him to divulge the secret of his charge. As they sat around the fire that evening, drinking the Colonel's wine, they toasted his liberality.[44] The owner of this residence, fearful of being named as a collaborator, had likewise taken steps to safeguard her own valuables and provisions, burying some in the fields, and concealing part of her meal in pillow-slips which were inserted into the inside of sacks of chaff. Finding no food in the house, the Highlanders turned their anger on their new landlady and her children. She too was forced to reveal the hidden material, and what she held back on was found by diligent search. The highlanders thrust their swords into all the sacks and middens to locate the concealed packages.[45]

With hindsight the officers learned not to carry so many valuable and unnecessary possessions with them, for they too could live off the land as the Highlanders had. "the officers dont care how little cash they have about them in these parts, especially in war; for every time we thought of a battle the officers' servants had all the regiment's cash, rings, and watches. I sold my watch a little before Falkirk's battle, and the dear lad that bought it was kill'd the first fire, so that he and all he had fell to those inhumane dogs. He was my particular friend".[46] Not all the aristocratic hierarchy were so concerned about their fellow men: James Masterton was still preoccupied with his own losses when he wrote: "Lieut.Col. Jordan of Cobhams Dragoons was Shott in ye Belly the Ball taken out, and I had a 14 Guinea Horse Shott under me".[47]

Alexander Grossett felt similarly aggrieved: "I have lost everything by my servants geting drunk & falling into their hand up with my things amongst which are all my books that were left ... & best herffurniture, but my glasses is what I repine most at as they will have a great advantage in them".[48] One of the main prizes of the battle had been the capture of the seven pieces of brass ordnance, along with the three covered wagons containing the associated supplies and three iron mortars or coehorns. These had been left on the hillside all day as the men were busy about their other tasks, but as it grew dark there was some concern that the locals might spirit them away over night. By then only the corpses on the top of the hill had been buried, the rain slowing progress. Johnstone returned from Dunipace and takes up the narrative:

> Having repaired to the Prince's quarters, about seven o' clock in the evening, I found no one in his anti-chamber; but when I was about to withdraw, Mr. Sullivan issued from the Prince's closet and informed me, that, from the badness of the weather, the cannon taken from the enemy had been left on the field of battle without any guard, and he requested me to go instantly with a guard of a serjeant and twenty men, and pass the night beside them. He added that I should find the guard below, ready to march. I set out with this detachment. The serjeant carried a lantern; but the light was soon extinguished, and by that accident we immediately lost our way, and wandered a long time at the foot of the hill, among heaps of dead bodies, which their whiteness rendered visible, notwithstanding the obscurity of a very dark night. To add to the disagreeableness of our situation from the horror of this scene, the wind and rain were full in our faces. I even remarked a trembling and strong agitation in my horse, which constantly shook when it was forced to put its feet on the heaps of dead bodies, and to climb over them. However, after we had wandered a long time amongst these bodies we at length found the cannon. On my return to Falkirk, I felt myself relieved as from an oppresive burden; but the horrid spectacle I had witnessed was, for a long time, fresh in my mind. How inconsistent is man! During a battle, we frequently see our dearest friends fall by our side, as has repeatedly happened to myself, without being sensibly affected with sorrow and regret at the moment of their unfortunate death; and yet, when we coolly proceed over a field of battle, we are seized with horror, at the sight of a spectacle repugnant to human nature, of dead bodies, though, when living, they may have been perfectly unknown to us. So much does man differ from himself, according to the situations in which he happens to be placed.[49]

At about this time the other leaders of the army were meeting in the room in which Captain Thornton was hiding. "The closet was only a yard and a half square; and the Captain's clothes being wet when he entered, made his situation the more uncomfortable, as he had got a severe cold, and sometimes could not forbear coughing, even when the rebels were in the room. Once in particular, hearing a cough, they said one to another "what is that?" but one of them answered, that it was somebody in another room; not in the least suspecting a door in the place where the closet was".[50] The matters being discussed were of the utmost importance to the future of the Jacobite cause. Lord George Murray and several of the clan leaders were for following up their victory by a rapid thrust towards Edinburgh to discomfort and disperse what remained of the demoralized government army and to remove the capital from its use as a staging post for the enemy. The port of Leith in particular was a strategic target as it provided the enemy with a base for future operations, supplying both provisions and reinforcements from England and the continent. The weather had detained them from an immediate pursuit, but it had also kept the enemy within striking distance at Linlithgow. Some of the officers present were more pragmatic and realized that their own army was in no fit shape to mount a full blooded pursuit. At best they could only hope to harry the enemy's retreat, if indeed they did not turn and fight! Prince Charles's own counsellors were convinced that Stirling Castle would now fall and that securing it should be the main priority as it would give them a major stronghold in which to detain their prisoners and open up communications with their heartland. In the end the weather won the argument and the decision was delayed.

New prisoners were still being brought in from the surrounding countryside. "some of the Rebel Officers being together in an Inn at Falkirk, a Serjeant came in & ask'd, What he should do with five of the troops whom he had prisoners? One of the Officers (said to be, either Hunter of Burnside, or one Capt Nairn) answer'd, What! have we no dirks? Upon this, the Serjeant retir'd, and caus'd murder, the 5 prisoners.[51] The reverend John Bisset, minister at Aberdeen, was "likewise pretty well informed, that, after the battell of Falkirk, the Highlanders killed, in a house, 16 militia men, in cold blood".[52]

The Jacobite forces had been kept on the alert all day, not knowing what had become of their enemy. They knew that Hawley was at Linlithgow, but he had withdrawn in pretty good order. Was he in a condition to return? The bridge at the river Avon was guarded by the Argyll Militia and it was necessary to procure information from intelligence reports brought in by spies travelling by other routes. This was a slow and dubious process. In the meantime, an officer and fifteen of Elcho's Horse and as many of Pitsligo's patrolled the road.[53] All the troops were ordered to provide themselves with enough provisions for a day.

Early that morning the government army had in fact marched out of Linlithgow and the main body arrived in Edinburgh at 4 o'clock that afternoon to the jeers of the Jacobite sympathizers there.[54] The citizens saw for themselves the bedraggled men, exhausted and despondent, and drew their own conclusions. They brought with them only four prisoners.[55] Yet the state of things in the capital was not too bad. Lord Semple's Regiment had arrived there from Newcastle on the day of the battle, and although it was relatively small it provided new and tried troops to replace the losses. As Hawley returned from Linlithgow a second regiment, the Scots Fusiliers, arrived at Musselburgh.[56]

Lieutenant-General Hawley gradually recovered his composure. Writing again to the Duke of Cumberland he wrote more optimistically:

> I am to report that I have given a severe check to the Highlanders. The evening being excessively raining I thought it proper to march the troops to Linlithgow and put them under cover there, otherwise we should have continued in our camp at Falkirk being masters of the field. There was too the danger that the rebels might push between us and Edinburgh. We lost 300 men but it is much worse for the Highlanders.[57]

He put his safe journey to Edinburgh down to the severe mauling he had given the enemy, whereas in reality the horrendous weather and the Jacobite's own disorder had been his saviours.

Two of Hawley's principal officers who had exerted themselves with such good effect the day before had developed serious ailments caused by their exposure and fatigue. Major-General Cholmondeley, the hero of the day, lost the use of his limbs and is said to have contracted a 'palsy'.[58] He was also dangerously wounded. Colonel Ligonier, who had been out in the rain until 1 am developed a fever or quinsy.[59] Both received medical attention in Edinburgh.

Everyone was exhausted. Like Alexander Grossett - "The fatiguie & Want of sleep for these three days past has been such will constrain me to give you a very abrupt acct of what hapnd yesterday ... in the meantime I remain in great hast & half asleep".[60] This was a sentiment echoed by most of those that had been at Falkirk on the eventful day. "I [George Stanhope] am extremely fatigued, not having been between sheets these four nights".[61]

Not a few of the Jacobite soldiers also suffered from the exposure. Prominent amongst these was the Earl of Kilmarnock who, like Ligonier, had been in harness until the early hours. He returned to Callendar House that evening to be nursed by his distraught wife. His part in the campaign was over for the moment.

The pattern of the next day started in the same way. Early in the morning about twenty-five more of the militia were taken prisoners by Major Gillies MacBean of the Mackintosh Regiment. "Mr Irvine of Burkla propos'd and urg'd, that they should all be dirk'd, But the Major and others detested the barbarous motion, and preserv'd their life".[62]

Auld Soulis from Kilmarnock had seen more than he had bargained for. What a tale he would be able to tell his compatriots back home, if he ever got there. He had had the satisfaction of beholding Prince Charles conducted by torchlight to his lodgings on the very night of the battle, but now he was trapped in the Prince's service. The Jacobites had decided that whatever their next move was to be it was advisable to remove the prisoners to Stirling on the 19th January and Auld Soulis was to march with a detachment of them. He was commanded to lead a horse on which were placed two wounded men and given a loaf of bread for their use. Afraid to act contrary to orders he took the men and the horse under his charge and proceeded slowly northwards. On coming to a turn in the road where an eminence concealed him from view he quietly slipped away leaving the two invalids to their own fate. When he felt it safe he then hurried homeward carrying with him the loaf. He had not gone far, however, when he was met by a separate party of hungry highlanders. It came as no surprise to him when they took the loaf back into the custody of their army, but he soon found himself shoeless as well. His life was spared and he gratefully proceeded barefoot, arriving in Kilmarnock three days later.[63]

Meanwhile, the prisoners continued their journey to Stirling where the churches were also pressed into use as prisons, along with the tolbooth.[64] Here they were given medical attention by George Lauder, a surgeon from Edinburgh. He had been taken from Edinburgh after Prestonpans and made to use his skills for his captors' benefit. Amongst the wounded were many militiamen, and Captains Fitzgerald of Munro's Regiment and Halley of Wolfe's.[65] He was probably able to make use of the chest of surgical instruments and the two chests of drugs left behind at Falkirk by the Surgeon Major of the government army.[66]

The burial of the dead continued. A new pit was dug for those lying towards the bottom of the hill (their remains were found near the High Station when work began on the railway tunnel in 1839) and the bodies finally put out of the reach of the stray dogs. It took much longer to deal with those corpses that lay dispersed further afield. Some littered the road to Linlithgow where they had been abandoned to their fate by the retreating government army. Others were scattered around the farmhouses or on the banks of the rivers Carron and Avon. Some weeks later a local woman was crossing the Carron Water in bare feet when she unknowingly stepped on the face of a dead Highlander! The shock of the experience mentally disturbed her and she never lived a normal life thereafter.[67]

The Jacobites never kept an overall tally of their own losses, though each regiment was asked to report them.[68] Over the following days the government spies brought in numerous distorted reports from eyewitnesses among the burial parties. They all gave the same picture of substantial losses being carefully masked: "When we came to the Field of Battle, the Country People that Buried the Dead, told us there were not above a Hundred and Fifty of the English killed. But a Gentleman who had counted them told us they wanted of Four Score... All the country People told us there were a Thousand of the Rebells Killed".[69] ...."and likewise heard the French officers say that they had lost 1000 men good in the late Engagment".[70]

he says a tenant of his on Sunday morning last was on the field of Battel and that the Rebels were driven away several Cart Loads of there dead to bury them in Different places to conceal there Loss that four of the Rebells told him they had already buried 1200.[71]

a miller there had two of his servants employed to helpe carry away theyr dead on carts and sledges as farr back as the old Colepitts at Bannockburn, where they buryed them, and he assures me to day that they counted above five hundred [72].

Walter Grindlay, a local man, was one of those who had carried his foot spade up the hill to help with the burials. He had been "curiose" to see the dead for himself, but whilst there could not resist pulling off some of the shoes from the slain horses with his spade. Iron was a useful commodity to have and in short supply so he also helped himself to a bracket that was "Hinging off" one of the carts. Indeed, between him and the other residents the cart seems to have been totally dismantled and removed piece by piece from the field.[73] In the eyes of the Erskine Church the crime was not so much the pilfering, but that it had taken place on the Sunday! Food in the locality of the town continued to be hard to come by and it is probable that the dead horses furnished meat for many a cooking pot.

The weather that Sunday was quite different from that of the previous two days. The rain ceased and the air was still and clear. The Jacobite soldiers came out of their shelters to stretch their limbs and walk in the warming sun. The streets of the town were full of groups of men talking over the earlier events and advocating new actions. Some of the highlanders were cleaning their equipment and preparing it for further use in the belief that they would soon be called to move forward once again. Upstairs in a room on the north side of the High Street[74] a Macdonald of Clanranald inspected a musket that he had obtained as spoil from the battle field. Finding it still loaded he carefully extracted the ball from the barrel. The gun was then pointed out of the open window and discharged in order to clear out the wedged cloth wadding and gunpowder. Alas, unknown to its handler the piece had been double-loaded, probably because it had failed to fire the first time due to the damp at the time of the battle. The remaining

Burns Court where the young Glengarry was taken after he was shot

ball pierced the body of Colonel Aenas Macdonell, young Glengarry, who had been standing in the street with a group of officers opposite to the house. Glengarry was seriously injured and his men carried him back to his nearby lodgings at the south side of Burns Court, then the property of the Burns family. As they carried him they kept saying "O hon! o hon!" Once there he was wrapped in his blood-stained cloak until the regimental surgeons were brought to examine him. Meanwhile, a party of his fellow officers had entered the house of his astonished assailant and seized him. Enraged, they demanded his life. Young Clanranald, the head of the clan, was brought to the scene and informed of the incident. Soon a large crowd gathered. Here was a dilemma indeed. Should Clanranald refuse to allow his clansman to be murdered he would immediately become embroiled in a feud with the Glengarry Macdonalds, and the latter would probably quit the Jacobite cause. They had proved themselves good fighting men and this would be quite a loss. On the other hand if the man were killed, then the MacDonells of Clanranald would become disaffected.

This was not a decision to be taken lightly and there was considerable discussion with Prince Charles's senior staff. Glengarry himself heard about the debate and expressed himself completely satisfied of the man's innocence and asked that no harm should come to him. He was, however, unable to dampen the ardour of his own clan. Reluctantly Clanranald was obliged to consent to their demand. Thereon, the man was taken out to the side of a park-wall, probably the Claddens at Callendar Park - the traditional execution ground. There a firing squad, which included his own father, poured a volley of shot into his body. The father wanted his death to be as instantaneous as possible.[75] Dougal Graham relates the incident in his own vivid manner:

> A man in plunder got a gun,
> Two balls from which he had new drawn,
> Judging in it there was no more,
> Yet another she had in store;
> Out at a window did her lay,
> Dreading no harm he did let fly,
> Which kill'd Glengarry as he past,
> Dead on the street it laid him fast.
> They seiz'd the fellow and did bang him,
> Would give no time to judge or hang him;
> But with guns and swords upon him drave;
> Which made him minch'd meat for the grave.[76]

Glengarry did not die that day. He spent a very painful night in his quarters and lingered on the next day too. Not everyone was convinced that his shooting was accidental: "I am also in great trouble for the murder commited on the person of my nephew, Coll. Macdonell, at Falkirk. His Enemys are too plain to doubt of the authors of the murder, which will surely be taken notice of by the Highest and Lowest of the Nation. The Gentleman's growing worth made him envyd by Beggers and hated by Traytors, which I never was".[77] The clan schisms were rearing their heads again.

Prince Charles, the clan chiefs and the regimental officers had been debating what their next course of action should be. Many were still for the advance on to Edinburgh, but Charles was now obstinately determined to continue the siege of Stirling Castle.[78] He was advised by his French engineer, Mirabelle, that it would be taken quite soon. The accidental shooting of Glengarry may well have dampened the resolve of the Highland chiefs at this critical moment and reluctantly they acquiesced in the move.

Inevitably this set the foundations for a crisis of confidence in the leadership and questions started to be asked. James Johnstone, who became a professional soldier, gives an indication of the mood:

> The friends of the Prince exhorted him to repair with all haste to the capital, to disperse this wreck of the English army, and resume the possession of that city. This, in the opinion of every one was the only sensible course which the Prince could adopt; but it was soon seen, that it is easier to gain a victory than to know how to profit by it. The gaining a battle is very often the effect of pure chance; but to reap all the advantages of which a victory is susceptible, requires genius, capacity, and superior talents; and it is in turning a victory to account that we particularly discover the great soldier. One thing is certain, and that is, that the vanquished will always have great resources in the negligence of the victorious party. We ought to have persued the English with the rapidity of a torrent, in order to prevent them from recovering from their fright; we should have kept continually at their heels, and never relaxed, till they were no longer in a condition to rally; without thinking of reaping the fruits of our victory, till their complete defeat should enable us to do so with safety, and with leisure and tranquillity.
>
> On the 19th, when the weather became favourable, it was natural to think we should take the route to Edinburgh. But, - what fatal blindness! - instead of persuing a vanquished and routed enemy, the Prince resolved to return to Bannockburn, to continue the siege of Stirling Castle.[79]

The decision having been made, Prince Charles returned to the comfort of Bannockburn House. He was suffering from a combination of malnutrition and exposure and as he took to his bed that evening he too developed an illness. Clementina Walkinshaw, his mistress, nursed and comforted him. Evidently he had not been clear headed enough to have reached a proper decision but his determination to maintain personal control of the campaign at all costs gave him no room for manoeuvre. He and Lord George were now constantly opposed to each other at their meetings.

Much to the further annoyance of Lord George the Atholl Brigade were taken to Bannockburn as the Prince's own guard,[80] leaving the clans at Falkirk and a party of horse at Westquarter.[81] A small advance party had even been pushed out as far as Linlithgow

Lord George Murray

once it had been learned that the government force had departed.[82] Lord George had probably sent these men in the belief that they would be the scouting party for the main body which should have followed. At Edinburgh Hawley was assessing his situation. Although badly mauled he still had a sizeable fighting force. If he could lick it into shape it would be feasible, with the reinforcements, not only to make a stand at the capital but to return to Stirling. A court-martial was set up under the presidency of Brigadier-General Mordaunt to try the men accused of cowardice and failure to do their duty. It was to sit for some time into the future. The government forces had made a quick calculation of their casualties, but it was impossible for them to determine at this stage the numbers of their dead. These lay at Falkirk, beyond their control, as did an unknown number of prisoners. There were also still men scattered about the countryside between the capital and the river Avon. Nonetheless Hawley duly reported "I send your Grace another return, but tis not yeat to be depended on, I shall come to the truthe at laste, for Mr Dundas has had ane answer from Ld George Murray, that as soone as he can, he shall send him a list of the Prisoners, I have ane account to day that there are moste of the men missing in the Royalls, and Batterau, seen withe white Cocards in theyr hatts, withe the Rebells. I shall be better informed as to that ...".[83] Colonel Campbell, commander of the Argyll Militia, was in a similar situation at Queensferry that morning. "I cannot" he wrote, "as yet give you an exact return of our men, but some of the companys have lost 35 & 40 men each, particularly Achnaba's company which consists of one Sert, one cor: & 7 men." Quite a lot considering that the companies consisted of only about 50 men each. He continues "I am to have all our men under arms to morrow & will then send you an effective return".[84]

Hawley and his staff set about re-equipping and supplying the army. Numerous letters were written to obtain these from the south. Foodstuffs were to be shipped up the east coast via Newcastle and Berwick, whilst the heavier materials, including a pay chest, were to be brought by road. The people of the borders contributed horses, and in Edinburgh more blankets were obtained. Meanwhile all claim to Linlithgow had been abandoned and in the restricted military circumstances an advance guard was posted at Corstorphine with the dragoons patrolling the roads to the west. They were all thankful for another undisturbed night.

Prince Charles had now committed his army to the siege of Stirling Castle. On the Monday after the battle his forces were further redeployed. The MacGregors returned to Stirling to help with the siege[85] and came under the inept supervision of Mirabelle. Cromarty's Regiment, along with the Frasers, was stationed at Larbert to be in readiness to support movement either to the north or south.[86] Lord George remained at Falkirk with a diminished covering force. Neither he, nor the clan leaders with him had accepted the redeployment easily.

That morning a brief account of the battle appeared in the Edinburgh newspapers. The printed version of events naturally minimized the Hanoverian party's difficulties and exaggerated those of their opponents. The resulting report produced a favourable outcome for the government whilst allowing that there had been a minor setback. Such propaganda was only to be expected and it seems to have worked in that it calmed many nerves and steadied support. Copies of the Edinburgh papers must have reached the Jacobite staff late that day. They came as no surprise, and probably raised a wry smile as well as an indignant exclamation. A longer narrative of the action had been prepared for their own purposes. They had thoughtfully brought a printing press, with all its accessories and men to work it, from Glasgow when they had first left that city [87]. It had already produced a journal of the expedition into England for them and now a quarto sheet was issued from Bannockburn. It too hides the cracks in the publisher's army, but was an important exercise. The main problem was that the Jacobites had already lost the initiative.

The Marquis d'Eguilles, the French ambassador, prepared his own report for his country. Prince Charles was keen to garner

French support in the form of direct aid and believed that the outcome of Falkirk would galvanize them into action. As well as sending his own accounts it was decided to direct a personal envoy to the French court. Captain Brown was chosen for this task. He was promoted to a colonel and given instructions to board the Hazard sloop at Montrose. Most of all a French landing on the south coast of England was needed, and had long been expected.

Whilst these political and propaganda moves were being attended to a start was made on the construction of a battery before Stirling Castle. This was not an activity that the Highlanders were willing to indulge in, nor did the lowlanders relish the task. The work therefore proceeded very sluggishly.

The inhabitants of Edinburgh were still digesting the newspaper accounts when their minds were further eased by the arrival of 170 government soldiers returning from the battle. They had taken ship from Bo'ness to Leith, and had been all but given up [88]. This was immediately followed by another propaganda coup for the government. A detachment of the Argyll Militia had been secretly shipped across the Forth and aided the release of the prisoners taken by the Jacobites at Prestonpans the previous September. These had been held on parole in Fife, but their guards were only minimal in number as the men were needed at Stirling and Falkirk.[89] Things were looking up indeed and all the attention was shifting towards the next clash.

That night Captain Thornton received his customary nocturnal visit from his fellow conspirator. She brought what food she could and was passing it into the cramped cupboard through the partially opened door when he said "I am determined to come out, let the consequence be what it may; for I will not die like a dog in this hole". This resolution evidently horrified the poor woman as there was little doubt that her role in the concealment would be discovered. She begged that he would bear his confinement for one more night and give her time to think of a way of getting him out safely. He agreed and the door closed for yet another unpredictable 24 hours.[90] The time passed slowly for Thornton as he crouched in the cramped dark space and mulled over in his mind the chances of escape and the consequences of discovery. Had he pushed his woman sympathizer too far? Would she betray him? She was running a great risk in helping him, a man that she had never even seen before. She "consulted an old carpenter", one true to the Royal cause, and he came the next night, removed the dresser, and liberated the Captain. They proceeded down the dark stairs to the woman's apartment, where she made tea whilst the carpenter concerted their plan of operation.

> They dressed him in a pladdie and brogues, with a black wig, and leaving his cloathes with the woman, and all that he had put by, he was scarce worth one penny, and the carpenter packed him up a bag of tools, as if he was going with his master to work as soon as it was light. The Captain had only ten guineas about him, (having lost his cash with his Lieutenant, Mr. Crofts) eight of which he gave to the woman who had so faithfully preserved him, and two to the carpenter, who, to secret them, put them into his mouth along with his tobacco, fearful of a search by the Highlanders, who would have suspected him had they found more than a shilling. Every thing being ready, they set out, the Captain with his bag of tools following his supposed master. On coming into a crowd, he looked about, and was rather behind; and although in disguise, did not look like a common workman; - which making the old man dread a discovery, he called out to him, "Come alang, ye filthy loon: ye have had half a bannack and a mutchkin of drink in your wame - we shall be too late for our day's wark." Whether this artifice served him or not, is uncertain; but they got safe through the throng, and, leaving the high-road, pursued their journey across the country. Having come to a rising ground, the Captain took a view of Falkirk moor, and said, "Yonder's the place where such a sad piece of work was made of it on Friday last." The old man at the same time looking the other way, saw two or three hundred Highlanders, who had been on plunder, coming down a lane which led from Callendar-House into the main road; and being desirous of passing the end of this lane before they came up, in order to avoid them, said, "We shall have a worse piece of work of it than we had on Friday, if you do not hasten your pace;" and begged the Captain to come forward, which he did; but walking briskly up a hill, he suddenly stopped, and said, "I am sick:" however they gained their point, and passed the Highlanders; for had they come up with them, the least injury would have been a march back to Falkirk, as prisoners. On going two miles farther, they arrived at a house belonging to a friend of the carpenter's, and which had been plundered: there the old man got an egg, but not being able to find a pan to boil it, he roasted it in peat ashes, and gave it to the Captain, to put in his wame, for so he called the stomach. Proceeding a few miles farther, they arrived at another house, where they procured a horse for the Captain.

He arrived at the English out-posts, and making himself known was permitted to pass, and reached Edinburgh in safety.[91] The route taken had evidently been a little devious in order to get around the Jacobite outposts. They had left Falkirk by the Glen Brae heading south and probably crossed the river Avon at Avonbridge or Slamannan. In the latter stages of his journey the captain was aided by a chapman, a travelling merchant named William Henderson, who evidently knew the locality well.[92] He arrived at Edinburgh on the 23rd January to the jubilation of his regiment and the newspapers who appreciated a good tale.[93]

By coincidence 25 soldiers who had made their own escape from the church in Falkirk also arrived in Edinburgh on that day. Falkirk was leaking prisoners like a sieve and there can be no doubt which side most of the inhabitants were on. The soldiers were debriefed by the government command in order to ascertain what conditions were like for the Highlanders in that town, and to gather some indication as to what their next step might be. There had been some 300 or so prisoners in the church provided with straw for bedding.[94] They reported that "it was with the greatest difficulty they could get any provisions whilst they were in custody, the greatest part of what had been ordered for their use having been forced from them by those who were their guards".[95]

This was just the type of news that Hawley had wanted to hear. Having recovered his composure he had ordered his ships to continue to harry the Jacobites by cutting off their communications across the Forth. Their success was considerable and several vessels laden with meal destined for the enemy were intercepted and some burnt.[96] One small boat got as far as Stirling when it was hit by a cannon from the castle! All the Jacobite supplies from the north therefore had to make the long and difficult trek round by the fords of Frew.

In response to the increased preasure on their supply lines the Jacobites intensified their foraging around Falkirk and Stirling, moving as far away as Glasgow. The local communities were drained of their resources yet again. Mr Todd, formerly a writer in Edinburgh, as the commissary general of provisions demanded 500 stone of hay, 10 bolls of meal, and 10 bolls of oats from the parish of Campsie, to be sent to Stirling.[97] The small farm of Stonerig set on the edge of Darnrigg Moss near Slamannan, some

5 miles south of Falkirk, was visited by a band of Highlanders. It was the home of the Stark family and the lady of the house was busy at the cradle with her child when they entered. They demanded a meal from her, but seeing her preoccupation with baby James one of them generously offered to rock the infant while she prepared the feast. "heestie wi' a pickle preed an' sheese, until ta petter meat was ready" they added. Having eaten they did not tarry long, the child was now crying loudly. Before they left, however, they paid a visit to the stable and finding amongst the horses a fine grey colt they walked off with it. Mr Stark could ill afford to loose the beast and upon discovering what had happened he took his staff in hand and doggedly tracked the villeins, determined to recover it. He followed them all the way back to Bannockburn where he was graciously granted an audience with an officer whom he believed to be Prince Charles. He related the purpose of his errand, upon which the officer asked to look at the horse. "Just be thankful, gudeman, that you have such a braw beast for Prince Charlie's men to take" was his only reply.[98] "All the Carse country was rifled and nothing paid for about Falkirk". What was not carried away was left in such a poor condition that it could not be used.[99]

> Commands they sent all round about,
> And searched all provisions out.
> Some of them paid like honest men,
> Others did not, I tell you plain:
> But this I have so far to say,
> They duly got their weekly pay;
> But yet when plunder came in use,
> They spared neither duck nor goose,
> Butter, cheese, beef, or mutton,
> All was theirs that could be gotten;
> Pocks of meal, hens and cockies,
> They made that country bare of chuckies;
> Made many a Carlin whinge and girn,
> By crowdie of her meal and kirn.[100]

In Falkirk it was the general practice of the Highlanders to enter the houses about the time when meals occurred. At breakfast time they would seize the dishes of porridge prepared for the families as they were laid out on the table. If the porridge dishes had been left on a window cill to cool then they had no need to go into the dwelling, merely emptying the contents into their own canteens and walking away with them. When verbal abuse was hurled at them for such an act they merely laughed and ate up. The populace was powerless to resist. At dinner time the Highlanders would make for the fireplace and search the kail-pots with their dirks for what solids they might contain. On one occasion an old woman, with precious few possessions, saw some of them making advances to her kail-pot. It was too much for her, she quickly seized the ladle and threatened to scald the first that approached the pot with its boiling contents. They were staggered at her boldness, and, from amusement at her ludicrous attitude, thought proper to retire.[101]

Food was the main item sought. The army had to be fed and so whilst the command disapproved of such behaviour they turned a blind eye. Some thought it justified as those with victuals either refused to sell or asked exorbitant prices. However, there were plenty of the local population, notably the townsfolk, who also had the greatest difficulty in procuring supplies. There were a number of receptacles in the town, called 'girnals', where the meal was stored. This grain had been taken in as rent by the landlords owning property in the neighbourhood. From here they normally retailed it to the common people. During the occupation of the town they had been carefully locked up. The poor consequently soon found it impossible to acquire their usual supplies and were in desperate straits. One old woman complained emotionally to a Highland officer, pointing out her plight. The officer was a shrewd fellow and took pity on her and her kind to quieten the situation. He broke open one of the sequestered stores, sold off all the meal it contained to the common people at a reduced price, and then walked off with all the money.[102]

The plundering did not stop at food. The day after the battle a small party of Highlanders had laid their hands on David Watt, a Jacobite supporter, in his own inn on the High Street. They took him out to the street where they eased his feet of a pair of new shoes with silver buckles. He protested his Jacobitism to save them, but they had heard it all before. The people of Falkirk had generally blown with the prevailing wind.[103] Watt's arguments went unheeded, save for the reply "Sae muckle ta better - she'll no grumble to shange a progue for the Prince's guid".[104]

Another house to receive their attention was known as Burnside, situated at the Bleachfield. It was the home of a man of some substance, John Muirhead, and his wife Elizabeth Miller. Among many objects looted here was a silver jug which had been a family heirloom.[105]

One of the main problems afflicting the occupying army was how to keep warm. For this most relied on the services of the residents with whom they were billeted. In the church, however, there was no facility for heating. So, what was left of the timbers that had been destined for the manse, along with the "tresses, tubs and stands", were broken up and burnt.[106] Furniture in the Grammar school also went missing at this time, doubtless meeting a similar end.[107] To many of the highlanders this long period of inactivity was even harder to bear than the fighting.

CHAPTER 8

The Aftermath
22nd January - 14th April 1746

After three days of suffering Glengarry finally died on the Wednesday. In a tribute written by Lord George that evening he was described as a modest, brave, and advisable lad. He added "it is more loss to us then all we suffer'd at the Batle".[1] Glengarry's shooting had coloured the Jacobite victory and his death divided them. Clan loyalties and animosities were stronger than the cause of the Stuarts. According to tradition Glengarry's body was buried in a place of honour in the churchyard, beside the grave of the Scottish hero Sir John de Graeme who had died in the Falkirk battle of 1298 for Wallace.[2] The best mort cloth was brought out again, for which a fee of £5 Scots was charged against the name "Col. M'Donald, Glengarry".[3] Prince Charles was unable to attend the funeral, ostensibly due to a cold. His absence did not go unnoticed and numbers of the Glengarry Macdonalds started to drift away from the army. Two days later the Duke of Atholl wrote to the boy's father desperately trying to maintain their unity and urging continued support.[4]

The next day Prince Charles made his excuses to Lord George, casually saying that the people at Bannockburn were continually teasing him about his cold.[5] His unfortunate choice of words evidently angered Lord George who wrote a blistering retort, undoubtedly pointing out the problems that would ensue. Charles's intention "always to take a particular care" of Glengarry's Regiment rang hollow, and his neglect at such a crucial stage was fatal.

The effect of Charles's absence on the morale of the Highlanders was significant. On the march to Derby he had won their admiration and respect by his manners, his actions, and the interest that he had shown in them. Now, by contrast, he was cosseted at Bannockburn House with his mistress and his favorite advisors such as O'Sullivan and the Marquis d'Eguilles. Far from showing his concern for the Highlanders he seemed to have shunned them in favour of the foreign sycophants.

The Tomb of the Scottish hero Sir John de Graeme from 1298 where the body of young Glengarry was laid.

There were grumblings too among the Highland officers. They had been discussing the events of the battle and it had not gone without notice that almost all of the fighting had been done by them and that the Lowland troops had fled the field. Now once more they were exposed to any enemy approach. The outcome of the battle appeared to be little more than a fluke and its conduct, on the whole, apalling. Worse still, the victory had been wasted by not following the enemy to Edinburgh. The Highland army was a mobile army unsuited to siege warfare. The McGregors had no taste for this work and had therefore started to desert in large numbers by way of Gargunnock.[6] They could see no point in wasting time on castles that they could pass by. The Highlanders needed to be kept occupied and here they were languishing in the God-forsaken town of Falkirk far from the centre of power and running out of provisions. By their previous rapid movements they had been readily able to live off the countryside, foraging as they went.

Cracks were developing in the army's unity. "They were deserting by Thirtys, Fiftys & Sixtys, in a Body. Twelve of their Hussars persued twenty four of these deserters, and returned with three Horses only, no men".[7] About thirty of Drummond's Irish Brigade deserted. They had been British officers fighting at the battle of Fontenoy and had been compelled to enlist in their enemy's forces when they lost that battle. Seeing the disarray around them they marched from Linlithgow where they had been posted since the 18th and surrendered to Hawley at Edinburgh. Hawley received them inhospitably, though he was glad enough to receive their up to date intelligence on the enemy. This confirmed the earlier reports of the total lack of provisions.[8]

Hawley passed such intelligence information on to the government's supporters to give them further assurances that all was well. His agents had told him that "The Rebells desert very fast in Bodys, and pass for Argyleshire Men to get over the hills".[9] Not all the messengers were successful in getting through the Jacobite cordon. One, sent to Stirling Castle by the sheriff of that shire, was detained for two days at Bannockburn and another two at Falkirk. When he finally escaped after his daring exploit and returned to Edinburgh his observations were of dubious quality, but who was to know that?[10] Similarly, blind John Metcalf who had returned to Falkirk in search of Captain Thornton stopped in Linlithgow and was later arrested in Falkirk on the 22nd, having first wined with Lord George. He was put into a drafty attic which a dragoon already inhabited. The bad weather had returned and the snow came through the gaps in the pantiles.[11] In these conditions he waited three days for a court-martial to hear him.

One particularly active agent somehow managed to set the Jacobite brig on fire. Having transported all the cannon the vessel was then full of coal for the forces besieging Stirling Castle.[12] The Jacobites too had their spies criss-crossing the country. One of them had accompanied Metcalf from Edinburgh in the belief that he had joined the cause. He was one of the many by whom "The Prince received news from Edinburgh every moment, with details of the consternation and panic-terror of the English in their flight. He was informed that, for several days after their defeat, they were still under the influence of their alarm".[13] News of the victory at Falkirk had revived the ardour of the Jacobite spirit in Edinburgh.

A considerable sum of money was raised to be transmitted to the Earl of Kilmarnock whom many credited with the command of Falkirk at this time due to his connections with the area. The money was entrusted to a messenger with implicit instructions to avoid a search at Linlithgow Bridge, which once again lay in the hands of the government troops. He got to Linlithgow, and was unable to proceed further. What happened to this man is unclear, but the money was discovered some seventy years later in a chest in that town.[14]

Lieutenant-General Hawley was increasingly confident. "We have very near repaired our Foot" he wrote on the 23rd, "two days more will finish it...We have fifteen Batallions, four Regimts of Dragoons, a Regimt of Horse coming, & Brigr Blighes, on their march for Scotland".[15] Mark Kerr's dragoons arrived that evening.

Hawley's reputation as a strict disciplinarian was well earned and over this period his men came to hate him even more than they had before. The courts-martial continued apace, although their first victim, Captain Cunningham of the artillery, slit his wrist on the morning of the 20th when he was due to appear.[16] Various enquiries were also being conducted to see what could be learned from the way in which the battle had been fought. The city of Edinburgh was in a sombre mood "There are constant desertions from them here to the Highlanders, notwithstanding the strict descipline kept here, for they are constantly whipping them for the loss of their arms and accoutrements, and this day they hung up four for desertion in the Grassmercate, and it's said as many more will be hanged to-morrow in the same place, and 7 more in chains at the Gallalee".[17]

News of the events at Falkirk travelled slowly. At noon on the 23rd expresses arrived at Whitehall from Lieutenant-General Hawley giving his version of the action. It was immediately published in the London Gazette to reassure those who had read the brief account published the day before which had left many questions open.[18] The court of St James was astonished at the turn of events. The first reports had arrived as the King was being attended by the Earl of Stair and Sir John Cope, amongst others. Only when subsequent accounts confirmed the news was the magnitude of the problem appreciated. Most had thought the rebellion over when the Jacobite army had fled back to Scotland. Only Cope was able to take any joy from the intelligence. His own defeat at Prestonpans at the hands of the same enemy but with only an inexperienced force was now put into perspective. It is said that he had placed a large bet on the outcome of such an encounter and was thus able to claim an immense sum of money.[19]

The situation was considered serious. The threat of a French invasion on the south coast of England having receded because of recent events on the continent, it was immediately decided to send the Duke of Cumberland to the north to sort out the problem. It is hard to exaggerate the Duke's popularity at this time with the Hanoverian supporters in general, but more particularly amongst the troops. He had been raised to a military career and had shared many of the hardships and dangers with the men. His very presence would be enough to animate the soldiers who had fled from Falkirk.[20]

On the 24th therefore, the Duke of Cumberland was brought to London where he received instructions and resources from his father and advice from Cope. His baggage was packed and at 2 am the next day, unobserved by most of the population he set out for that wild unruly part of the island that still appeared from London as though it were only partly civilised. As he did so the government lost another of its most loyal supporters as Colonel Ligonier finally succumbed to his ailments.

The loss of Falkirk had galvanised the government into a unity of action and purpose and all their resources were now directed at the suppresion of the rebellion in the north. Their focus was quite clear and their other concerns in England and on the continent were placed on hold. The army in Edinburgh was supplied from England and reinforced by further troop movements. By contrast, altercation, contention and animosity had crept into the irregular and undisciplined army of the Jacobites, exacerbated by Prince Charles' continued neglect and inaction. The Jacobites by remaining stationary and dormant had once again lost the initiative.

Relations between Prince Charles and Lord George were growing even worse by the day and desertions were increasing. Many of the highlanders returned to their homes in the north with the material they had looted during the campaign.. Such pickings would be of no use to them in the advent of another battle. Eight days after the battle and the Jacobites had made little progress in their siege of the castle. Indeed, things were going badly wrong in this task. Men, time and effort had been wasted with no reward. The reports from Edinburgh showed the enemy getting stronger and their presence on the Forth was ever felt. As a precaution the prisoners were transferred to the near-ruined castle at Doune and Charles's baggage went to Leckie. These motions were seen by the government spies and in Edinburgh they were interpreted as preparation for the long anticipated advance to that city. The Argyll Militia were put on a state of high alert and extra patrols of dragoons arranged. Nothing disturbed them that night, although a party of highlanders was reported at Linlithgow.[21]

On the 26th January Edinburgh welcomed the arrival of sixteen brass cannon from Newcastle. They came complete with stores and 40 gunners and matrosses.[22] The last piece in Hawley's jigsaw was in place, but now he had news to wait for the arrival of the Duke of Cumberland himself. Preparations went on apace. At the battle the government army had been greatly incommoded by the large number of spectators, and before that at Linlithgow they had given away a promising manoeuvre. There had been several thousand present, principally from Edinburgh and Glasgow. Their treatment on the field by the Jacobites was not felt by the government to have been a sufficient deterent and so the opportunity was taken, it being a Sunday, to have notices read from the pulpits of the churches in Edinburgh that the like was not to recur. The next day, the 27th, the full text was placed in the newspapers:

> Whereas it has been found by experience, that the army's being followed by great numbers of idle or ill-designing people, is attended with great inconvenience to it, and may prove fatal to themselves, and whereas the attendance of such great numbers upon the army, is not only a great incumbrance, but consumes very much of the provisions and forage which may be necessary to support the army; these are therefore to give notice, that whoever shall presume to come within one mile of the army after its march from Edinburgh, without being duly furnished with a pass from the Rt.Hon. the Lord Justice-Clerk, his Excellency General Hawley, or one of the General officers, they shall be punished, and must blame themselves if they be fired upon; excepting such as bring provisions and forage to the army, who are to be paid ready money for what they bring, to whom all protection is to be given; and excepting also whose information may be useful to the army. [23]

William Augustus, Duke of Cumberland (1721-1765)

Reports of the church readings had reached Lord George at Falkirk and on the following day he received the written confirmation. Another battle was inevitable within the week. Could it possibly be fought with all the advantages that they had been fortunate enough to have at the last meeting? The terrain, wind, rain, element of surprise and the reaction of the enemy had all been to their advantage and yet they had only just managed a victory.

A review of the regiments at Falkirk had been expected for some time, but it was the 27th before Prince Charles was well enough to attend.[24] This parade worried Lord George yet more. The clans were then seen to be well short in numbers.[25] That night he wrote to his brother, the Duke of Atholl:

> I am quite dispirited by your men's going off and deserting their coullers; for God Sake make examples or we shall be undone ... We had a review here this day and made a fine appearance; it was only those of our first line that were at the last battle. The enemy say they will be soon with us again. [26]

The writing was on the wall and even the 19 year old Robert Forbes of Newe recognised it. He deserted from the Jacobite army and sought refuge with Patrick Dundas, a surgeon in Airth, who later vouched for the strength of his Whig principles.[27] Some of the men were actually out with the forage parties and others were intending to return once they had unloaded their battle trophies, but the impression of large scale desertion remained. The sick and wounded were sent on to Dunblane for their safety.[28]

Reassuring letters were reaching Hawley from London showing that the royal family did not blame him for the recent setback.[29] He confidently continued to prepare the ground for his return. The 'Vulture' sloop was sent up the Forth to reinforce the small fleet already there and to harass the Jacobites along the shores. This, he knew from earlier experience, would draw significant numbers of the enemy soldiers to Airth, Elphinstone Pans and the areas adjacent for fear of a landing by seaborne troops. The Jacobites thus deployed would then be unavailable in the main arena.

LIEUTENANT-GENERAL HAWLEY TO
THE DUKE OF CUMBERLAND
Edinr 28th Jan 1746.

I had the honour of your Graces's letter of the 24th this morning at eight a clock, which has sett my heart at rest, to finde that his Majesty is so gracious, and so good, as not to blame me for what is passed in so fatall a manner, occassioned by the Pannicke which when it comes, is too well knowne, to be irretreavable for the time. what I mostly feared was, that his Majesty should have thought me rashe to undertake a battle before the Hessians came, but withe suche foot as the old Regts: here, who I knew and had seen behave so well, and being sure wee had the superiority.

HAWLEY[30]

The day after the poor turnout at the Falkirk review Lord George received word that the Duke of Cumberland himself would soon be in Edinburgh.[31] This information was passed on to Prince Charles at Bannockburn who despatched Secretary John Murray of Broughton to Lord George to lay his proposals for their future action. It was Charles's intention that the clans should remain at Falkirk until the enemy appeared at Linlithgow. Then, the rest of the army would join him there for the ensuing combat.[32] The scheme mortified Lord George. He felt that it would leave him and the clans too exposed. If the Duke of Cumberland was at Linlithgow, the clans at Falkirk, and the rest of the Jacobite army at Torwood and Bannockburn, then it would be easily possible for the Hanoverian army to reach him before he obtained support. He strongly urged that they should instead repeat the previous manoeuvre and fall back on Torwood on the approach of the enemy in order to give battle on the famous field where Robert Bruce had been victorious. Early next day Broughton left Lord George promising to put his views to the Prince.

Charles received Broughton's report in a meeting with his party of advisors. It was they that had helped to formulate the first policy, and so not surprisingly they did not appreciate Lord George's interference. Determined to follow their initial plan O'Sullivan set out for the other camp. He found Lord George and represented to him the

> Ill consequence of it, if he retired, how much it wou'd discourage the men, & the little danger he underwent haveing such a post as the Torwood behind him, where the Prince cou'd send him imediat succor if he was pursude; & to the Contreray if he kept his ground, how much it wou'd incourage the whole army, & discourage the enemy who was not yet cured of their Pannic. Ld George promis'd to stay, & seemed to relish all the reasons yt Sullivan gave him, made very much of him, made all the fine complyments yt cou'd be on his beheavior the day of the battle, conducted him to see him a horse back, & embrassed him most kindly before all the Chiefs. Sullivan parted as satisfied of his reception, & of haveing gained upon Ld George as if he had gained a battle, & came full of it to the Prince, assureing him, yt when things were represented to Ld George in a right light yt he understood reason, yt he was a very usefull man, yt he began to have credit wth the chiefs, & yt he was a man to be maneged".[33]

Charles was well satisfied with the outcome of the mission. He had recovered from his illness and was once again taking an interest in affairs. He looked forward to what he evidently believed would be the decisive encounter with the opposing army, particularly as it would be commanded by the Duke of Cumberland.[34]

O'Sullivan had left Falkirk at 4 o'clock that afternoon leaving behind him a worried general. Lord George required a few moments peace t~ consider his next course of action. He retired to his room and started a letter to his wife:

My dearest Friend,

It is a great comfort to me to think that my Dearest Life is in so good a way of recovery. I have all along had but faint hopes of our success, as we have the very worst regulations in all partes of our conduct. You know in parte, but not wholly what a Burden I have had upon my hands, & often was I resolved to demit & retyre into some corner of the earth, if I could not find a fitt occasion of falling in the field, which was what I most wanted, as I imagin'd to myself by that means to save my Familie from forfetry. But I resign myself wholy to providence, who has indeed most remarkably protected & favour'd me hitherto, and you have prevail'd with me to take a more proudential care of myself then I have done for some time past; but God knows what efect that may have, for human proudence is but folly at best, & when I expos'd my self, I may say rashly, I was safe; the contrary measures may have a contrary afect. Be all this as it will, I shal endeavour to conform to your advice, as I look upon you as my good genius.
One reason which wegh'd amongst many with me not to give up my Command, was the persuasion I found evry body had (tho' I believe it was being too partiall to me) that I was of absolute use to the Service, and could not be spear'd, add to that I could not leave so many brave men who were Ingag'd in the same botome. All this besides my duty to my King and country.

I have been the more particular in this as I expect in two or three days we may have another Batle, which will assuredly be more decisive then the last, tho' a more reall Victory cannot be obtean'd ... I am persuaded the French will now atempt a landing in Ingland, but will it come in time?

Adieu, my Life & Love, yours whilest

GEORGE MURRAY [35]

The animosity between Charles and his advisors on the one hand, and Lord George and the clan chiefs on the other, had grown as a consequence of the failures of command since the battle. The clan leaders had lost almost all confidence in their council at Bannockburn. Moderates, like the Earl of Kilmarnock, Lord Elcho, and Lord Pitsligo, had been side-lined because of their quarters covering Falkirk from the east. Murray of Broughton, Hay of

Rastelrig, William O'Sullivan and Sir Thomas Sheridan had the Prince's ear. This was very much resented. These men had little to lose personally, and it was the clans that were taking all the risks and bearing the brunt of the fighting.

The gloomy situation at Falkirk worsened when news arrived from Stirling that the gun batteries, which had taken the Jacobites so long to construct, had been destroyed with great loss of life in just a few hours firing from the castle. Lord George and the clan chiefs sat down at a meeting that evening to discuss their predicament. The weather had continued cold and as they gathered in the candlelight they must have had a sense of foreboding. They had been in that town for twelve days since the battle and watched as their ranks slowly depleted whilst their enemy grew in strength. Desertion from the ranks was increasing daily, some even thought it to be as high as a third of their fighting men.[36] After almost two hours discussion they all agreed to sign a paper which more or less demanded a withdrawal beyond the Forth. There is no doubt that the decision to do so was unanimous and that by putting their signatures to the document each supported the other in a bond that they knew to be unbreakable. One can almost imagine the silence of this solemn occasion as they came up, one by one, to place their name at the bottom of the sheet. The town of Falkirk little suspected what a momentous event was taking place in that concealed room off the High Street.

The deed done, Lord George quickly penned a covering note and handed the package over to his aide-de-camp to be delivered to Charles at his headquarters in Bannockburn House. It was late, about eleven o'clock, when John Hay, Charles's secretary, took delivery of it. Charles was already in bed and Hay would not let him be disturbed despite the urgency of the message.[37] The missive was instead handed over to Murray of Broughton who consulted O'Sullivan. Both were stunned. In an attempt to retrieve the situation Broughton rode straight to Falkirk, which he must have reached about midnight, the hollow dull thuds of his horse on the street breaking the silence of a town in slumber.

He found a resolute Lord George unwilling to consider the possibility of change. To him the bond once made could not be broken.[38] Left alone again Murray returned to the letter he had written to his wife and added a foonote:

shall now tell you our situation is changed since what I wrote yesterday. Our men are Impatient to be home, & numbers have left us; so we are in an absolut necessity to retyre northwards, & the season hinders the taking of Stirling Castle.

I expect to see you, were it for a moment, in a few days. We will be able to make a stand with those who will abide with us for a winter campagne towards the confines of Atholl, on this side of that country, & are posetive in a litle time to bring a much greater Army out of the Highlands than ever. Duke Cumberland came about three this morning to Edr. Adieu.

... I have once more had it in my power to do esenciall service, which you will know more off at meeting. Take care of yourself & be in good spirats. All may yet be well. Fairwell.[39]

In the morning, when Charles awoke he was given the declaration by John Hay.

LORD GEORGE MURRAY TO THE PRINCE'S SECRETARY

Falkirk, 29th Jany 1746.

Dr Sr,

The Gentlemen who sign the enclosed representation Intreat you would take the most prudent method to lay it before His Royall Highness without loss of time. We are sensible that it will be very unpleasant, but in the Name of God what can we do? It is as we apprehend our indispensable duty to spake our minds freely. One thing we think of the greatest Consequence, what ever His Royall Highness determine, let the thing be kept as secret as the nature of it will allow; and only those consulted who may be depended upon for their Prudence and probity.

> I am Dr Sr with great esteem,
> Your most Humble and Obedient Servant,
>
> GEORGE MURRAY
>
> [Endorsed] 29th Jany 1746

ADDRESS FROM THE CHIEFS TO CHARLES, AFTER THE
BATTLE OF FALKIRK, ADVISING A RETREAT TO THE NORTH.

Falkirk, 29th January, 1746.

We think it our duty, in this critical juncture, to lay our opinions in the most respectful manner before your Royal Highness.

We are certain that a vast number of the soldiers of your Royal Highness's army are gone home since the battle of Falkirk; and notwithstanding all the endeavours of the commanders of the different corps, they find that this evil is encreasing hourly, and not in their power to prevent: and as we are afraid Stirling Castle cannot be taken so soon as was expected, if the enemy should march before it fall into your Royal Highness's hands, we can foresee nothing but utter destruction to the few that will remain, considering the inequality of our numbers to that of the enemy. For these reasons, we are humbly of opinion, that there is no way to extricate your Royal Highness and those who remain with you, out of the most imminent danger, but by retiring immediately to the Highlands, where we can be usefully employed the remainder of the winter, by taking and mastering the forts of the North; and we are morally sure we can keep as many men together as will answer that end, and hinder the enemy from following us in the mountains at this season of the year; and in spring, we doubt not but an army of 10,000 effective Highlanders can be brought together, and follow your Royal Highness wherever you think proper. This will certainly disconcert your enemies, and cannot but be approved of by your Royal Highness's friends both at home and abroad. If a landing should happen in the meantime, the Highlanders would immediately rise, either to join them, or to make a powerful diversion elsewhere.

The hard marches which your army has undergone, the winter season, and now the inclemency of the weather, cannot fail of making this measure approved of by your Royal Highness's allies abroad, as well as your faithful adherents at home. The greatest difficulty that occurs to us is the saving of the artillery, particularly the heavy cannon; but better some of these were thrown into the River Forth as that your Royal Highness, besides the danger of your own person, should risk the flower of your army, which we apprehend must inevitably be the case if this retreat be not agreed to, and gone about without the loss of one moment; and we think that it would be the greatest imprudence to risk the whole on so unequal a chance, when there are such hopes of succour from abroad, besides the resources your Royal Highness will have from your faithful and dutiful followers at home. It is but just now, we are apprised of the numbers of our own people that are gone off, besides the many sick that are in no condition to fight. And we offer this our opinion with the more freedom, that we are persauded that your Royal Highness can never doubt of the uprightness of our intentions. Nobody is privy to this address to your Royal Highness except your subscribers; and we beg leave to asssure your Royal Highness, that it is with great concern and reluctance we find ourselves obliged to declare our sentiments in so dangerous a situation, which nothing could have prevailed with us to have done, but the unhappy going off of so many men.

<blockquote>
Signed by   Lord George Murray,
Locheil,
Keppoch,
Clanronald,
Ardshiel,
Lochgary,
Scothouse,
Simon Fraser, Master of Lovat.[40]
</blockquote>

Charles was transfixed with rage and vexation, striking his head against a wall till he staggered, and all the while exclaiming loudly against Lord George [41].

Sir Thomas Sheridan was sent to continue the shuttle diplomacy [42]. His letter of authority gave him considerable latitude in the negotiations:

Bannockburn Jan 30th 1746.

I send the bearer Sir Thomas Sheridan in whom you all know I have entire Confidence to talk with you on the subject of your last nights memorial as likewise to concert with you what measures Will be judged most proper to be taken at this juncture. I desire you may give entire Credit to him and whatever shall be determined I shall readily agree to.

Charles PR.[43]

He also carried a reply from the Prince himself:

Bannockburn, Jan, 30th.

GENTLEMEN, -I have received yrs of last night and am extremely surprised at the contents of it, wch I little expected from you at this time. Is it possible that a Victory and a Defeat shou'd produce the same effects, and that the Conquerors should flie from an engagement, whilst the conquer'd are seeking it? Shou'd we make the retreat you propose, how much more will that raise the spirits of our Ennemys and sink those of our own People? Can we imagine, that where we go the Ennemy will not follow, and at last oblige us to a Battel which we now decline? Can we hope to defend ourselves at Perth, or keep our Men together there, better than we do here? We must therefore continue our flight to the Mountains, and soon find our selves in a worse condition than we were in at Glenfinnen. What Opinion will the French and Spaniards then have of us, or what encouragement will it be to the former to make the descent for which they have been so long preparing, or the latter send us any more succours? I am persuaded that if the Descent be not made before this piece of news reaches them, they will lay aside all thoughts of it, cast all the blame upon us, and say it is vain to send succours to those who dare not stay to receive them. Will they send us any more Artillery to be lost or nail'd up? But what will become of our Lowland friends? Shall we persuade them to retire with us to the Mountains? Or shall we abandon them to the fury of our Merciless Ennemies? What an Encouragement will this be to them or others to rise in our favour, shou'd we, as you seem to hope, ever think our selves in a condition to pay them a second visit? But besides what urges us to this precipitate resolution is as I apprehend the daily threats of the Ennemy to come and attack us; and if they shou'd do it within two or three days our retreat will become impracticable. For my own Part I must say that it is with the greatest reluctance that I can bring my self to consent to such a step, but having told you my thoughts upon it, I am too sensible of what you have already ventured and done for me, not to yield to yr unanimous resolution if you persist in it. However I must insist on the Conditions wch Sr Thomas Sheridan the Bearer of this, has my orders to propose to you. I desire you wou'd talk the matter over with him and give entire credit to what he shall say to you in my name.

Your assured friend.

Charles PR. [44]

The arguments were to no avail. Sheridan returned with Keppoch and Cluny who put the case directly to Prince Charles. The meeting was evidently a stormy one and even the compromise of repeating the previous tactic of withdrawing to Bannockburn was rejected:

> I doubt not but you have been inform'd by Cluny & Keppoch of what passed last night and heard great complaint of my despotick temper, I therefore think it necessary to explain my self more fully to you. I can't see nothing but ruin and destruction to us all in case we should think of a retreat. Wherever we go the Ennemy will follow, and if we now appear afraid of them their spirits will rise and those of our men sink very low. I cannot conceive but we can be as well and much more safely quarter'd in and about Falkirk than here. We have already tried it for several days together, and tho' the men were order'd to be every day on the field of Battle early you know it was always near noon before they cou'd be assembled. Had the Ennemy come upon us early in ye morning, what wou'd have become of us? and shall we again wilfully put our selves in ye same risk? Believe me ye nearer we come to the Forth the greater the Desertion will prove. But this is not the worst of it. I have reason to apprehend that when we are once here it will be proposed to cross the Forth it self, in wch case we shall be utterly undon and lose all the fruits of ye success providence has hitherto granted us. Stirling will be retaken in fewer days than we have spent in taking it, and prove a second Carlile for it will be impossible to carry off our Cannon, etc. In fine why we should be so much afraid now of an Ennemy that we attacked and beat a fortnight aso when they were much more numerous I cannot conceive. Has the loss of so many officers and men killed and wounded and the shame of their flight still hanging upon them made them more formidable? I would have you consider all this and represent it accordingly, but shew my letter to no mortal. After all this I know I have an Army yt I cannot command any further than the chief Officers please, and therefore if you are all resolved upon it I must yield; but I take God to witness that it is with the greatest reluctance, and that I wash my hands of the fatal consequences wch I foresee but cannot help.[45]

It was this day, the 30th January, that the Duke of Cumberland arrived in Edinburgh. His coach had travelled through the night and he entered the city at 3 o'clock in the morning after completing the arduous journey from London in only five days. He immediately went to bed, but at 8 o'clock that same morning had a meeting with Hawley and then with the other commanders. After Hawley's rigid rule the common soldiers were elated by the presence of their old hero from earlier battles. His effect on their morale, and on that of the general populace, was inspiring. One volunteer wrote:

> Our whole Army expects to morrow (His Royal Highness commanding) to march against the Rebels, who are destroying every thing they can lay Hands on about Falkirk, where the Battle happened, and it is thought there will be a Famine in the Country soon: unhappy, of consequence, must our Troops be, in going after these Rebels, if we get nothing to eat, but what we must be supplied with from England. But however we are all in high Spirits, by means of his Royal Highness's Presence, who also gives new life to the Soldiers, and we want nothing, but to meet with our Enemy speedily.[46]

These sentiments were echoed throughout the forces. One of Cobham's dragoons asked his bother to "Pray for the young British hero, for had he been at Falkirk those brave Englishmen that are now in their graves had not been lost, his presence doing more than five thousand men"[47]. The scourge of the Highlanders, the Duke, was admired by his own men.

The dragoons of Hamilton and Ligonier were ordered to patrol the roads to Linlithgow and to detain anyone they found using them. The enemy were not to be given any certainty concerning the main body's movements. At about half past four on the day appointed the Hanoverian army moved out of Edinburgh in two columns consisting of fourteen battalions of foot, the Argyll Militia, and the dragoons of Cobham and Lord Mark Ker. It had been only 18 days since they had first taken this route, and two weeks since they had hurriedly retreated from the Battle of Falkirk. Regrouped, resupplied, reinforced and now rejuvenated their spirits were high. Major-General Huske led the van, and the artillery brought up the rear. Again the Earl of Hopetoun sent money to each of the regiments, twelve guineas for the foot and twenty-five to the Argyll men. Hopetoun also provided the Duke of Cumberland with a carriage and at 9 o'clock, after only 30 hours in the city, he followed the army westward. He caught up with them after seven or so miles and switching to a horse put himself at the head of the Royal Scots.

The Hanoverian forces encountered no opposition that day and reached their designated targets. Major-General Huske and eight battalions, with the Duke, proceeded to Linlithgow. Brigadier-General Mordaunt made for Bo'ness with the other six battalions. The Argyll Militia quartered by the bridgehead over the river Avon, and the dragoons were posted to the neighbouring villages. In all there were some 10,000 men. The government army was back in force.

Despite their best endeavours their movements were closely monitored by the Jacobites. Even their marching order was known in advance. Spies concealed such information on minute scraps of paper which were then rolled up and hidden anywhere on their person where they might remain undetected.[48] The clans had been under arms all day and at around 4 o'clock in the afternoon it was confirmed that the enemy was at Linlithgow. The planned withdrawal began after sunset.[49] One by one the foot regiments marched off to Bannockburn, their rear protected by the horse regiments of Pitsligo, Kilmarnock and Elcho.[50] These straggling parties were seen from Linlithgow and the retreat went undetected that night. At 10 o'clock these too retired, all being quiet on the road between Falkirk and Linlithgow.[51] They passed through Falkirk at 11 o'clock[52] on their way to Bannockburn. Their departure left the town ominously empty. For 27 days the town had been occupied by one of the two opposing armies. Now the townsfolk could only wait apprehensively for another change of garrison followed by another period of uncertainty and perhaps another bloody battle. How long would the government army be here this time? It was patently obvious that the Jacobites would hold Torwood as less than a century before King Charles II had held the mighty Cromwell at bay from there.[53] As one correspondent put it: "The government army has moved to Linlithgow. The rebels are at the Torwood, whence it may be difficult to force them without setting the wood on fire".[54] It could take some time. Surely the Jacobites would be back to collect the cannon that they had left at Falkirk, including a 9-pounder near the battlefield.[55] Then again, 200 draught horses had just been sent from this area up to St Ninians without taking them.[56] In fact, the cannon had been rendered useless by having their touch-holes nailed. On their way from Falkirk the clans had joined up with Cromarty's Regiment which had been ordered from Larbert to Torwood Head at dusk. They then continued on and reached Bannockburn together around 9 o'clock.[57] After supper a council of war was convened in Bannockburn House. Only those that had been party to the declaration made two days earlier at Falkirk knew that the meeting was to discuss the manner of their retreat beyond the Forth. To the others it came as a complete surprise. Lord Macleod had thought that the council had met "only to deliberate on what was the properest place to give battle to the Duke of Cumberland's army, which was then advancing against us, for I did not dream of a retreat".[58]

It was agreed to make a general review of the army at 9 o'clock the next morning on a field to the east of St Ninians [59] according to a planned battle line. The Prince and his party hoped that this would show that the desertion was not as bad as it had been painted, and that the retreat might still be cancelled. If desertion was found to be as considerable as was supposed then an orderly retreat would commence at 10 o'clock [60]. In this event Lord George would take a detachment of a hundred out of each battalion (or an equivalent number of clan regiments) from the review to form a rearguard.[61]

The meeting broke up about midnight and Lord George made for his quarters at Easter Greenyards. There he found his aide-de-camp, Colonel Kerr waiting for him with the report that the cavalry from Falkirk had arrived in camp instead of continuing their patrols along the river Carron to guard the fords as instructed.[62] Lord George immediately ordered them back telling them that the safety of the whole army depended upon their vigilance that night. He also found two troops of Life Guards who, though they had been on duty for 48 hours already, likewise agreed to return to Larbert Bridge.[63]

For the rest of the night Lord George was only able to snatch short periods of sleep. At 2 o'clock he was up again directing Colonel Kerr to check upon the various posts along the Carron. With him went 12 bottles of brandy which Lord George had promised to the cavalry for their service that frosty night. Kerr arrived at Larbert before 3 o'clock and found the outpost very much on its guard. The drink was distributed and Kerr too remained until first light.[64]. Riders kept Lord George informed of the situation every hour, or two at most. Some of the cavalry even went the length of

Falkirk around 2 o'clock and found it still quiet. Part of Kilmarnock's Horse watched over the ford at Dunipace from the house of Sir Archibald Primrose who was with them. His wife and eleven children spent the next few hours in his company not knowing what would befall them.[65]

The Duke of Cumberland was totally ignorant of all this frantic activity and was still convinced that the enemy lay not ten miles from him between Falkirk and the Avon. In his campaign strategy he had determined to break camp early each morning to reduce the ability of the enemy to undertake night marches, and to give them little time to muster their whole force together. In this he still had a considerable advantage as the Highlanders refused to make use of the tents that they had captured[66] and so were widely dispersed at night. At 4 o'clock the government army started to form up.[67] Soon an alarm was raised and the soldiers formed into battle order waiting to receive the Highland charge at break of day. As they waited the sky was partly lit up by the melancholy sight of Linlithgow Palace in flames. No attempt was made to douse this torch, the men had other things on their minds.[68]

The dragoons and the Argyll Militia crossed Linlithgow Bridge first and, under cover of darkness, were followed by the rest of the army. Once across they formed into battle order again and slowly advanced. To raise their spirits the Duke walked on foot at the head of the Royal Scots. Several more false alarms occurred.[69] Then the Duke received intelligence that the clans had withdrawn to Torwood where they were to make a stand, the tension eased and the march continued.[70]

Meanwhile, Stirling was a scene of utter confusion. Those commanders that had not experienced the successful retreat from Derby pannicked and at first light made for the Fords of Frew with no thought to the review. Even the regular troops, the Irish Picquets and Drummond's, stationed in the town left precipitately with little consideration for their comrades protection. So quickly did they leave that no guards were left on the town's gates to ensure that all got away safely, and the townsfolk closed and barred them trapping a number of Jacobites that had not been apprised of the unscheduled change in the retreat.[71] Officers were sent to stem the tide and bring back the renegade regiments, but it was too late. Charles, seeing that nothing could be done to prevent the flight,

The Aftermath

The church tower at St Ninians which remained when the church was blown up on 1st February 1746

marched off with some of the chiefs and those few troops that were with him.[72] Lord George, leaving his quarters to the south-east of the town, was oblivious of the mass exodus. At about 8 o'clock he heard a loud noise which he believed to be firing from the castle, though it seemed closer than usual. What had actually occurred was the blowing up of the Jacobite ammunition store at St Ninians church.[73] The detonation was so loud that it was heard by the Government army on the other side of Falkirk. Cumberland was worried lest it should prove to be the Castle itself. Colonel Kerr, having waited at Larbert until it was light rode to Green Yards to report to Lord George. All was still quiet in Falkirk, but to Kerr's great astonishment he saw that most of the Jacobite army was on the road to the Fords of Frew. Having made his report he asked Lord George the reason for the premature retreat. However, it was news to Lord George and together they went to the place arranged for the rendezvous and sought the truth. On the way they passed the ruins of the church. The body of the building had disintegrated leaving the tower isolated. A few villagers had gathered around searching the wreckage for their friends and relatives and around them the tattered shreds of the tents taken from Falkirk still burned. The two companions quickly surveyed the scene of destruction and rode on. They were alone at the appointed place at the appointed time. The situation was now critical. Although they both knew that the main government army still lay beyond Falkirk a sally from the Castle could easily turn the flight that they now perceived into a rout. Lord George acted quickly, catching up with Glengarry's Regiment he managed to persuade Lochgarry to remain at St Ninians for an hour to cover any sortie from the direction of the town. This enabled the stragglers to get away safely. Meanwhile, Kerr went to Prince Charles and informed him that the Duke of Cumberland was still a long way off. Charles was helpless to prevent the flight and so Kerr mentioned that the horse patrols had been told to stay at Larbert Bridge and the fords across the Carron without specific orders. One of Charles' aides-de-camp was therefore sent to Larbert to bring them away, and a second was despatched to the Head of Torwood to be of assistance. Kerr returned to Lord George and St Ninians and was then sent on by this now distrusting general to retrieve the cavalry himself. On his way Kerr met them.[74] Lord Elcho, the commander of one of the troops of Life Guards, was fast growing disillusioned with the leadership shown by Charles. His troop which had been "order'd to wait at the Bridge of Carron untill further orders was forgott, so that at two o clock when they left it, they had near been intercepted by a Sally from the town and Castle of Sterling".[75] Further down the river Lord Kilmarnock's Horse also got away, taking with them the hapless Primrose.[76]

Proceeding with caution the Duke of Cumberland's army could see Stirling Castle on their march which temporarily ended around 10 o' clock that morning when they arrived at Falkirk.[77] It had taken them five hours to get there from Linlithgow Bridge because they had fully expected to encounter the enemy on the way. It came as something of an anti-climax therefore when they entered the town unopposed. Those prisoners that had been too badly injured in the late battle for the Jacobites to move were thus liberated, but where were the enemy? Sightings of the Horse Guards at Larbert confirmed they were still intent on holding Torwood. After the fatigues of the day the army was therefore allowed to camp just outside of the town.[78]

The Jacobite cavalry withdrew from the river Carron around noon and shortly afterwards the Duke of Cumberland started receiving accounts of a disorderly withdrawal by the Jacobites from Stirling. Brigadier Mordaunt was despatched towards that town with the dragoons and the Argyll Militia to confirm this at first hand, and if it proved to be true to harry the retreating enemy. A little after 5 o'clock these advance guards reached Stirling.[79] The siege of the castle was over. Had Cumberland known earlier about the Jacobite's flight he might well have tried to reach Stirling that night with the main force to stay on their heels. He desperately hoped to engage them before they reached the difficult terrain that the Highlands provided. The secrecy concerning the declaration of the 29th had held, and Lord George had done just enough to delay them by a vital day.

How Cumberland spent that afternoon we are not told, but we may assume that he visited the battlefield and the graves of his men. It was now Cumberland's turn to seek quarters in the war weary town of Falkirk. He is said to have enquired for the house which "his cousin had occupied", being sure that it would be the most comfortable and best provisioned.[80] The room that Charles had used was thoroughly searched before the Duke would use it, and the man-servant of Mr Menzies the owner was ordered to stay awake all that night in the adjoining room. Sentries were posted at the door. It seems that an assasination plot was suspected, or was it perhaps that Cumberland merely felt a little uncomfortable beyond the civilised part of Britain.[81] Before retiring to bed Cumberland wrote to Andrew Fletcher the Lord Justice Clerk in Edinburgh keeping him informed of the days happenings.

DUKE OF CUMBERLAND TO THE LORD JUSTICE CLERK

Camp at Falkirk, Feb 1, 1746.

This morning early word was brought, that the rebels had retired to the Torwood, and intended to make a stand there ... I reviewed the whole army this morning, before we marched; who were in the highest spirits. The advanced parties of the rebels retired with precipitation on the approach of ours and our foremost scouts brought in some stragglers, who said the rebels were repassing the Forth in a good deal of confusion; being afraid, as they said, of another battle, because of the increase of our strength, and the great desertion there had been amongst the clans, which had much diminished their numbers. On our march we heard two great reports, like the blowing up of some magazine ... On my arrival here, I found all our wounded men whom they had made prisoners in the late action, and in their retreat had been obliged to leave behind them men, and all the dragoons, in pursuit of them ... One circumstance is particular, that Lady Kilmarnock, who till last night had always staid at Callender-house, went off with them. I propose to march to morrow to Stirling.[82]

Fletcher was elated by this news and wrote that same night to the Duke of Newcastle:

> The Arrival of his Royal Highness the Duke has done the Business, animated our Army, and struck the Rebels with Terror and Confusion. He lost no time to improve these Advantages, marched the whole Army Yesterday to Linlithgow, and the adjacent Places, and continued his March this Morning to Falkirk, the Rebels always flying before him. This Morning the Rebels renew'd their Firing against Stirling Castle; but General Blakeney continuing to make a good Defence, they raised the Siege, and have blown up their Magazine of Powder, and, as believed, have spiked their Cannon, and the whole Army of Rebels have fled with Precipitation, and crossed the Forth at the Ford of Frew; and his Royal Highness has sent on the Dragoons and Argyleshire Men to take Possession of Stirling, and remains with the Foot this Night at Falkirk. Wishing your Grace Joy at this great and good News".[83]

In Falkirk there was celebration too. That night a son was born to John Adam, the master of the Grammar School, and given the Christian name of 'Cumberland' in honour of the Duke's stay.[84]

A soldier in the government camp there was not so happy. He complained about the unseasonable weather "under our Tents, and cold Lodging we had, for it was a hard Frost; we were now pretty sensible of the Hardships we had endured for several Days past, when we could get nei-Victuals nor Drink for our Money, the Rebels having consumed all the Provisions, and had just left the Town as we entered".[85]

At 4 o'clock the next morning the man-servant woke the Duke of Cumberland and the preparations for the day's march to Stirling began.[86] "After decamping, we left Falkirk, and hastened to Stirling, which we had in full view, at four Miles distance... passed by Torr-Wood, which served as a Harbour for the Rebels, before the late Battle; it is chiefly composed of Firs and Beech. We expected to meet with some lurking Rebels now here, but did not".[87] On reaching Stirling more of the wounded prisoners were found, including Captain George Fitzgerald of Munro's whom it had been believed was dead. He was now able to give them his account of the battle and its consequences for him:

CAPTAIN GEORGE FITZGERALD OF MONRO'S ACCOUNT

Dated Jan 18 1746.

I commanded the Platoon next to ye grenadier Platoon on the left of our Regt att the Battle of Falkirk and Blakeney's Regt being put into some disorder on the left of ours by being Attack'd on their Flank by the Rebeles, occasion'd ours likewise to give way, it was att that time I was knock'd down by a musket ball wch went threw my hatt & wig & graz'd my head but I rose again being only stunn'd by it, and perceiv'd the left wings of both had broke & retreating down the Hill I observ'd the ... army still form'd on the right and was endeavouring to make that way, but was surrounded again by a party of the Rebells who cut me in the head & knock'd me down a 2d time when they began to rob me, & as I immagin'd wou'd have afterwards murder'd me, but I calld out to a French soldier going by and desir'd he wou'd not suffer those Villians to kill me, and he immediatly came to my assisstance & prevented their doing me any further mischief, but they said I was their Prisoner & they wou'd carry me to their P. wch they did over a Muir that was, as I thought 2 miles from the field of Battle where the Pretender's son was, with a number of horsemen abt hin standing with his back to an Hutt to shelter them from the weather, it raining & blowing excessively hard. He said nothing to me but desird those fellows that brought me to him to secure me. They carried me into that Hutt, where I staid for some time, & Ld Lovatt's son with severall others coming in, carried me with them to the House of one Sir Archibald Primrose of Dunnypace as their Prisoner, where they kept me that night & the next day, being very unwell, having no ...... nor cloaths of any kind to shift me; I observ'd there were severall of their chiefs att the smae house on the night of the battle, as Ld Lewis Gordon, Cluny, MacPherson one Farquarson & c who seem'd to me to be apprehensive that our Dragoons were pursuing them, nor did they know till next morning that the Pretender's son was att Falkirk by severall things I heard them say. On the Sunday following they carried me with one of their wounded officers to St Ninian's, from whence I was to be mov'd to the Tolebooth att Stirling, but Mr Mackay the Minister of St Ninian's having some Rebell officers quarter'd on him, prevaild with them to speak to Lovatt's son not to remove me till I was mended, being in a very miserable condition with rheumattick pains & c not able to stand nor move occasion'd by the Violent cold I contracted the night of the Battle.

On the Wednesday before they fled from H.R.H. the Duke, I was carried to Stirling to Ld Perth in order as they told me to be sent to the Tolebooth with the other Prisoners, but he seeing the condition I was in, order'd me to be carried back again, to St Ninians under a guard till further orders.

On the morning of their flight, Ld Lovatt's son came into the room where I lay & told me they were going over the Forth, & that I must rise and goe off with them. I told him I had taken physick and that it was not possible for me in the condition I was in to stirr, but that if I must goe they shou'd dress me, and throw me over an horse, for I was not able to do it my self. The Pretender's son came att that time and satt on horseback att the door talking to Mrs Jenny Cammeron, till abt five minnetts before the Church of St Ninians was blown up, when he & his whole rabble gallop'd away. Abt two hours after they were gone I sent to Genl Blakeney to let him know I was left there & Brigadier Mordaunt coming that evening to Stirling I sent to him likewise, who sent me word he woud send a Party for me that night or the next morning, w'ch he did, but Genl Husk's Aid d. Camp Mr Davis, coming to see me in the morning, told me the Genl wou'd soon march that way, & that I may goe with him, w'ch I accordingly did, & had the Honour to wait on his R:H: the Duke who was pleas'd to tell me I did my Duty & behav'd like an officer.

As for my not joyning the Regt sooner wch I was very impatient to do the reasons are known by many in Stirling, having been violently afflicted with rehmattick pains & an ague for a long time, wch has cost me a great deal of money, and what is worse I shall feel the pain during my life.

Geo Fitzgerald[88]

Ironically, at the same time as Stirling was being occupied by the government foot the Jacobite delegation was having an audience at the French court to deliver the good news about their victory on the 17th January. They greatly exaggerated the scale of the victory and played down the need for more aid: "Ce prince ne manque jusqu'a present ni d'argent ni meme de chevaux; ses troupes ont grande confiance en lui, et il a une artillerie considerable; il est cependant vraisemblable que sa cavalerie n'est pas nombreuse".[89] So naturally the French did not send any!

Cumberland and his army remained a few days at Stirling, during which time Major Lockhart of Cholmondeley's Regiment made his escape from Doune Castle and rejoined the army. However, there were a few questions concerning his conduct to be cleared up. Rumours had circulated suggesting that he had surrendered a little sooner than was necessary and that he had thrown his lot in with the enemy. Enquiries were made before he was allowed to join his regiment.[90] As soon as the bridge over the Forth was repaired the army set off in pursuit of their enemy, but by this time they had gone well ahead. The weather worsened and the government army halted a while at Perth. The after-shocks of the Battle of Falkirk were still being felt amongst their rank and file. On the 15th February, for example, we learn that "Lt Ballwin Latton of Major Genll Blakney Regt Lt Wm Skipton and Ens Aircort of the same Regt and Ens John Love of Brigr Clamons Regt having been try'd for misbehaviour or Cowardice at the akshan at Fowcirk and Sentense to be Suspended during the Plasur of Genll Hawley".[91] Hangman Hawley was to see many more swing from the gallows before he was through with them.

It was also essential to gather as much intelligence about the enemy's mode of fighting as they could so that methods could be developed to combat them. February 16th: "If thair be aney Soldars hear who was taken Prisners at Falkirk and have Since maid thair Askape from the Rabells are to Com this After Nouen at 2 a Clock and anser Such Questen's as Major Wolff Shall Ask them".[92]

As a consequence of such information new tactics for use in battle were indeed forthcoming. Training in these soon began. The infantry were to thrust their bayonets at the exposed underarms of the clansmen attacking their comrades on the right rather than the body of the Highlander immediately in front of them which would be defended by his targe. This reliance upon one's fellow soldiers to defend the individual took much discipline to instill, but was to be applied with deadly effect at their next encounter.

Falkirk had taught the government army many things that they were to find of use in their next major engagement. For example, more people were assigned to the artillery in order to help transport it across rough ground. Perhaps the most important lesson had been that regiments, such as Barrel's and Ligonier's, which stood their ground and kept up a regular fire by platoons could keep the Highlanders at some distance from them and deny them the opportunity to make use of their broadswords. "Barrells & Legoniers Regiments of Foot have found out an easy way to destroy the Hyland Rebells, by fireing in platoons, and the first line's kneeling & droping their Bayonets to the ground, thereby keeping up their fire".[93] This instilled the men with great self-confidence: "They talk of doing mighty matters with their broad swords, but that is a mere humbug, and two of our weak battalions stopped them at Falkirk, after the disorder was begun.".[94] Encouragement to take this line of action had come from Hawley's gallows which had dealt with 31 dragoons and 32 infantry back in Edinburgh. Others were broken, including the recovered captain of the artillery. At Montrose in the last week of February Cunningham was "brought under guard to the head of the artillery, had his sword broke over his head by the provosts, his sash thrown to the ground, and was order'd to quit the army for cowardice and misbehaviour in action".[95] More apposite was the knowledge that the losses of the two regiments that had behaved so well at Falkirk had been significantly less than any other regiment and that they had been treated as heroes.

    The government army had paid but a fleeting visit to Falkirk on February 1st, but the town had been left impoverished by military occupation since January 4th, a period of four whole momentous weeks. The Duke of Cumberland must have left a small unit in the burgh to restore order and to safeguard his communications with the capital. Messengers would have been a common sight reporting the latest events in the war as the government army moved northwards. On 17th February the Duke with a small bodyguard again passed through the slumbering town on his way to Edinburgh to meet his brother-in-law, the Prince of Hesse, who had landed at Leith with a force of almost 4,000 men. Later the townsfolk watched as this army of tall fair men marched north to guard the passes at Stirling and Perth. The worst was over.

CHAPTER 9

Mopping Up
14th April 1746 and After

On the 14th April James Paterson the Sheriff-Depute of Stirlingshire issued the following proclamation: "These are ordering and comanding the haill heritors, fewars, and tenants, within the Shire of Stirling, immediately to bring in to the magasine at Stirling, all straw they presently can spare for the use of the armie, and such as have wheat, oat or bear forthwith, to thresh out the same, and bring in the straw for what they are to be paid at the magasine - with certification to such as neglect or refuse, the same will be taken from them by the troups and the offenders punished for contempt. Given at Stirling, this fourteen day of Aprile, 1746".[1] It was then sent to William Henderson, the new postmaster at Falkirk, for intimation there. Henderson had been active in the town on behalf of the government giving advice and organizing accommodation.[2] John Hardie, one of the sheriff's officers in the town called upon his fellow officers, John Callander, William Aitken and John Lithgow to assist him in the execution of the order, but they all refused. The district, they knew, was in no fit state to contribute.[3]

Two days later, on April 16th, the two opposing armies met for the decisive final clash. The Jacobites were overwhelmed on the field of Culloden and their cause came to an ignominious end. The earlier defeat at Falkirk had been constantly in the minds of the government soldiers and, three days after it, a death pact had been formed: "some Regts: have shooke hands and vowed all to dye nexte time".[4] Pride therefore dictated that Munro's Regiment, which had behaved so despicably on the former occasion, withstood some of the fiercest hand to hand fighting at Culloden when rushed by Lord George and the Jacobite right wing. The main shock of that attack, however, was borne by the one regiment that was most likely to keep its head in the midst of the fury, as it had at Falkirk, and that was Barrel's. The Earl of Kilmarnock repeated Macdonald of Tiendrish's fatal error. In the heat of the battle he

212 *Falkirk or Paradise*

The execution of Lord Kilmarnock on Tower Hill in August 1746

mistook a body of the enemy horse for that of Fitzjames's regiment and was thereby taken prisoner.[5] As he was being led across the field, a dejected and forlorn captive, his bare head soaked by the drizzle, his eldest son boldly stepped from the ranks of the Hanoverian army and placed his own hat on his father's head.[6]

Immediately after the battle Ninian Dunbar was hung from a tree in the red uniform that he had taken from Major Lockhart at Falkirk. The Duke of Cumberland and Lieutenant-General Hawley both found this an amusing irony, but Lockhart did not. His subsequent persecution of the Highlanders was his personal retribution for the disgrace and humiliation that he had suffered. Many of his fellow Scots acted in a similar fashion, perhaps remembering what they had been told of the way in which Sir Robert Munro and his brother had been killed in cold blood.[7]

The prisoners too had to be dealt with. One of those appointed to this task for his loyalty was Patrick Haldane of Bearcrofts, Grangemouth. On 15th March, before Culloden, he had taken up the post of one of the two solicitors to King George for the realm of Scotland. After Culloden, at the desire of the Duke of Cumberland, he was appointed Sheriff-Depute of Perthshire and carried out the examination of the rebel prisoners there.[8] He became a most unpopular figure as a result.

Throughout the rest of the year army detachments were to unsettle the people of Falkirk as the victorious regiments moved through the area on their return and their replacements marched northwards. With the army were often small groups of prisoners under escort.[9] Kilmarnock was taken to London by sea. His wife left Callendar House and made the long journey over land to be with him, leaving the townsfolk to speculate on her fate as well as his. At his show trial Lieutenant George Cumming, who had been captured at Falkirk, spoke of Kilmarnock's good conduct to the prisoners.[10] The verdict, however, was predictable. On 18th August 1746 he was beheaded along with Balmerino on Tower Hill.[11]

While in the Tower of London Lord Kilmarnock had repented for his part in the rebellion. He may have hoped that by doing so it would make life easier for his family. Anne continued to be harassed, and it was many years before his son, Charles, was permitted to return. Charles Boyd escaped to the island of Arran where he picked up some medical knowledge from books and worked among the islanders before finding safety in France.[12]

The unfortunate Sir Archibald Primrose was finally captured near Aboyne, Kincardineshire, in the middle of July 1746. He was taken to Carlisle for trial where he had the privilege of residing in the town gaol rather than the more squalid castle dungeons where the other rebels lay.[13] He pleaded not guilty to the charge of treason, but on legal advice changed it to guilty and put in a special plea for clemency.[14] He was recommended for this by Lord Stair.[15] While awaiting the verdict two of his children died. His plea failed:

> the said Sir Archibald Primrose to return to the Gaol of the said County of Cumberland from whence he came and from there be drawn to the place of Execution and when he Cometh there that he be hanged by the Neck but not till he be dead and that he be therefore Cut down alive and that his Bowels be then taken out and Burnt before his face and that his head be then Severed from his Body and that his Body be divided into four Quarters and that those be at the Disposal of our said present Sovereign Lord the King [16]

On 15th November he too was executed and his body buried at Carlisle. Within the month his wife was dead, and a few weeks later was followed by her only son. A tragic family indeed![17]

The fate of the other Jacobites from the Falkirk area varied. Most were captured and taken to Carlisle, Chester, York, Lincoln or Southwark. Those that went to trial did so at Carlisle and Southwark. Some, like John Auld the fourteen year old drummer from Kilmarnock's Horse, were transported. Others were forced to enlist in the government's army and served overseas. A few were released under the General Pardon issued in 1747.[18] James Livingston was specifically exempted from this last Act, probably because of his enthusiasm for the cause. He had been one of the first to rally to the Stuart army. The proofs against him, however, were not particularly concise. The witnesses against him were James Gaff, messenger in Falkirk; Thomas Christie, the town clerk of Stirling; Andrew Turnbull, a tailor in Stirling; John Wilson, a Falkirk merchant; John Hopkins, a portioner of Falkirk; George Wilson, a surgeon in Edinburgh and Robert McPherson of Calder. They had little to say other than that they had seen him sporting his weapons and wearing Highland dress. He had also served as a commissary of supply for the Jacobite army in March and April.[19]

At any rate, he evaded capture and escaped to Holland. His friend Walter Graham, the Falkirk surgeon, also found exile in that country where he practised his profession, dying there in 1793.[20] They may have met Lord George Murray in Holland, for he too ended his life there in 1760. Alexander MacLeod of Muiravonside eventually took refuge abroad as well. For several months he had been on the run, spending part of his time hiding at Muiravonside. He was pardoned in 1778.

The pardoned Jacobites were able to return to a normal life. James Adamson, a gardener by trade, actually came out of the rebellion with a profit. He had returned home after the battle of Falkirk with his share of the spoil and this became the foundation of his future prosperity.[21] Another outsider, Major James Rattray of Ranagulzion in Perthshire, settled down in Falkirk. He had fought in the Atholl Brigade at both Falkirk and Culloden, after which he was captured but was aquitted due to contradictory evidence at his trial. He returned to farm part of the lands of Mungal for the Ramsay family. He died in 1774 at the age of 70 years and was buried in the north-west corner of the parish churchyard, only a stone's throw from Sir Robert Munro.[22]

To the professional soldier on the government side Falkirk became just another in a long list of battles. Lieutenant-General Hawley never forgot it. It stunted his career, though most of his colleagues thought that it should have ended it. "Cope is actually going to be tried; but Hawley, who is fifty times more culpable, is saved by partiality: Cope miscarried by incapacity; Hawley, by insolence and carelessness",[23] an opinion shared by the general public.[24] In the event, Hawley was diplomatically superseded by the Duke of Cumberland and given command of the cavalry which he despised so much. At Culloden these cavalry butchered the retreating enemy in great numbers. After the campaign in Scotland was over Hawley led a more comfortable life as governor of Portsmouth. He died in 1759. John Huske took the credit for saving the government forces from the rout at Falkirk. He became a full general in 1756, and governor of Jersey where he died in 1761. Lieutenant-Colonel George Stanhope, known as "the preserver of the Troops at Falkirk", never did receive his just reward. Despite the backing of Brigadier-General Cholmondeley [25] and Lord Chesterfield [26] he never achieved the rank of colonel which he had so

Kinneil House, Bo'ness

much wanted. In 1747 he was wounded at Lafeldt and resigned his commision. He died in 1754 at the age of 37 years. By comparison, Brevet-Major Wolfe's rise was rapid. He became a Major-General, which rank he possessed when he was killed in action at Quebec in 1759.

Slowly life in East Stirlingshire returned to a kind of normality. Services at the parish church of Falkirk had resumed five weeks after the battle and the Kirk Session met again to wield its influence over the congregation. Part of their duty was to supply the poor with relief. Typical offerings included : "To a soldier's wife in poverty . . 18d", "To a distressed soldier . . 18d".[27] The town too was to suffer from its economic effects for some considerable time. Many of the assets of the residents had been destroyed or removed by the occupying forces and it would take a considerable amount of effort and investment to bring things back to what they had been. The roof at Kinneil House was so bad that the Duke of Hamilton had the leadwork replaced in October 1746[28], and his private chapel there was left in ruins.

Alexander Niven, a carter in Falkirk, had his horse stolen by the retreating Jacobite army placing his income in jeopardy. He struggled on until in November he caught up with his charge, which he found at Stirling. There then followed a legal dispute over ownership.

> Unto the Magistrates of Sterling The Petition of Alexr Niving Carrier in ffalkirk Humbly Sheweth
>
> That in January last your Petitioner had a white Horse belonging to him intromted with and carried off by the Rebells then lying in ffalkirk, which Horse the Petitioner did never discover till this Day the Eigth of November 1746, when he found him in the Custody of William Leckie Burges in Stirling who refuses to deliver him up. Notwithstanding the Petitioner offers to instruct his Property in him.
>
> May it therefore please you to conveen the said William Leckie before you and examine him how he came by the foresaid Horse. And mean time to secure the Horse till the Petitioner brings up his Proof concerning him According to Justice & c.
>
> ALEXANDER NIVEN.
>
> Sterling 8th November 1746.
> The Baillie having considered the above Petition and having caused conveen the above designed William Leckie before him, and interrogate him concerning the above mentioned Horse. He, the said William judicially Declares, That he bought the white horse now in his Custody from the Lord Elchoe, when he was in this Town in Jany last with the Rebells, and that he payed half a Guinea for the horse, beside a Crown.
>
> WILLM DEINSKIN[29]

Another Falkirk trader had been more fortunate. A brewer by trade, he had succeeded in securing one of the unmounted dragoon horses which had raced down the hill into the town after the battle. It was a handsome beast

> which he afterwards reduced to the humble labour of dragging his professional sledge. One day, some years after the battle, when the once-spirited animal had become a patient and worn out drudge, the brewer was filling the barrel with which it was loaded at the public well, when a troop of dragoons, which happened to be in the town, was called into order by the sound of the trumpet, close to the spot where it was standing. No sooner did the poor old hack hear that

lively point of war, than, totally forgetting its present duties, it scampered off along the street, rushed up to the troop, which was then just falling into line, and, with irresistible force clearing room for itself among the bystanders, took its place, sledge, barrel, brewer and all, in the midst of the ranks. The commander of the troop, highly amused at the scene, patted it kindly on the head, observing, 'Ah, I see you've been a soldier in your day;' and gave orders for its being gently led out of the line.[30]

Claims for compensation were submitted to the Lord Justice Clerk. One of these was for the artillery horses that had been killed at Falkirk, and another for the forage taken from Linlithgow.[31] At the end of the year money was still owed by the exchequer for the transportation of the Glasgow Militia from Bo'ness to Edinburgh and for the subsequent hire of the ship.[32]

The port of Bo'ness had suffered directly at the hands of the Jacobites. The town had been pillaged on four or five separate occasions. Yet the trade there soon picked up. The town's merchants had gained some influence with the civil authorities for their tenacious support of the Hanoverian government. They had also acted wisely to preserve their ships and crews intact, retaining the requisite skills and expertise. The local salt and coal industries were expanding and the moves to improve the harbour facilities attracted more business. Airth, on the other hand, never recovered. At least two ships had been burnt at their moorings and a third taken by the Jacobites before being destroyed by a government agent. "The trade in Airth, prior to the year 1745, was very considerable, but had since been on the decline, owing to a number of vessels being burnt at that period ... The loss of these vessels were severely felt by the trading people in Airth" wrote the parish minister in 1793.[33] The wood from the shipbuilding yards had also gone, used for fuel during the Jacobite occupation. However, the trade at Airth had already been in decline and it did continue for some time after the rising. There are numerous examples of smuggling attempts connected with the town.[34] As the century progressed the harbour became less desirable due to the reclamation of land in its vicinity which reduced the access to the wharfs and barred the larger ships from using it. Shipping simply moved to the better facilities at Bo'ness and Carronshore.

At first it looked as though the Falkirk Tryst would never recover from the disruption to trade. The victorious government army had rampaged across the highlands stealing cattle and burning homes as an act of vengeance. Thousands of cattle were disposed of, flooding the market and deflating prices. In August 1746 when the trysts resumed the attendance was consequently low, nor did it pick up in October. People still moved with unease through the country and the loyal McLeods felt it necessary to take their cattle to the market under escort: "Two Droves of Black Cattle went thro' this Town Yesterday [Stirling, 26th August 1746] to the Fair at Falkirk; they belong to the McLeods, and were Escorted by Men with Arms as Your Lordsps Pass directs, otherwise their Arms should have been taken from them, and the Men Secured for a further Examination".[35] Highlanders in the south were treated with suspicion. The drovers' exemption from the Disarming Acts of 1716 and 1746 permitted them to continue to carry weapons on their long droves though Scotland, and reassured them of their personal safety even if it worried others. The sale of these cattle was one of the most important sources of revenue from Scotland and had to be safeguarded. In December the Sheriff-Depute of Argyll issued a similar permit of safe-conduct to James Macnab of Glenorchy to buy cattle in Kintail and Skye "to pass to and from these countries with their arms alwise behaving themselves as Loyall subjects of His Majesty".[36]

English dealers must have been thin on the ground at the Falkirk Tryst that year. Some drovers risked taking their charges through England itself to find their markets. A drover from Ross-shire took his cattle to Craven in Yorkshire; while a Dumfriesshire man had nearly 1,500 beasts for sale in East Anglia. Both of these speculations proved unprofitable. In Yorkshire the shortage of hay had lowered the price to 35s a head, while the drove in East Anglia fell victim to a widespread cattle disease. However, in the following years the market bounced back. The shortage of cattle in the highlands and disease in England caused prices to soar.[37] In 1747 the roads were busy again and Richard Pococke was turned off the road by droves on their way to Falkirk.[38] The trysts, and Falkirk, were back in business.

CHAPTER 10

A Tale to Tell - a Yarn to Spin

Falkirk had just gone through a very traumatic episode in its history and its inhabitants were well aware of the historical importance of the events which they had witnessed. Soon they found themselves recounting the incidents in which they had been involved to people from outside the district as well as amongst themselves.[1] On the 1st February 1746, when Cumberland's army had passed through in pursuit of the recently departed Jacobite force, the battlefield had attracted many interested soldiers. "we passed by the Place where the late battle of Falkirk happened, which Curiousity tempted me to spend some time in remarking; and I met with a Countryman, just on the Spot, who lived close by, was an Eye-witness, and gave me its History".[2]

Such visits continued. Towards the end of April that year we hear from James Pringle that "Sir Robert and I, according to our resolution, have made out our Expedition the length of Stirling, which I think has been very well worth while, for at Falkirk we saw the Field of Battle, which is certainly the most extraordinary that ever any general led his Troops to".[3] Likewise, Richard Pococke visited the area on his tour of Scotland the following year. Here the story was related to him "by a person I met with on the spot and showed me the whole scene of the battle".[4] No doubt a gratuity was involved! At Stirling in 1760 he saw the brass cannon, with the name Sidney on them, which had been taken at the battle of Falkirk.[5] By then the rebellion had become the centre of a small tourist industry.

A couple of rudely dressed stones were erected on the small hillock from which Prince Charles had nervously watched the battle himself. At a later date, probably in the 1820s, double sets of the initials CR were carved on each stone, and the little path leading to them became a public right of way. Charlie's Hill became a regular feature visited by Sunday walkers. Slowly the landscape around them changed. Gilpin in 1788 noted the beginning of this

The stones which mark the spot on the battlefield where the Prince stood.
The initials CS were carved there in the early years of the 19th Century.
The place is still known as Charlie's Hill

process: "Within less than a mile from the Carron works was fought the battle of Falkirk. The workmen pointing out the place on a moor; bad us observe, upon the highest part of it two small houses together, and one at a distance: between these, they said, the principal attack was made: tho I believe, now Falkirk moor is inclosed, and cultivated; and the scene of action perhaps scarcely to be traced".[6] However, the land was still of a poor quality and in this century the hill was planted with conifers.

Each family in Falkirk had its own gruesome tale to tell and over the years the young children listened intently to these stories of a bygone age. Even in 1746 the Jacobite interlude was seen as the death throes of an obsolete feudal and clan system, and to following generations who had grown up in peaceful times, during which the agricultural and industrial revolutions had taken hold, the events appeared far away. In the 1820s a promising young man, the son of a Falkirk clockmaker, gathered some of these stories together. Some he gleaned from folk who had been small children at the time of the rebellion, most came from their descendants. Robert Kier was very interested in this local history, but to him the events of 1746 were as far removed as the first world war is to us now. The collection was sent to Robert Chambers in Edinburgh and part of it was finally published in Chambers's great work on the rebellion in 1827, the very year in which Kier died at the age of only 20. By this means these stories have come down to us today.

Not all of the traditional tales connected to the battle can be taken at face value. Some were corrupted in the telling and re-telling; some were expanded to make the yarn more interesting; and others came about as deliberate propaganda or mistaken assumptions. Amongst these latter we must include the anecdote that relates how Anne Livingston, the Countess of Kilmarnock, deliberately entertained Lieutenant-General Hawley at Callendar House on the afternoon of the battle of Falkirk, thus delaying his actions.

The seeds which gave rise to the story can easily be found. The Duke of Cumberland appears to have held a great hatred of the Earl of Kilmarnock, and when asked which out of Kilmarnock, Balmerino and Cromarty should be pardoned, he replied that it could be any except Kilmarnock.[7] After the retreat of the Jacobites from Falkirk and its occupation by his own army he wrote from that town to the Lord Justice Clerk "One circumstance is particular, that Lady Kilmarnock, who till last night had always staid at Callendar-house, went off with them".[8] This letter was published shortly afterwards[9] and appears to have been the foundation upon which the legend was built.

Anne, it would seem, had good reason to accompany her husband at this time. Lord Kilmarnock was still suffering from the fever that he had developed after the battle and the illness that he had reported to the Prince on the 14th January. Rather than riding with his horse regiment with Lord George's column along the long coastal route north, Lord Kilmarnock was given the comfort of a carriage. This he shared with the French ambassador, forming part of Charles's column taking the shorter inland route.[10] However, Anne did not remain in their company long, for by the 12th February she was back in Falkirk. From her ancestral house she wrote to the Lord Justice Clerk to staunch the rumours which the Duke of Cumberland's letter had sparked off concerning her conduct.[11]

LETTER FROM ANNE LIVINGSTONE TO LORD JUSTICE CLERK

My Lord

I was very uneasy to hear that it had been represented to your Lop that I should have left Calander upon hearing of the Dukes coming, I assure you my Lord, that was very far from being my reason, and I beg you woud not believe that I woud have done any such thing, if your Lop will be so good as let me know if you get this, and I shall write the reson of my leaving home, I give you my word I am intirely innocent of all the Transactions of late, as my Lord Rosse can assure your Lop, I offer my respectfull Compliments to My Lady, & the young Ladys and I am with great regard,

My Lord
yr Lops most Obedient most humble servant

Feby 12th 1746   A. KILMARNOCK

if I had not had many instances of yr Lops friendship I durst not have ventured to have given you this trouble which I beg you'll forgive.

Postmark FALKIRK [12]

The rumours continued unabated. Anne's backgound made her a Jacobite whatever her actions might be, or have been. She was the daughter of a strong Stuart supporter who had lost his estates in 1715 when he had gone out in the Jacobite cause. At the beginning of the 1745 rising she was therefore only the tenant of what had once been the family's estates. Yet, as Lord Kilmarnock explained, "tho she was bred in different sentiments, that he thought her now more inclined to whiggish than jacobite principles".[13] Just as bad, in the public's eye, she was an episcopalian. Already she had caused a great deal of scandal by building meeting houses at Falkirk and Linlithgow which were attended by most of the Jacobite families in the neighbourhood. Here again this seems to have been reasonable behaviour and even Robert Wodrow of the established church noted the mitigating circumstances: "the Lady Kilmarnock usually goes to a Meeting-house ... but it's so distant, and she was in such hazard going to it when last with child, that she is very active to get one near her. I belive in all these, though the people who attend are Jacobites, yet the King is prayed for, and the act of Tolleration is the foot upon which they go".[14]

The episcopalian support for the rebellion was well known. Two of its adherents, Dr Drummond of Edinburgh and the Reverend Robert Forbes of Leith, the author of The Lyon in Mourning, had set off in September 1745 to join the Jacobite army. They passed through Falkirk only to be arrested at St Ninians on 7th September on suspicion. They were then confined at Stirling Castle until February the next year when the Duke of Cumberland ordered them out. They were then "kept standing in the streets of Stirling from 9 a.m., till 2 or 3 p.m. a gazing-stock for all".[15] Lord Albemarle asked why those prisoners were not roped, and their warder, a Captain Hamilton, replied that they were gentlemen. "Gentlemen!" said Albemarle, "Damm them for rebels." He ordered them to be roped for the march to Edinburgh, despite the remonstrances of Captain Hamilton who declared that they had only been apprehended on suspicion and that nothing could be proved against them. The fact that they were episcopalians was damming enough. However, once out of Stirling Hamilton untied them and so unencumbered they retraced their steps through Falkirk after five months imprisonment.

The episcopalian minister at nearby Bothkennar, William Harper, was described after the rebellion as having been "very active in aiding & assisting the rebels of the Pretender's Son at Falkirk",[16] though he seems to have come out of the episode unimpeded for he afterwards became minister of St Paul's in Edinburgh until his death in 1785.[17]

There are several peripheral variations to the main story which present considerable problems of plausibility. One Jacobite song makes Anne's maid the focus of Hawley's attention that fateful day:

> Gae dight your face, and turn the chase,
> For fierce the wind does blaw, Hawley,
> And Highland Geordie's at your tail,
> Wi' Drummond, Perth, and a', Hawley.
>
> Had ye but staid wi' lady's maid
> An hour, or may be twa, Hawley,
> Your bacon bouk, and bastard snout,
> Ye might have saved then a', Hawley.

Up and rin awa, Hawley,
Up and rin awa, Hawley;
The philabegs are coming doon,
To gie your lugs a claw, Hawley.[18]

There is even a tradition that Lady Ogilvy was with Anne,[19] though surely this cannot have been the case, for whilst Anne had been openly espousing the Hanoverian cause Lady Ogilvy had been down to Derby with her husband. The latter's presence could not therefore have been countenanced by the brutal Hawley.

Nor does it seem possible that Anne could have known that the battle was to occur that particular afternoon. The decision for the Jacobite army to advance from Skeoch Muir was only taken after noon, from which moment it was in rapid motion until the action commenced at quarter to four o'clock. Hawley had rejoined his troops by 3.15 pm, leaving no time for Anne to receive any news of the advance.

Anne was left at liberty, though she was roughly treated. The Scottish authorities seem to have been satisfied by her conduct, but her name was connected with the battle in most of the histories of the rebellion that were published in the following years. Apart from these rumours Anne also had to struggle with a financial crisis. Her husband had depleted the livestock on the estate to aid the uprising. The horses had gone as cavalry mounts and the sheep and cattle as fresh meat. He must also have taken what little reserves of cash he could lay his hands on. Anne needed money to pay for her stay in London to visit Lord Kilmarnock in the Tower, and just as pressingly to pay the annual rent to the York Buildings Company. Towards the end of 1746 it became clear that she could not raise any funds from her few assets. Her Ross relatives stood surety for her, as did James and George Lockhart. Unable to repay them a detachment of dragoons was sent to Callendar House to take possesions of some of its contents in lieu of payment.

INVENTARY OF THE EFFECTS CARRIED OUT OF THE HOUSE OF CALLENDAR by Captain Ferrie of —— Regiment of Dragoons being the Property of Lord Ross Sir James Lockhart and George Lockhart having been assign'd to them by Lord & Lady Kilmarnock in Security of their Obligations to the Annuitants of the York Building

Company for payment of the yearly Tack Duty out of the Estate of Callendar.

It. 31 Silver table Spoons & a dividing Silver one
It. 10 Silver hafted Knives & thirteen Silver fforks
It. Two pair Silver Standing Candlesticks and one pair Silver Soled ones
It. One pair Silver Candle Snuffers & Silver Dish
It. One pair Silver Servers
It. One pair Silver Salts
It. A Silver Lamp for a tea kettle
It. A Sett of Silver Instruments wt a Shagreen Case
It. A Silver Stock Buckle wt Bristol Stones
It. In a Trunk; one Dozen Shirts
It. In Do   9 Shirts & two Riding Shirts
It. In Do   22 yards fine linnen Cloath
It. In Do   three Dozen Damask Nappery cutt & uncutt
It. In Do   three Silk Gowns
It. In Do   One pair pink Silk Stockings

Taken away by Serjeant Beck

Imp. The whole Books in the Library
It. Taken out of the Best Bed Chamber the whole Curtains of a fine Silk Bed of needlework lined wt Sattine
It. Taken out of Do Room 2 peice of Arras Hangings
It. Taken out of Do Room Shovel Tongs & Pocker
It. Taken out of a Dining Room 2 peice of Arras Cloath
It. Taken out of a Bed Room the Curtains of a bleu Bed being fine blew Cloath & the Tester of the Bed
It. Two peice of Arras Hangings
It. Taken away out of a Room above stairs four peice of Damask Curtains
It. A whole Bed Cover
It. A Damask Table Cloath & napkin which was laid for Capt Ferries Supper and was not returned
It. Taken out of a Sewed Bed a twilled Reoff & tester & the Linning torn out of ye hangings of Sd Bed
It. Carried away two Coach Mares one Bay Mare & fole and a black Saddle horse
It. Ane open Chaise Harness & Briddle
It. 5 Briddles & a hunting Stock

It. 3 Currie Combs and two Brushes
It. Taken away belonging to the Coachman One pair Fleems, blood stick & Jockie Belt
It. Belonging to the house keeper one brocade Silk Gown lined wt blew Silk
It. Taken away from Thomas Leishman Clservant betwixt 2 & 9 yards of Drab Cloath just new uncutt wt severall books & his name on them.

Dated 1746 [20]

In March 1747 another blow fell on her. The government decided to take over the tenancy of the Callendar estates. Bitterly she complained:

TO THE RIGHT HONOURABLE MY LORD JUSTICE CLERK AT HIS HOUSE EDINR

My Lord
The long experience I've had of your Lops Goodness and Friendship to this unhappy family, induces me to give you this trouble, and beg your assistance and advice in an affair that troubles me a good deal, I'm informed by my doer at Calendar that their is order read out in Church by the Sheriffs order, desiring the Tennants there to pay no money to any body concern'd with me, but henceforward to the Government. your Lop has the Tack of the Estate of Calr in your hands and if you'll take the trouble to look to it you'll see that its in my name, I beg for God sake your Lop will be so good as let me know what I shall do in this matter, it creates me a great deal of uneasiness as I have more to do for than my self, I beg leave to offer my sincere and humble Compts to My Lady Milton and with the utmost regard, My Lord your Lops most Obedt most humble Servt

Kilk March 22nd 1747   A. KILMARNOCK [21]

The decision was reversed, but by this time Anne had suffered much from depression; in August 1746 she had seen her beloved husband executed; she had been persecuted by the populace and by the government. On 16th September 1747 she finally succumbed to her illness. No longer there to contradict them the rumours and legend could now take free flight. Soon there was a popular account of her death to add. It was said that she had spent the last

The Stained-glass windows from the Howgate shopping centre. They were first displayed in South Bantaskine House in the 1860s

few months of her life at Kilmarnock. Broken hearted, she shut herself up in an apartment lighted only by a dismal lamp. The walls were hung with black to suit the gloom of her mind, and she vowed never again to look upon the light of day. Here she is said to have wept herself blind, and eventually to have died of grief.[22] So much for romantic fantasy! Within a few months her story had became part of the attraction of Kilmarnock.[23] The web of fiction was encompassing everyone connected with the rebellion, not just the Bonnie Prince and Flora Macdonald.

On the same level as this story we might include one collected by Robert Kier which held that Prince Charles was present at Glengarry's funeral. It was said that Charles had been the chief mourner, holding the rope which consigned Glengarry's head to the grave.[23] However, it is clear that Charles was in Bannockburn at the time and did not make the journey to the Falkirk Parish Churchyard. It is far more probable that Lord George Murray had been the chief mourner that day, and perhaps that dignitary was mistaken for the Prince.

In the years following the battle the simple wooden grave markers in the churchyard were replaced with grandiose stone edifices celebrating the military achievement of the Hanoverian army. In October 1750 the church accounts record a "Present for the poor from Sir Henry Munro, five guineas, for the priviledge of a Tomb upon Sir Robert, my Father, in the Church yeard".[24] Another of these spurious legends recalls that on application being made to a gentleman in the neighbourhood for permission to take the necessary stone from his quarry, he answered "Monuments! 'od, on ye like, I'll gi'e ye monuments for them a'!".[25] The retort is as likely to have been a sign of his business acumen as that of his Jacobite sympathies. It was some time after, in 1765, before Captain-Lieutenant Edmonstone's grave was marked with a standing stone, the sum of £1.1.9 1/2 being paid for the privilege. The present memorial was erected by the philanthropist Robert Dollar earlier this century. Of Colonel Whitney's memorial nothing is known. Nor is it likely that the two Jacobite officers received any further recognition.

There is little left to remind us of the daring deeds performed on that cold wet January afternoon. The chair in the room where Charles stayed that night was kept as a souvenir, though its whereabouts now is unknown. The overmantle from the same room survived the demolition of the building and is now in safe keeping. The cloak in which Glengarry died was kept for many generations by the Burns family, who may still have it!

In June 1927 a monument was erected on the field of battle following a public fund raising campaign. It was unveiled by the Duke of Atholl whose ancestor Lord George Murray had played such a prominent part in the affair. In Falkirk's new Howgate shopping centre visitors admire the handsome stained-glass windows depicting the Lord George, Lord John Drummond and the Prince. They were originally made for South Bantaskine House which stood near the battlefield and whose owners, the wealthy Wilson family, were proud of their Jacobite ancestors who had fought at Falkirk. The broadsword carried by one of them is still in the possession of a family descendant in Linlithgow. At a safe distance in time from the battle the Victorians liked to remember the part they had played in the great events and the old coat-of-arms of the burgh included two highlanders who can still be seen high up on the Glebe Street wall of the old burgh buildings. Two other swords were found on the battlefield; the one pictured here, was picked up on the site some years ago and is now in the National Museum in Edinburgh.

And what of the ghosts of the past? Although many apparitions of doom were seen during the rising, only two are said to have manifested themselves regularly thereafter. One was the poor lad from Skye, so unceremoniously tipped into the gaping tomb. On a bleak winter's night it is said that his tormented moans can still be heard [26]. The second refers to the headless trunk of Sir Archibald Primrose which, on the 15th November every year walks round the Hill of Dunipace seven times.[27]

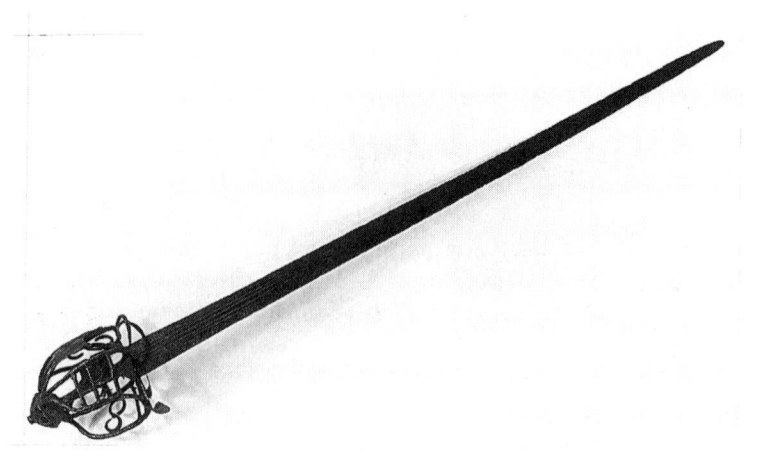

The basket hilted broadsword from the Falkirk battle now in the National Museum in Edinburgh

The Battle of Falkirk Monument
The inscription says:

THE BATTLE OF FALKIRK WAS FOUGHT AROUND HERE 17TH JANUARY 1746

Photograph by Roy Earle

NOTES

Chapter 1: The Storm Clouds Gather

1. Livingston, E. 1920; but see Abbotsford Club 1858 p.33
2. Doddridge, P. 1764.
3. Wodrow, R. 1842, i p.218.
4. Blaikie, W. 1916.
5. NRO 324/f2/38.
6. Lockhart, G. 1817, p.486.
7. Doddridge, P. 1764, p.144.
8. Henderson, A. 1752.
9. Henderson, A. 1766, p.188.
10. Graham, d. 1812, p.13.
11. Doddridge, P. 1764; SP 54/26/23.
12. Taylor, A and H. 1938.
13. Lockhart, G. 1817, p.444,486.
14. Taylor, A and H. 1938.
15. Doddridge, P. 1764, p.144.
16. Atholl, 1908, p.214; Lockhart,G. 1817, p.444; Bell, R. p.188.
17. SHS. 1958, p.214.
18. Graham, D. 1812, p.14.
19. MacGregor, A. 1901, p.366.
20. Bell, R. 1898.
21. SHS. 1958, p.144; Lockhart G. 1817.
22. PRO TS 20/95/17
23. Blaikie, W. 1916.
24. Atholl, 1908, p.27.
25. Bell, R. 1898.
26. Atholl, 1908.
27. ibid; Bell, R. 1898.
28. ibid; Lockhart, G.1817 p.444.
29. Volunteer. 1747, p.96.
30. Blaikie, W. 1916.
31. Salmon, T. 1913, p.398; Mounsey, G. 1846, p.19.
32. MacGregor, A. 1901, p.367.
33. Fraser, W. 1869. vol 2 p.232.
34. MacGregor, A. 1901, p.367.
35. Blaikie, W. 1897.
36. MacGregor, A. 1901, p.367.
37. Carlyle, A. 1860, p.131.

Chapter 2: The Eye of the Storm

1. Chambers, R. 1840, p.143.
2. Wilkins, F. 1993, p.51.
3. Chambers, op cit, p. 154.
4. SHS. 1890.
5. Chambers, op cit, p. 161.
6. PRO KB 33/4.
7. Graham, B. 1890, p.25.
8. Livingstone et al.1984.
9. Walpole, H. 1955, p.281/285; Graham, B. 1980, p.19; Foster, J. 1746, p.201.
10. Paul. J. 1875.
11. NLS ms 16604 f108.
12. Walpole, op cit, p.283.
13. NLS, op cit, f 107.
14. ibid.
15. NLS, op cit, f 108.
16. ibid.
17. Wodrow, R. 1842, p.415.
18. Thomson, K. 1846, p.391.
19. NLS, op cit, f110.
20. ibid.
21. Elcho, D. 1973, p.283; Sullivan's Account, p.87.
22. Foster, J. 1746, p.23.
23. ibid.
24. ibid.
25. PRO KB 33/4.
26. McKay, A. 1909, p.75; Chambers, op cit p.163.
27. Trial, 1746, p.32.
28. Seton and Arnot. 1929; SHS 1890.
29. Livingstone, Aikmam and Hart. 1984.
30. PRO KB op cit.
31. PRO TS 20/101/22.
32. NLS ms 16604, f 107.
33. ibid, f108.
34. Murray, K. 1908, p. 324.
35. Abbotsford Club. 1840, p.129.
36. Lockhart, G. 1817, p.453.

37. Abbotsford Club.1840, p.134-4.
38. Lockhart, op cit, p.453.
39. Chambers, op cit, p.166.
40. Steuart, A. 1907, p.84.
41. Mure, W. 1854. p.69.
42. HMC. 1913, p.116.
43. Love, J. 1928, p.76; Kirk, E. 1987, p.10.
44. Mure, op cit, p.70.
45. PRO TS 20/101/22.
46. Spalding Club,. 1841, p.352.
47. Mure, op cit,. p.169.
48. NRO ZRI 27/4/28.
49. PRO SP 54/26/94a.
50. Bisset, A. 1850.
51. Dennistoun, J. 1830, p.40.
52. ibid, p.48.
53. Chambers, op cit, p.213.
54. NRO 324/f2/38.
55. Hunter, R.
56. SHS 1890; Seton & Arnot, op cit.
57. Love, op cit, p.72.
58. NLS ms16608 f27.
59. NLS ms 16608 f27
60. Blaikie, W. 1916, p.388.
61. ibid, p.348.
62. ibid.
63. NLS ms16604 f104.
64. Blaikie,op cit, p.348.
65. Dennistoun, J. 1830, p.51.
66. Blaikie, op cit, p.385.
67. ibid, p.348.
68. Dennistoun, op cit, p.46.
69. NLS ms16608 f130.
70. Hunter, op cit.
71. NLS ms16608 f130.
72. Blaikie, op cit.
73. Dennistoun, op cit, p.59.
74. CP 9/13.
75. Blaikie, op cit, p.388.
76. ibid.
77. ibid.
78. ibid, p.350; NLS ms16608 f109.

Chapter 3: The Storm Approaches

1. SRO GD 61/113.
2. ibid.
3. Johnstone, J. 1821.
4. Atholl. 1908.
5. Johnstone, op cit; SP 54/27/6.
6. Forbes, J. 1903, p.250.
7. Blaikie, W. 1916.
8. Stewart Society. 1952, p.150.
9. Elcho, D. 1973, p.363; Maxwell, J. 1841 p.94.
10. Paul, J. 1875.
11. Forbes, op cit, p.252.
12. Atholl, op cit.
13. Elcho, op cit.
14. Blaikie, op cit.
15. Henderson, A. 1752.
16. ibid; Marchant, J. 1746, p.280; Fraser, W. 1876.
17. Forbes, op cit, p.252.
18. Stewart Society, op cit, p.162; SRO GD158/2579.7.
19. SRO GD158/2579.7.
20. Stewart Society, op cit, p.162.
21. Atholl, op cit.
22. Fraser, W, op cit.
23. Marchant, op cit.
24. SP54/27/18c.
25. ibid; Fraser, op cit.
26. Lockhart, G. 1817.
27. HMC. 1913, p.160; Blaikie,op cit
28. Prevost, W. 1963 p.247.
29. CP 9/43.
30. Atholl, op cit, p137.
31. Elcho, op cit,; Marchant, op cit.
32. Johnston, A. 1723, p.327.
33. Maxwell, J. 1841. p.94.
34. NLS ms17514 f185.
35. Fraser, op cit.
36. SP 54/27/58; Marchant, op cit.
37. Blaikie, op cit.
38. SP 54/27/58; Marchant, op cit.
39. SP 54/27/57
40. SP 54/27/58; Marchant, op cit, Scots Magazine.
41. Blaikie, op cit; Marchant, op cit.
42. Elcho, op cit; Taylor, H. 1948.

43. Marchant, op cit.
44. SP 54/27/19; Elcho, op cit.
45. NRO 324/f2/38.
46. Henderson, op cit.
47. Elcho, op cit; Blaikie, op cit; Marchant, op cit.
48. Blaikie, op cit.
49. CP 9/196.
50. CP 9/199.
51. PRO SP45/27/18c.
52. NRO 324/f2/38.
53. Blaikie, op cit; Fraser, op cit.
54. NLS ms 17514 f185.
55. SP 54/27/19; Marchant, op cit.
56. Elcho, op cit.
57. Maxwell, op cit.
58. Elcho, op cit.
59. Atholl, op cit.
60. Lockhart,1817; NLS ms 17514 f193.
61. NLS ms 17514 f193.
62. Blaikie, op cit; Taylor, op cit.
63. SP 54.27/18a.
64. Fraser, op cit.
65. Blaikie, op cit; SP 54/27/18a.
66. Blaikie, op cit.
67. NLS ms17514 f193.
68. NLS ms 17514 f186.
69. CP 9/208.
70. Elcho, op cit.
71. NLS ms17514 f193.
72. Elcho, op cit.
73. Stewart Society, op cit, p. 163.

Chapter 4: The Storm Begins

1. Scots Magazine.
2. Tomasson and Buist,1962, p.104
3. SP 54/27/22b.
4. SP 54/27/22c.
5. CP 9/210.
6. Atholl. 1908.
7. Maxwell, J. 1841.
8. Atholl, op cit.
9. Lockhart, G. 1817.
10. Atholl, op cit.
11. Forbes, D. 1815, p.265.
12. Corse.
13. Browne, J. 1838.
14. Elcho, D 1973.
15. Atholl, op cit.
16. Blaikie, W. 1916.
17. Inshwen's Vindication.
18. Elcho, op cit.
19. NRO 324/f2/38.
20. Henderson, A. 1752; Forbes, op cit and many others.
21. Fraser, W. 1876.
22. SP 54/27/22b.
23. SHS 1890.
24. NLS ms17514 f193.
25. Chambers, R . 1834, p.97.
26. McKay, A. 1909, p.76.
27. Lockhart, op cit.
28. SP 36/84 pt 1/46.
29. Corse, op cit.
30. CP 9/102.
31. Blaikie, op cit.
32. CP 9/91.
33. SP 36/84 pt 1/46.
34. ibid.
35. Ferguson, J. 1951 p.66.
36. CP 9/84.
37. Haldane, J. 1929.
38. Elcho, op cit.
39. Stewart Society. 1952.
40. ibid.
41. Fraser, op cit.
42. Salmon, T. 1913, p. 397.
43. Elcho, op cit.
44. Cholmondeley.
45. Haldane, op cit.
46. Corse, op cit.
47. Mitchell, J. 1825.
48. Murray, G. 1887.
49. NLS ms16614 f120.
50. Atholl, op cit.
51. Elcho, op cit.
52. Stewart Society, op cit.
53. SP 54/27/28.
54. Taylor, H. 1948, p.62.
55. Cholmondeley, op cit.
56. Chambers, R. 1840 p.224.
57. Corse, op cit.

234

Chapter 5: The Tempest

1. Forbes, D. 1815.
2. Metcalf, J. 1804.
3. NLS ms3733 f199.
4. Haldane, J. 1929.
5. Taylor, H. 1948.
6. NLS ms17514 f193.
7. Elcho, D. 1973.
8. Fraser, W. 1876.
9. Elcho, op cit.
10. Fraser, op cit.
11. Metcalf, J. 1804; Veitch, J.1894.
12. Forbes, op cit.
13. NRO 324/f2/38.
14. Henderson, A. 1752; HMC 1885.
15. ibid; Ferguson, J. 1948, p.134.
16. NLS ms3736 f1020.
17. Forbes, op cit.
18. Henderson, op cit.
19. NLS ms3736 f1010.
20. Atholl, op cit.
21. Lockhart, G. 1817.
22. Seton, B. 1923.
23. Elcho, op cit.
24. NLS ms295 f23.
25. Forbes, op cit.
26. Taylor. op cit.
27. Maxwell, J. 1841.
28. Taylor, A and H. 1938.
29. Atholl, op cit.
30. ibid.
31. NRO 324/f2/38.
32. Forbes, J. 1903, p.252.
33. NLS ns3736 f1020.
34. NRO 324/f2/38.
35. Atholl, op cit; Lockhart, op cit.
36. NLS ms295 f198.
37. Metcalf, op cit.
38. NLS ms295 f23.
39. Home, J.1822.
40. Forbes, D. 1815.
41. Chambers, R. Volume 1, 1827.
42. Haldane, op cit.
43. HMC 1885
44. ibid.
45. NLS ms3733 f199.
46. HMC, 1895.
47. HMC, 1885.
48. Home, op cit.
49. Chambers, R. 1840, p.227.
50. Metcalf, J. 1804; Veitch, J. 1894.
51. CP 9/102.
52. Reid, J. 1992.
53. Blaikie, W. 1916; MacGregor, A. 1901.
54. Blaikie, op cit.
55. Elcho, op cit.
56. Home, op cit.
57. PRO SP 54/27/55b.
58. Henderson, op cit; Chambers, R. 1827.
59. Atholl, op cit.
60. Graham, D. 1812.
61. Marchant, J. 1746.
62. HMC 1895.
63. Home. op cit.
64. Dunbar, E. 1865.
65. Blaikie, op cit.
66. MacGregor, A. 1901.
67. Elcho, op cit.
68. Blaikie, op cit.
69. Forbes, D. op cit.
70. Graham, op cit.
71. Johnston, J. 1812.
72. HMC 1895.
73. Metcalf, op cit.
74. Scott, W. 1828.
75. Taylor, A and H. 1928, p.170.
76. Marchant,op cit; Mure, W. 1854.
77. Johnstone, J. 1821.
78. Eguilles.
79. Mackintosh, A. 1914. p154.
80. ibid. p162
81. ibid. p 81
82. Menzies, D. 1894.
83. Dunbar, E. 1865, p.351.
84. Volunteer 1747; PRO SP 54/27/55b.
85. Johnstone; Macgregor, op cit.
86. Atholl,op cit.
87. Forbes, D. op cit.
88. SRO GD158/2582; SHS 1933 p.349.
89. HMC 1934, p.54.

235

Chapter 6: The Storm Rages

1. Forbes, D. 1815.
2. Graham, D. 1812, p.49.
3. Lockhart, G. 1817.
4. MacGregor, A. 1901.
5. Henderson, A. 1752.
6. Collins, W. 1925.
7. Veitch, J. 1894; CuRo dHud 8/49/3/16.
8. PRO SP 54/27/55b.
9. HMC 1885.
10. Forbes,op cit.
11. Chambers, R. 1827 Vol 2, p.11.
12. Home, J. 1822.
13. Taylor, A and H. 1938.
14. Chambers,op cit.
15. CP 9/102; Metcalf, J. 1804.
16. Graham, D. 1812.
17. Doddridge, P. 1746.
18. Mackenzie, A. 1898, p.136.
19. Forbes, W. p.267.
20. Blaikie, op cit.
21. Chambers, R. 1840, p237.
22. Prebble, J. 1961.
23. Marchant, J. 1746.
24. Findlay, J. 1928, p.74.
25. Forbes , op cit.
26. HMC 1885.
27. Fraser, W. 1876.
28. Blaikie,op cit.
29. Elcho, op cit.
30. Fraser, op cit.
31. Forbes, R. 1896.
32. Atholl. 1908.
33. Taylor, op cit.
34. Henderson, op cit.
35. Marchant, op cit.
36. ibid.
37. Chambers, R. 1827, Vol 1, p.32.
38. Hughes, M. 1747, p.23.
39. Cameron, A. 1753.
40. Taylor, op cit.
41. Johnstone, J. 1821.
42. Taylor, H. 1948.
43. Eguilles.
44. Taylor, op cit.
45. Atholl, op cit.
46. Chambers, op cit, 1827.
47. NLS ms3733 f215.
48. PRO SP 54/28/34f.
49. HMC 1885.
50. Johnstone, op cit.
51. Chambers, op cit, 1827.
52. Home, op cit.
53. Atholl, op cit.
54. Fraser, op cit.
55. Johnson, S. 1775, p.199.
56. Forbes, R, op cit.
57. HMC 1885.
58. Johnstone, op cit.
59. NLS ms295 f23.
60. CuRO D/Hud 8/49/3/16.
61. NRO ZRI 27/4/53.
62. MacGregor, op cit.
63. Anon. 1746, p.30.
64. Johnstone, op cit.
65. Maxwell, J. 1841.
66. Blaikie, op cit.
67. Eguilles.
68. Maxwell, op cit.
69. Eguilles.
70. Metcalf, J. 1804.
71. Kier, R. 1827 p.151.
72. Blaikie, op cit.
73. Atholl, op cit.
74. Fraser, op cit.
75. Taylor, H, op cit.
76. Athol, op cit.
77. Chambers, R. 1827, Vol 2, p.302.
78. Ferguson,J. 1948.
79. Henderson, op cit.
80. Home, op cit.
81. Henderson, op cit; Nimmo, W. 1777.
82. Eguilles.
83. Henderson, A. 1766.
84. Chambers, R. 1827, Vol 2, p.13.
85. NLS ms 3733 f200.
86. Metcalf, op cit.
87. ibid.
88. Henderson, op cit, 1766
89. Eguilles.
90. Blaikie, op cit.
91. Maxwell, op cit.
92. Metcalf,J, 1804; NRO ZRI 27/4/53.
93. Love, J. 1928, p.64.

94. McLuckie, J. 1869. p.15.
95. Chambers, R. 1827, Vol 2, p.14.
96. Johnstone, op cit.
97. Chambers, op cit, 1827, p.302.
98. Home, J, op cit.
99. Gentleman's Mag .1746, p.61.
100. Volunteer 1747.
101. McIntyre, D; Scots Mag. 1746.
102. Chambers, R, 1827, Vol 2, p.302.
103. Thomson, D. 1896, p.14.
104. Forbes, D. op cit.
105. NLS ms 3733 f200.
106. ibid.
107. Prebble, J. 1961, p.22.
108. Blaikie,op cit.
109. Forbes, D. op cit.
110. Blaikie, op cit.
111. Fraser, op cit.
112. Blaikie, op cit.
113. Forbes, D. op cit.
114. Blaikie, op cit; PRO SP 54/27/55b

Chapter 7: Storm Damage

1. Johnstone, J. 1821.
2. Taylor, A and H. 1938.
3. Fraser, W. 1876.
4. Veitch, J.. 1884.
5. Stewart Society. 1952.
6. Taylor, op cit.
7. Elcho, D. 1973.
8. Atholl. 1908.
9. NLS ms3736 f1010.
10. Home, J. 1822.
11. Crammond, W. 1887, p.11.
12. Livingstone et al.1984; PRO SP54/27/38a.
13. Daniel.
14. Anon. letter; Crammond, op cit.
15. Metcalf, J. 1804.
16. Chambers, R. 1827, p.15.
17. ibid, p.303.
18. Taylor, op cit.
19. Graham, D. 1812.
20. NLS ms3736 f1020.
21. Stewart Society, op cit.
22. Chambers, op cit, p.24.
23. ibid, p16.
24. Forbes, D. 1815, p.268.
25. PRO SP 54/27/41c; NLS ms3733 f221.
26. Falkirk Monthly Advertiser, 26th October 1841,in McLuckie, J. 1869, iv p.18.
27. PRO SP 54/27/39.
28. Chambers, op cit, p.24.
29. Taylor, H. 1946, p159.
30. Spalding Club, 1841.
31. Chambers, R. 1834.
32. NLS ms17514 f193.
33. Chambers, op cit, 1834, p.97.
34. McLuckie, J. 1869, p.19.
35. Love, J. 1928, p.72.
36. ibid, p.93
37. CP 10/313.
38. Scots Magazine 1746.
39. Blaikie, W. 1916, p.205.
40. Taylor, A and H. op cit.
41. Steuart,A. 1927, p.26.
42. CP 10/313.
43. Taylor, A and H. op cit.
44. Chambers, op cit, 1827, p.29.
45. ibid.
46. Forbes, R. 1894 1,p.380 Letter from Enoch Bradshaw
47. PRO SP 54/27/55b.
48. NRO 324/f2/38.
49. Johnstone, op cit.
50. Metcalf, op cit.
51. Taylor, H.1944
52. Spalding Club, 1841, p.380.
53. Stewart Society, op cit.
54. GD 158/2579.9.
55. PRO SP 54/27/55b.
56. Home, op cit.
57. State.
58. Anon. 1746, p.31.
59. HMC, 1913.
60. NRO 324/f2/38.
61. CKS U1590 C708/2.
62. Taylor, H. op cit.
63. MacKay, A. 1939, p.76.
64. Henderson, A. 1752.
65. Warrand, D. 1929. p.145.

66. Atholl, op cit.
67. Chambers,R, 1827, p.302.
68. Stewart Society, op cit.
69. PRO SP 54/27/41c.
70. PRO SP 54/27/41e.
71. PRO SP 54/27/39.
72. PRO SP 54.27/38a.
73. Love, J, p.78; Kirk, E. 1987, p.10.
74. Love, op cit, p. 63. The building stood betweem Mathiesons Bakery and the Victoria Inn.
75. Chambers,R, 1827, p.25.
76. Graham, op cit.
77. Athol, op cit, p.165.
78. Elcho, op cit.
79. Johnstone, op cit.
80. Atholl, op cit.
81. Elcho, op cit.
82. Taylor, H.1944.
83. PRO SP 54/27/38a.
84. NLS ms3733 f215.
85. MacGregor, A. 1901.
86. Fraser, op cit; Atholl, op cit.
87. Chambers, R, 1827, p.33.
88. Scots Magazine 1746; PRO SP 54/27/34.
89. Ferguson, J. 1951.
90. Metcalf, op cit.
91. ibid.
92. Henderson, A. 1766.
93. Scots Magazine 1746.
94. Volunteer's Letter.
95. Scots Magazine 1746.
96. Marchant, J. 1746.
97. GD 61/144.
98. Gillespie, R. 1868, p.39.
99. SHS 1890, p. 400.
100. Graham,op cit.
101. Chambers,R, 1827,p.29.
102. ibid, p.27.
103. Metcalf, op cit.
104. Chambers, R, 1827, p.28.
105. Love, op cit, Vol. 4, p.72.
106. ibid.
107. Murray, G. 1887.

Chapter 8: The Aftermath

1. Atholl, 1908.
2. Chambers, R. 1827, p.25.
3. Love, J. 1928, p.69.
4. Atholl, op cit; Lockhart, G. 1817.
5. Atholl, op cit.
6. PRO SP 54/27/41d.
7. PRO SP 54/27/41c.
8. HMC 1913 p.8; Henderson, A.1766.
9. NLS ms3733 f221.
10. NLS ms17514 f191.
11. Metcalf, J. 1804.
12. Blaikie, W. 1916; PRO SP 54/27/51b.
13. Johnstone, J. 1821.
14. Love, op cit, P.305.
15. NLS ms3733 f227.
16. PRO SP54/27/35.
17. Veitch, J. 1884.
18. Scots Magazine 1746.
19. Chambers, op cit, p.308.
20. Henderson, op cit.
21. Blaikie, op cit.
22. Henderson,A. 1752.
23. Scots Magazine 1746.
24. Maxwell, J. 1841.
25. Lockhart, op cit; Atholl, op cit.
26. Atholl, op cit.
27. Taylor, A and H,1928, p.191.
28. Home, J. 1822.
29. PRO SP 54/27/51a.
30. ibid.
31. Lockhart, op cit.
32. Maxwell, op cit.
33. Taylor, A and H, 1938.
34. Maxwell, op cit.
35. Atholl, op cit.
36. ibid.
37. Home, op cit.
38. Taylor, A and H. 1938.
39. Atholl, op cit.
40. Duke, W 1927; Home, J. 1822.
41. Home, op cit; Chambers, R 1827.
42. Taylor, A and H, 1938.
43. PRO SP 36/80 pt 3/485.
44. ibid, pt 3/499.
45. ibid.
46. Volunteer, 1747.
47. Forbes, R. 1896, p.380.

48. NLS ms14267.
49. Atholl, op cit.
50. Chambers,R,1840, p.253.
51. Maxwell, op cit.
52. Brown, G.1856.
53. Bailey, G. 1992.
54. HMC 1913.
55. ibid, p165.
56. Atholl, op cit.
57. Fraser, op cit; Atholl, op cit.
58. Fraser, op cit, p.395.
59. Atholl, op cit.
60. Maxwell, op cit.
61. Atholl, op cit.
62. Lockhart, op cit.
63. Atholl, op cit.
64. Lockhart, op cit; Atholl, op cit.
65. Forbes, J. 1903, p.252.
66. Gentlemans Magazine.
67. Henderson, A. 1766, p.227.
68. Volunteer 1747.
69. ibid; Metcalf, op cit.
70. Scots Magazine 1746.
71. Atholl, op cit.
72. Maxwell, op cit.
73. Atholl, op cit.
74. ibid; Lockhart, op cit.
75. Elcho, D. 1973.
76. Forbes, J. op cit.
77. Henderson, op cit, 1752.
78. Volunteer 1747.
79. NLS ms17514 f193; Chambers, R, 1834.
80. Chambers, op cit,1827, p.42.
81. Forbes, R. op cit.
82. Scots Magazine; PRO SP 54/28/1b.
83. Marchant, J. 1746, p.324; PRO SP 54/28/3.
84. Love, op cit, p.65.
85. Volunteer 1747.
86. Forbes,R. op cit.
87. Volunteer 1747.
88. CP 9/110.
89. Albert, C. 1861, p.221.
90. ChRO DCH/X/9a/59.
91. Cholmodeley's Order Book.
92. ibid.
93. PRO SP 54/27/36a.
    Letter from Andrew Fletcher.
94. Findlay, J. 1928, p.98.
    Letter from Aberdeen
95. Gentlemans Mag. Vol XVI p.168.

Chapter 9: Mopping Up

1. Love, J. 1928, p.306.
2. CP 9/84.
3. ibid.
4. PRO SP 54/27/35.
5. Foster, J. 1746.
6. Thomson, K. 1846.
7. Hughes, M. 1747.
8. Haldane, J. 1929, p.153.
9. Terry, C. 1902, p.183.
10. Foster, op cit.
11. ibid; Walpole, H. 1955; Bradstreet, D. 1755.
12. Love, op cit, p.86.
13. Prevost, W. 1964.
14. PRO SP 36/91/7.
15. ibid.
16. PRO KB 8/69/632.
17. Forbes, J. 1903.
18. SHS 1890; Seton and Arnot,1929.
19. PRO TS 20/101/22.
20. Love, op cit, p.87.
21. Taylor, A and H. 1928, p.121.
22. Love, op cit, p.83.
23. Walpole, op cit, p.295.
24. Mounsey, G. 1846, p.184; NLS 1696 f26.
25. HMC 1885, p.441.
26. Lodge, R. 1930, p.140; CKS U1590 C708/1.
27. Murray, G. 1887, p. 156.
28. RCAHMS 1929, p.191.
29. CRC Archives B66/27/779/6.
30. Chambers,R. 1827. Vol 2, p.302.
31. NLS 17527/5.
32. ibid.
33. Ure, R. 1991, p.114.
34. Wilkins, F. 1993.
35. Terry, C. 1902, p.183.
36. Haldane, A. 1952, p.25.
37. ibid, p.57.
38. Kemp, D. 1887.

Chapter 10: A Tale to Tell, a Yarn to Spin

1. GD 220/5/1618.5.
2. Volunteer 1747.
3. SHS. 1933, p.348.
4. Kemp, D. 1887, p.296.
5. ibid, p.295.
6. Gilpin, W. 1973, p.79.
7. Foster, J. 1746.
8. PRO SP 54/28/1b.
9. Scots Magazine 1746.
10. Graham, D. 1980, p. 28; Foster, op cit, p.318.
11. NLS ms16614 f122.
12. ibid.
13. Foster, op cit, p.23.
14. Wodrow, R. 1842, p.415.
15. Ingram, M. 1907, p.66.
16. SHS. 1890.
17. Ingram, op cit, p.66.
18. Jesse, J. 1883, p.238.
19. Wilson, W. 1924.
20. NLS ms 17527 f176.
21. NLS ms16640 f128.
22. Chambers, R. 1827., Vol 2, p.334.
23. ibid, p.25.
24. Love, J. 1928, p.92.
25. Chambers, op cit, 1827, p.303.
26. McLuckie, J. 1869.
27. Forbes, J. 1903.

GENERAL BIBLIOGRAPHY

Abbotsford Club *Jacobite Correspondence of the Atholl Family* (1840)
Abbotsford Club *Memoirs of the Insurrection in Scotland in 1715 by John Master of Sinclair* (1858)
Albert, C. *Memoires du Duc de Luynes.* vol 7 (1861)
Allardyce, J. *Historical Papers relating to the Jacobite Period. 1699-1750.* New Spalding Club 14 (1895)
Anonymous *A Compleat and Authentick History of the Rise, Progress, And Extinction of the Late Rebellion* (1746)
Atholl *Chronicles of the Families of Atholl and Tullibardine* (1908)
Bailey, G *The incident at Larbert Bridge and the siege of Callendar House* in Calatria vol 3 (1992)
Bell, R.F. (ed) *John Murray of Broughton - Memorials* S.H.S.(1898)
Blaikie,W *Itinerary of Prince Charles Edward Stuart.* S.H.S.(1897)
Blaikie,W. (ed) *Origins of the Forty-Five.* S.H.S. (1916)
Boyse, S. *An Impartial History of the Late Rebellion in 1745* (1748)
Bradstreet, D. *The Life and Uncommon Adventures of Capt. Dudley Bradstreet* (1755)
Brown, G. *Diary of George Brown: Merchant in Glasgow 1745-1753* (1856)
Browne, J. *A History of the Highlands and of the Highland Clans* (1838)
Calder, G. *The Poems of Duncan Ban MacIntyre* (1912)
Cameron, A. *An Historical Account of the Life of Dr Archibald Cameron* (1753)
Campbell, J. (ed) *Highland Songs of the Forty Five* (1994)
Carlyle, A. *Autobiography of the Rev Dr Alexander Carlyle, minister of Inveresk* (1860)
Chambers, R. *History of the Rebellion 1745-6* (1827 and 1840)
Chambers, R. (ed) *Jacobite Memoirs of the Rebellion* (1834)
Charles, G. *Transactions in Scotland in the Years 1715-16, and 1745-46 vol 2* (1817)
Charteris, E. see Elcho, D (1973)
Collins,W. *President Witherspoon: A Biography* (1925)
Constable. *Constable's Miscellany of Original and Selected Publications in the Various Departments of Literature Science, and the Arts* (1827)
Cramond, W. *The Plundering of Cullen House by the Rebels* (1887)
Crooke,W. (ed) *The Battle of Falkirk* in The Stirling Antiquary vol. III (1904)
Dennistoun, J. (ed) *The Cochrane Correspondence regarding the Affairs of Glasgow.* Maitland Club vol 37 (1830)
Doddridge, P. *Some Remarkable Passages in the Life of the Honourable Colonel James Gardiner* (1764)
Duke, W. *Lord George Murray and the Forty-Five* (1927)
Dunbar, E. *Social Life in Former Days* (1865)
Elcho, D. *A Short Account of the Affairs of Scotland in the Years 1744, 1745, 1746. ed. Charteris, E.* (1973)
Ewald, A. *The Life and Times of Prince Charles Stuart, Count of Albany commonly called the Young Pretender* (1883)

Ferguson, J. *John Fergusson 1727-1750* (1948)
Fergusson, J. *Argyll in the Forty-Five* (1951)
Findlay, J. *Wolfe in Scotland* (1928)
Forbes, D. *Culloden Papers* (1815)
Forbes, J. *Sir Archibald Primrose of the '45* in Scottish Art & Letters. vol. II no3 (1903)
Forbes, R. *The Lyon in Mourning* (S.H.S.) ed Paton, H (1896)
Foster, J. *An Account of the Behaviour of the Late Earl of Kilmarnock, after his Sentence, and on the Day of his Execution* (1746)
Foster, J. (attrib) *Observations and Remarks on the Two Accounts Lately Published, of the Behaviour of William Late Earl of Kilmarnock, and of Arthur Late Lord Balmerino, while under Sentence of Death* (1746)
Fraser, W. *The Chiefs of Colquhoun and their Country* (1869)
Fraser, W. *The Earls of Cromartie, their Kindred, Country and Correspondance* (1876)
Fraser, W. *The Chiefs of Grant* (1883)
Gentleman's Magazine 1746
Gillespie, R. *Round about Falkirk* (1868)
Gillespie, R. (ed) *The History of Stirlingshire*. Nimmo.3rd ed (1880)
Gilpin, W. *Observations on the Highlands of Scotland* (1973)
Graham, B. *William Boyd, Fourth Earl of Kilmarnock* in The Boyds of Kilmarnock (1980)
Graham, D. *Impartial History of the Rise, Progress, and Extinction of the Late Rebellion in England and Scotland, in the Years 1745 & 1746* (1812)
Haldane, A. *The Drove Roads of Scotland* (1952)
Haldane, J. *The Haldanes of Gleneagles* (1929)
Haynes, M. *Alloa Port, customs and excise accounts* in The Forth Naturalist and Historian vol 3 (1978)
Henderson, A. *The Edinburgh History of the Late Rebellion, 1745 and 1746* (1752)
Henderson, A. *The Life of William Augustus, Duke of Cumberland. Historical Manuscripts Commission Reports* (1766)
Home, J. *The History of the Rebellion in the Year 1745* (1822)
Hughes, M. *A Plain Narrative and Authentic Journal of the Late Rebellion begun in 1745* (1747)
Hunter, R. *The Kirk of Kinneil* (no date)
Ingram, M. *A Jacobite Stronghold of the Church* (1907)
Jesse, J. *Memoirs of the Pretenders and their Adherents* (1883)
Johnston, S. *A Journey to the Western Islands of Scotland* (1775)
Johnstone, J. *Memoirs of The Rebellion in 1745 and 1746* (1921)
Kemp, D. (ed) *Tours in Scotland 1747, 1750, 1760 by Richard Pococke* S.H.S. (1887)
Kier, R. *History of Falkirk* in The Falkirk Monthly Magazine (1827)
Kington Oliphant, T *The Jacobite Lairds of Gask*. Grampian Club (1870)
Kirk, E. Annals of Erskine (1987)
Kitzmiller, J. *In Search of the Forlorn Hope* (1988)
Livingston, E. The Livingstons of Callendar and their Principal Cadets (1920)
Livingstone, A., Aikman, C. & Hart, B. (ed) Muster Roll of Prince Charles Edward Stuart's Army. 1745-46 (1984)

Lockhart, G. *The Lockhart Papers* (1817)
Lodge, R. (ed) *Private Correspondence of Chesterfield and Newcastle 1744-46*. Royal Historical Society (1930)
Love, J *Local Antiquarian Notes and Queries*. vol 4 (1928)
MacGregor, A. *History of the Clan Gregor* (1901)
McKay, A. *The History of Kilmarnock* 5th ed (1909)
Mackenzie, A. *History of the Macleods* (1889)
Mackenzie, A. *History of the Munros of Fowlis* (1898)
Mackintosh, A. *The Muster Roll of the Forfarshire or Lord Ogilvy's Regiment* (1914)
McLuckie, J. *The Principal Memorials in the Falkirk Parish Churchyard* (1869)
Mahon, L. *The Forty-Five* (1851)
Marchant, J. The History of the Present Rebellion (1746)
Maxwell, J. *Narrative of Charles Prince of Wales' Expedition to Scotland in the Year 1745*. Maitland Club (1841)
Menzies, D. *The Red and White Book of Menzies* (1894)
Metcalf, J. *The Life of John Metcalf, commonly called Blind Jack of Knaresborough* (1804)
Miller, T. *The origin of the Falkirk Trysts* in Proceedings of the Falkirk Archaeological and Natural History Society vol 1 (1936)
Mitchell, J. *The Scotsman's Library; being a Collection of Anecdotes and Facts* (1825)
Mounsey, G.G. (ed) *Carlisle in the 1745* (1846)
Mure, W. (ed) The Caldwell Papers. Maitland Club (1854)
Murray, D. The York Buildings Company (1883)
Murray, G. *Records of Falkirk Parish*: A Review of the Kirk Session Records of Falkirk, from 1617 to 1689 (1887)
Murray, K. *A Military History of Perthshire, 1660-1902* (1908)
Nimmo, W. *A General History of Stirlingshire* (1777)
Norrie, W.D. *The Life and Adventures of Prince Charles Edward Stuart* vol III.
Paton, H. (ed) see Forbes, R. (1896)
Prebble, J. *Culloden* (1961)
Prevost, W. *Mr George Clerk and the Royal Hunters in 1745* in Transactions of the Cumberland and Westmorland Antiquarian and Archaeological Society. vol 63.(1963)
Prevost, W. *Two Jacobite prisoners in Carlisle in 1746* in Transactions of the Cumberland and Westmorland Antiquarian and Archaeological Society vol 64 (1964)
Ray, J. *A Compleat History of the Rebellion* (1749)
Reid, J. *The muir of Falkirk* in Calatria vol 3 (1992)
Rose, G. (ed) *A Selection from the Papers of the Earls of Marchmont* (1831)
RCAHMS Inventory of Monuments and Constructions in the Counties of Midlothian and West Lothian (1929)
Ruvigny, Marquis *The Jacobite Peerage* (1904)
Salmon, T. *Borrowstounness and District* (1903)
Scots Magazine 1746
Scott, W. *The Tales of a Grandfather* (1828)

243

S.H.S. *List of Persons Concerned in the Rebellion* Transmitted to the Commissioners of Excise (1890)
S.H.S. *Cordora's commentary on the Expedition to Scotland made by Charles Edward Stuart Prince of Wales* in Miscellany of the SHS vol 4 (1926)
S.H.S. *Marchmont Correspondence Relating to the '45* in Miscellany of the SHS vol 5.
S.H.S *Scottish Population Stats including Webster's Analysis of Population 1755* (1952)
S.H.S. *An Account of Proceedings from Prince Charles' Landing to Prestonpans* in Miscellany of the SHS vol 9 (1958)
Seton, B. *The Orderly Book of Lord Ogilvy's Regiment in the Army of Prince Charles Edward Stuart* (1923)
Seton, B. & Arnot, J. (ed) *The Prisoners of the '45* (1923)
Sheridan,T. *Copia d'Una Lettera del Cavalier Sheridan a Mr D'Obrien* (1746)
Sheridan,T. *Relazione della Vittoria Riportata in Scozia da Sua Altezza Reale Carlo Eduardo Principe di Galles su le Truppe Inglesi Commandate dal Generale Hawley* (1746)
Spalding Club *The Miscellany of the Spalding Club. vol 1* (1841)
Stanhope, P. *The Forty-Five* (1869)
Steuart, A. *The Woodhouselee Manuscript: A Narrative of Events in Edinburgh and District during the Jacobite Occupation, September to November 1745* (1907)
Steuart, A. *Patrick lindesay: The Jacobite* (1927)
Stewart Society *The Order Book of the Appin Regiment* in The Stewart Mag. Vol 9 (1952)
Taylor, A. & H. *Jacobites of Aberdeenshire and Banffshire in the Forty-Five* (1928)
Taylor, A. & H. *Jacobite Letters of Lord Pitsligo* (1930)
Taylor, A. & H. *1745 and After* (1938)
Taylor, H. *History of the Family of Urquhart* (1946)
Taylor, H. (ed) *The History of the Rebellion........1745 and 1746.* Roxburghe Club (1944)
Taylor, H. (ed) *A Jacobite Miscellany.* Roxburghe Club (1948)
Terry, C. *The Albemarle Papers.* New Spalding Club (1902)
Thomson, D. *Memories of Wallacestone* (1896)
Thomson, K. *Memoirs of the Jacobites of 1715 and 1745. Vol 3* (1846)
Tomasson, K. & Buist, F. *Battles of the '45* (1962)
Trial 1746 *The Whole Proceedings in the House of Peers upon the Indictments against William Earl of Kilmarnock, George Earl of Cromartie, and Arthur Lord Balmerino; for High Treason.*
Ure, R. *The Old Statistical Account of Scotland* in Calatria vol 1 (1991)
Veitch, J. *Side lights on the Battles of Preston and Falkirk* in Blackwood's Mag. (1894)
Volunteer 1747 *A Journey through part of England and Scotland along with the Army Under the Command of His Royal Highness the Duke of Cumberland.*
Walpole, H. *The Yale Edition of Horace Walpole's Correspondence.* vol 19 (1955)
Warrand, D *More Culloden Papers* (1929)
Wilkins, F. *The Smuggling Story of Two Firths* (1993)
Wilson, W. The House of Airlie (1924)
Wodrow, R *Analecta: or Materials for a History of Remarkable Providences; mostly relating to Scotch Ministers and Christians.* Maitland Club 60 (1842)

MANUSCRIPT SOURCES

National Library of Scotland (NLS)
Scottish Records Office (SRO)
Public Record Office (PRO)
Northumbria County Records Office (NCRO)
Cheshire County Records Office (ChCRO)
Cumbria County Records Office (CuCRO)
Centre for Kentish Studies (CKS).
Cumberland Papers (CP) on microfilm and
Cholmondeley's Order Book at Edinburgh Castle.

INDEX

Abbot's Ford 5
Abbot's Moss 109
Aberdeen 7,49
Achnabar's Company 152
Adam, John teacher 206
Adams, Rev John 3,4,8,36,86
Airdrie 81
Airth Castle 37
Airth 20,30,33,34,36,37,38,47,56,57,58, 59,65,66,68,190,218
Aitken, William 211
Alloa 6,7,8,20,30,31,32,34,38,48,53,57, 58,62,64,65,67,75,77,78
Almond, River 17
Alves, Andrew 24
Ancrum, James 36
Anderson of Whitburgh 110
Angus Og of Glengarry 95
Angus Regiment 118
Antonine Wall 93
Appin Regiment 46,72,164
Ardshiel's Regiment 12,143,196
Argyll Militia 74,81,91,102,112,125,136, 137,145,148,152,155,165,168,177,185, 188,199,200,204
Atholl, Duke of 31,183,189,229

Atholl Brigade 30,46,95,110,122,129,174, 215
Auld Soulis 78,169
Auld, John 29,214
Avon, River 2,11,50,69,75,84,147,170, 175,200
Avonbridge 179

Baad, William of Letham 20
Balmerino, Lord 22,213
Balmerino's Regiment 29,37,83,97,110
Bannockburn 10,46,62,79,94,163,176, 183,185,191,197,198
Bannockburn House 174,183,193
Bantaskine House 10,46,50,68,78,83,102
Bantaskine 93
Bantaskine Port 145
Barrel's Regiment 64,79,111,129,131, 132,134,139,140,209,210,211
Battereau's Regiment 43,74,81,135,142
battle monument 229,231
Beith Militia 86,87
Bennet, Rev 86
Berwick 43
Blakeney, General 39,41,163
Blakeney's Regiment 5,81,125,161

245

Bleachfield 182
Bo'ness 7,12,14,15,19,31,37,38,40,
41,43,50,66,73,79,82,85,126,152,177,
200,218
Bonhard Pans 36
Bonny, River 101
Bonnybridge 39,104
Bothkennar 224
Boyd, James 21
Boyd, William 22
Boyd, Charles 22,28,30,213
Brand, Major 49
Burnfoot 3
Burns Court 172
Burnside 182

Cambuskenneth 48
Callander, John 211
Callendar House 2,3,10,11,16,17,18,
22,23,30,39,47,49,54,86,90,94,102,105,
151,152,158,159,205,202,225
Callendar estate 10,135,138,145,173
Cameron of Lochiel 95,133,145,147,148,
Cameron, Dr Archibald 133
Camerons 65,95,126,127,145,159
Campbell Regiment 91
Campbell, William of Succoth 153
Carlisle 41,79
Carmuirs 9,102
Carnegie, James 118
Carriden 3
Carron, River 9,38,42,69,79,84,86,88,94,
98,99,101,107,137,170,201,204
Carronshore 218
Carsie Neuck 33,39
Castle Downie 20
Chambers, Robert 222
Charles II, King 91,200
Charlie's Hill 220,221
Chisholms 95
Cholmondeley 94,104,125,135,136,154,
215
Chomondeley's Regiment 74,79,122,128,
129,132,139,209

Claddens 173
Clanranald 20,196
Clanranald's Regiment 12,46,72,95,110,
117,171
Cluny Macpherson's 46,72,83
Cobham's Dragoons 91,114,118,122,124,
135,136,138,139,165,199,
Cope, General John 4,6,7,17,18,89,105,
143,153,186,187,215
Corstorphine 176
Cow Wynd 144,146,149,
Cromarty, Earl of 161
Cromarty's Regiment 48,62,79,84,92,95,
155,176,200,
Cross, William 35,116
Cross Well 145
Culloden 132,211,213
Cumberland, Duke of 127,153,168,187,
188,189,190,191,194,198,199,201-206,
210,213,215,220,213
Cumbernauld 44
Cumming, Lieutenant George 118,213
Cunningham, Captain 79,81,106,126,
186,210

Dalderse 42
Dalkeith 20,34
Darnrigg Moss 179
Denny 46,94,99,100,101
Derby 37,41,48,51,54,183
Dollar, Robert 229
Dorrator 91,112,155
Doune Castle 188,209
Dovecote Croft 49
Drummond, Lord John 38,44,48,59,
62,77,88,92,94,95,96,97,100,101,104,
107,138,141,145,148,185,202,230
Dumyat Drive 163
Dunbar, Ninian 213
Dunblane 48,50,190
Dundas, Patrick of Airth 190
Dunipace House 99,157
Dunipace 44,45,49,92,97,100,99,102,104,
112,137,144,151,157,202

Dunipace, Steps of 99,100,137
Dutch soldiers 38

Earn, Loch 38
East Burn 144
East Bridge Street 144,145
Easter Greenyards 79,201
Edinburgh Castle 35,79
Edinburgh 2,8,9,14,17,43,44,45,47,46,47,
48,49,66,70,71,74,19,24,27,31,33,35,36,38,
41,42,98,104,105,135,153,173,183,185,
198,199,
Edinburgh Volunteers 125
Edmondstone, William 161,164,229
Eguilles, Marquis de 30,122,134,176,183
Elcho, Lord David 23,137,192,204
Elcho's Regiment 44,46,47,59,63,69,72,
73,74,110,157,168,200
Elphinstone 31,33,60,65,66,67,72,77,190
episcopalianism 26
Erskine Church 159,171
Erskine, Rev Ebenezer 5,39
Erskine, Rev Henry 6

Falkirk 1-6,9-13,16,20,21,28-39,44,48-54,
58,60,64,65,71-89,93,95-107,112,119,120,
124-127,137,143-167,171-205,209-224,
229,230
Falkirk cattle trysts 219
Farquharson's 95,116,137,155
Faulkener, Captain 56,57,64,66
Fitzgerald, Captain George 206,207,208
Fleming's Regiment 81
Fletcher, Andrew 43,88,205
Fontenoy, Battle of 127,185
Fontenoy, Battle of 185
Forbes, Duncan 21
Forbes, Robert of Newe 189,224
Forth, River 19,45,46,48,53,54,55,56,57,
58,59,64,67,84,179,193,188,209
Fraser, Simon of Lovat 196
Frasers 83,95,122,176
Frew, Fords of 20,47,48,179,203
Gardiner, Colonel James 3,4,5,8-13,17,18,
22,86
Gardiner's Dragoons 35,164
Gargunnock 184
Gartcows 104
Glasgoe, Major of Ogilvy's 118
Glasgow 2,6,10,15,17,19,35,41,43,44,81,
83,87,99,102,176,179,
Glasgow Militia 35,42,74,90,98,112,119,
121,123,130,218
Glebe Street, 230
Glen Burn 109,128
Glen Brae 179
Glenbucket 20,41
Glencairn, Earl of 35
Glengarry 46,72,145,183,229
Glengarry's Regiment 95,110,143,183,203
Glengyles 128
Gordon, Duke of 21,137
Gordon, Lord Lewis 20,21,49,79,88,95,
134,137
Graeme, Sir John de 183,184
Graham, James of Airth 12,37,46
Graham family 149
Graham, Dougal 173
Graham, Walter surgeon 215
Grammar School 182,206
Grangepans 29,36
Grant Regiment 95
Grant, Colonel 58,60,63,65
Great Lodging 149,150
Grindlay, Walter 171
Grossett, Alexander 7,94,99,100,166
Grossett, Walter 7,12,14,38,42,43,45,48,
53,57,59,62,75,76,153,154
Guest, General Josiah 39,40,41

Haddington 17
Haldane, Patrick of Bearcrofts 213
Hamilton, Duke of 36,216
Hamilton's Dragoons 8,29,35,36,74,119,
199
Happy Janet, ship 33,40
Hardie, John 211
Harper, Rev William 224

247

Hawley, General Henry 49,54,67,70,71, 75,76,79,91,94,100,102,105,106,110,113, 114,119,124,125,129,143,144,153,154,164, 168,175,179,185,186,187,190,199,210,213, 215,222,224,225
Hay, John 193
Henderson, William 211
Hesse, Prince of 210
Higgin's Neuck 20,32,33,39,98
High Street 147,171,149,150,171,181,193,
Holland 7
Holyrood 27
Home, Earl of 35,42,74,119
Home, John 158,159
Hopetoun, Earl of 70,199
Horse Guards 204
Howard, Colonel 101,102
Howard's Regiment 79,101,134,135,140
Howgate Windows 228
Huske, General John 45,74,76,79,81,82, 84,94,102,122,135,139,154,199,200,215

Irish Picquets 138,140,143,146,147,157, 185
Inverkeithing 53

Jean, ship 39
Jinkabout Ford 85
Johnstone, Chevalier James 136,166,174

Keppoch Macdonalds 12,72,95,112,121, 129,143,145,196,198,
Kerr, Colonel 31,50,53,96,110,132,138, 201,203,204
Kersie House 30,46,59,60
Kier, Robert 222,229
Kincardine 6,53,56,58,64
Kilmarnock, Earl of 3,11,12,13,16,22-29, 34,45,46,47,49,54,80,146,158,159,169, 186,191,211,212,213,222,223
Kilmarnock's Horse 29,72,97,99,118,143, 151,152,158,200,202,214,
Kilsyth 39,44,46,74,98
Kinghorn 59

Kings Park 9
Kinneil 36,39,216
Kinneil House 216
Kirkcaldy 7
Kirkland 92,100
Kirkliston 16,17

Larbert 87,94,101,102
Larbert Bridge 83,86,87,91,92,97,101, 102,201,204,
Lauder, George surgeon 170
Leighton, Colonel 58,59,62,65
Leishman, James 151
Leith 7,12,19,40,42,53,66,210,224,
Life Guards 34,46,201
Ligonier's Regiment 125,135,140,164,209, 210
Ligonier, Colonel 109,112,114,169,187,
Ligonier's Dragoons 74,110,112,118,151, 152,199
Ligonier's Foot 35,37,136,129,131,132, 134
Linlithgow Bridge 12,22,47,73,75,76,77, 85,152,157,186,202,
Linlithgow 2,3,10,11,13,14,20,24,39,41, 42,50,71,73,74,75,76,78,79,84,86,91,119, 135,144,145,151,155,167,168,170,176,185, 186,188,191,200,218,230
Linlithgow Palace 13,202
Lithgow, John 211
Livingston, Lady Anne 3,11,23,25,26,27, 28,39,40,94,86,90,213,222,223,224,225, 227,228
Livingston, James 30,214
Livingston, James Earl of Callendar 2,28
Lochgarry 145,151,196,203
Lochiels 12,46,47,62,65,68,75,78,79,196
Lockhart, George 225
Lothian volunteers 41
Louden's Foot 91,92
Lovat, Lord 20,21,137

MacBean, Major Gillies 169
Macdonald of Tiendrish 130,138,139,211

Macdonald, Alexander 121
Macdonald, Sir Alexander of Skye 20
Macdonald, Sir John 89
Macdonald of Torbrex 164
Macdonalds of Lochgarry 95
Macdonalds 106,115,118,121,124,129,130,161,
Macdonell, Aeneas 172
MacDonnells 115,172
MacGillies, Rev Aeneas 110
MacGillivray of Dunmaglass 95
MacGregors 95,109,118,121,129,176,184,
MacGregor, Captain Evan 11,18
Mackenzies 95,122
Mackintosh Regiment 95,155,169
MacLachlans 95
Macleod, Lord John 48,58,59,62,67,95,130,157,201,
MacLeod of Muiravonside 20,78,215
Macpherson, Cluny 30,198
Maggie Wood's Loan 104
Manchester Regiment 46
Manse Place 144
Masterton, James 106,110
McDonald, Captain Rev Allan 110
Melford's Company 152
Menzies 95,122,129,
Menzies of Grahamsfield 149
Metcalf, Blind Jack 84,106,185
Mordaunt, General 87,135,140,175,200,204
Muiravonside 78,215
Mungal Burn 85
Mungal, lands of 215
Munro, Sir Robert 127,153,161,170,213,215,229
Munro's Regiment 74,111,153,206,211
Murray, Lord George 30,31,91,95,106,107,108,109,110,112,115,118,119,121,122,129,130,131,136,137,139,141,145,147,148,164,174,175,183,185,187,189,190,191,192,193,194,195,201,203,205,211,229,96,98,99,101,104
Murray of Broughton 63,190,191,192

Musselburgh 17,168

Newcastle 176,188
Newcastle, Duke of 206
Niven, Alexander 216,217

O'Sullivan, John 63,68,72,98,122,126,134,144,165,166,191,193
Ogilvy, Lord 23,30,143
Ogilvy's Regiment 95,96,118
Old Kirk of Falkirk 127
Oliphant of Gask 110,112,143,145

Paisley 11,35,112
Paterson, James 211
Paterson, Hugh 46
Perth, Duke of 53,103,159,163
Perth 6,8,20
Pikes 49,51
Pitsligo, Lord 20,192
Pitsligo's Regiment 46,47,65,67,72,83,97,98,157,168,200
Plean Muir 69,82,83,89,92,97
Pococke, Richard 220
Polmaise 64,67,68,77,84,92
Polmont Hill 49
Ponsonby, General 127
presbyterian ministers 130
Prestonpans 3,17,19,105,110,143,177,
Pretty Janet, ship 39,40
Price's Regiment 35,135
Primrose, Sir Archibald 44,45,47,49,99,137,202,214,230,
Pulteney's Regiment 64,79,124

Queensferry 37,40,152

Rattray, Major James 215
Red Lion Inn 33
Redding 152
Robert's Wynd 147
Robertsons 95
Royal Company of Archers 47
Royal Scots 43,129,199,202

249

Sauchie 9
Scots Fusiliers 22
Seafield 108,112
Secession Church 5,6,33
Semple's Regiment 168
Shaw, Captain Alistair 118
Sheddon, Charles 28
Sheriffmuir 2,75
Sheridan, Sir Thomas 145,193,196
Silver Row 159
Simpson, John brewer 20
Skeoch Muir 78,84,225
Slamannan 29,179,
South Alloa 62
Sprewell, Robin of Ormiston 101
St Andrews 37,46,144
St Clair's 81
St Ninians 92,201,203,207,208,224
Stair, Earl of 186
Stanhope, Colonel George 129,169,215
Stapleton, Brigadier Walter 99,134
Stenhouse Ford 85
Stewart, Colonel John Roy 109,110,111, 112,122,134,161,
Stewarts of Appin 95,122
Stewart of Ardshiel 95
Stewart, Captain Robert 164
Stirling Bridge 32
Stuart, Prince Charles Edward 1,9,10,12, 13,14,17,19,22-27,37,39,41,44-47,51-55, 58,68,72,77-80,85,96,98,145,149-151,158, 159,162,166,167,172174,176,180,181,183, 187,190-199
Stirling 4,5,7,8,8,9,10,14,19,20,34,35,36, 37,38,47,48,57,67,72,85,87,91,93,163,169, 177,204,208,210,211,
Stirling Castle 20,34,39,40,45,66,69,70, 88,92,163,167,173,174,177,185,194,224
Stonerigg 179
Stormonth, James of Kinclune 118
Strathallan, Lord 145
Sunnyside 91

Tamfourhill 104
Thornton, Captain 84,106,148,149, 177,185,
tolbooth steeple 127,149,158
Tor Burn 91
Torwood 3,10,69,82,83,91,92,94,97,99, 100,101,191,200,201,202,203
Touch House 9
Tullibody House 78

Vicars Loan 4
Vulture ship 190

West Burn 85
Walkinshaw, Clementina 174
Walpole, Horace 22,24
Watt, Bailie David 33,181
West Bridge Street 144
Westquarter 174
Whitney, Colonel Shugbrough 18,110, 111,114,161
Wilson family, of South Bantaskine 228
Wolfe, Major James 129,216
Wolfe's Regiment 84,122

York Buildings Company 2,225
Yorkshire Blues 84,126,148